Iain W. Provan

Hezekiah and the Books of Kings

Iain W. Provan

Hezekiah and the Books of Kings

A Contribution to the Debate
about the Composition
of the Deuteronomistic History

Walter de Gruyter · Berlin · New York
1988

Beiheft zur Zeitschrift für die alttestamentliche Wissenschaft

Herausgegeben von Otto Kaiser

172

Printed on acid free paper (pH 7, neutral)

Library of Congress Cataloging-in-Publication Data

Provan, Iain W. (Iain William), 1957—
Hezekiah and the books of Kings.
(Beiheft zur Zeitschrift für die alttestamentliche Wissenschaft ;
172)
Revision of thesis (Ph.D. — University of Cambridge, 1986)
under the title: The David and bamot themes of the books of
Kings.
Bibliography: p.
Includes index.
1. Bible. O.T. Kings — Criticism, interpretation, etc. 2. D
document (Biblical criticism) 3. Hezekiah, King of Judah. I. Title.
II. Series: Beihefte zur Zeitschrift für die alttestamentliche Wissen-
schaft ; 172.
BS1335.2.P76   1988   222'.5066   88-3808
ISBN 0-89925-461-6

CIP-Titelaufnahme der Deutschen Bibliothek

Provan, Iain W.:
Hezekiah and the Books of Kings : a contribution to the debate
about the composition of the deuteronomist. history / Iain W.
Provan. — Berlin ; New York : de Gruyter, 1988
(Beiheft zur Zeitschrift für die alttestamentliche Wissenschaft ;
172) Zugl.: Cambridge, Univ., Diss., 1986
ISBN 3-11-011557-3
NE: Zeitschrift für die alttestamentliche Wissenschaft / Beiheft

To my family

PREFACE

This monograph represents a revision of my doctoral thesis, *The David and* במות *Themes of the Books of Kings*, presented to the University of Cambridge in September 1986. Of the people mentioned in the foreword to that original volume, I should particularly like to thank once more my supervisor at Cambridge, Dr. Hugh G. M. Williamson; and Dr. Douglas R. de Lacey, who has provided invaluable assistance with the technical aspects of the project over a number of years. In the course of the revision, I received helpful advice from Professors Otto Kaiser, Ronald E. Clements and Andrew D. H. Mayes, and also from Dr. Graham I. Davies, who was particularly generous with his time. Finally, I should like to thank the editor of BZAW and the publishers Walter de Gruyter and Co. for accepting my manuscript for publication in this series.

Scholars' views about the date, extent and purpose of the original books of Kings have always influenced in a fundamental way the positions which they have adopted in the debate about the composition of the Deuteronomistic History. Yet often in this debate there has been little real interaction between those who differ on these basic issues. It is my hope that this study will once more demonstrate the importance of resolving the problem of Kings if a scholarly consensus is to be reached with regard to the history as a whole, and by doing so will stimulate further research in this area.

Iain W. Provan
King's College, London,
September, 1987.

CONTENTS

METHOD OF CITATION AND ABBREVIATIONS

In the notes, commentaries on Kings are cited on their first appearance by author and title, thereafter by author only. Standard introductions to the Old Testament are cited first by author and title, then by author and short title. Other books and articles are cited first by author, title and primary subtitle, thereafter by author and short title. The Hebrew Old Testament text of K. Elliger and W. Rudolph (eds.), *Biblica Hebraica Stuttgartensia* (Stuttgart, 1967-1977) is assumed throughout. English translations of the Hebrew are my own. The abbreviations used follow those listed in "Instructions for Contributors", *Journal of Biblical Literature* 95 (1976) 331-346, with the addition of:

"Dtr" for "Deuteronomistic" or "the Deuteronomistic author/editor"

"Dtn" for "Deuteronomic"

"DH" for "Deuteronomistic History"

"Chr" for "the Chronicler"

and the following supplements to the "List of Abbreviations of Commonly Used Periodicals, Reference Works and Serials":

AASF	Annales academiae scientiarum fennicae
AJBI	*Annual of the Japanese Biblical Institute*
ANVAOH	Avhandlinger Utgitt av det Norske Videnskaps-Akademi i Oslo, 2: Historisk-filosofisk klasse
ASORSVS	American Schools of Oriental Research, Special Volume Series
AThD	Acta theologica danica
ATSAT	Arbeiten zu Text und Sprache im Alten Testament
BAT	Botschaft des Alten Testaments
BFT	Beiträge zur Förderung christlicher Theologie
BKAT	Biblischer Kommentar: Altes Testament
CAB	Cahiers d'archéologie biblique
CenB	Century Bible
CNEB	Cambridge Bible Commentary on the New English Bible
COHP	Contributions to Oriental History and Philology
ConBOT	Coniectanea biblica, Old Testament Series
CT	Cahiers théologiques
EET	Einführung in die evangelische Theologie

EF	Erträge der Forschung
EHS	Europäische Hochschulschriften
ErF	Erlanger Forschungen
ETB	Evangelisch-theologische Bibliothek
FzB	Forschung zur Bibel
GaR	*Greece and Rome*
GTW	Grundriss der theologischen Wissenschaften
HDB	J. Hastings (ed.), *A Dictionary of the Bible*
Hen	*Henoch*
HSAT	Heilige Schrift des Alten Testamentes
IBT	Interpreting Biblical Texts
ITL	International Theological Library
IEUS	International Encyclopedia of Unified Science
JHNES	John Hopkins Near Eastern Studies
JSOT	*Journal for the Study of the Old Testament*
JSOTSup	JSOT Supplement Series
KB	L. Koehler and W.Baumgartner, *Hebräisches und aramäisches Lexikon zum Alten Testament* (3rd ed.)
KHC	Kurzer Hand-Commentar zum Alten Testament
MRS	Mission de Ras Shamra
NCB	New Century Bible
NDCT	A. Richardson and J. Bowden (eds.), *A New Dictionary of Christian Theology*
NTG	Neue theologische Grundrisse
OBO	Orbis biblicus et orientalis
OTG	Old Testament Guides
OTL	Old Testament Library
SAT	Schriften des Altes Testaments
SBOT	Sacred Books of the Old Testament
Ser	*Serapis*
SHVL	Skrifter utgivna av Kungl. Humanistiska Vetenskapssamfundet i Lund
SKGG	Schriften der Königsberger Gelehrten Gesellschaft: Geisteswissenschaftliche Klasse
SMHVL	Scripta Minora: Studier utg. av Kungl. Humanistika Vetenskapssamfundet i Lund
SThT	Studia Theologica-Teresianum
TBC	Torch Bible Commentaries
ThS	Theologische Studien
TICP	Travaux de l'Institut Catholique de Paris

TRE	G. Krause and G. Müller (eds.), *Theologische Realenzyklopädie*
TW	Theologische Wissenschaft
TynBul	*Tyndale Bulletin*
UCNES	University of California Publications: Near Eastern Studies
WBC	Word Biblical Commentary

1. THE DEUTERONOMISTIC HISTORY: THE CURRENT DEBATE

1.1 Introduction

In the history of the study of Deuteronomy and the Former Prophets, the year 1943, which saw the publication of Martin Noth's *Studien*[1], stands as a watershed. That this work occasioned a major "paradigm shift"[2] within biblical scholarship is plain from the most cursory glance at the literature. The general consensus among scholars in the pre-*Studien* period was, as any survey of the major introductions of the time will illustrate[3], that the sources JEDP of the Pentateuch could also be found in the book of Joshua, and thus that it was correct to refer to a Hexateuch[4]. A comment by Cornill catches well the general opinion of the age:

> ... Josua und Pentateuch gehören so untrennbar zuammen [sic], dass man jetzt vielfach lieber von einem Hexateuche redet[5].

As late as 1938, indeed, von Rad[6] could assume the existence of the Hexateuch as the starting point for his study of the traditions contained in Genesis-Joshua. It was regarded as the fundamental unit of the whole literary complex Genesis-Kings. The Dtr contribution to the development of Deuteronomy-Kings was limited to the composition or editing of Judges,

---

[1] M. Noth, *Überlieferungsgeschichtliche Studien, 1: Die sammelnden und bearbeitenden Geschichtswerke im Alten Testament* (SKGG 2; Halle, 1943).

[2] On the concept of paradigm shifts, cf. above all T. S. Kuhn, *The Structure of Scientific Revolutions* (IEUS 2/2; Chicago, 1962). For a brief, but useful discussion of paradigm in Kuhn's thought, cf. J. Habgood, "Paradigm", in A. Richardson and J. Bowden (eds.), *A New Dictionary of Christian Theology* (London, 1983) 427.

[3] S. R. Driver, *An Introduction to the Literature of the Old Testament* (ITL; 9th ed. revd.; Edinburgh, 1913); C. H. Cornill, *Einleitung in das Alte Testament* (GTW 2/1; 2nd ed.; Freiburg, 1892); E. Sellin, *Einleitung in das Alte Testament* (ETB 2; Leipzig, 1910); O. Eissfeldt, *Einleitung in das Alte Testament* (NTG; Tübingen, 1934); W. O. E. Oesterley, and T. H. Robinson, *An Introduction to the Books of the Old Testament* (London, 1934).

[4] The most influential works in forming this consensus were, of course, those of J. Wellhausen (*Die Composition des Hexateuchs und der historischen Bücher des Alten Testaments* (2nd ed.; Berlin, 1889); idem, *Prolegomena zur Geschichte Israels* (6th ed.; Berlin, 1905); idem, *Skizzen und Vorarbeiten, 2: Die Composition des Hexateuchs* (Berlin, 1885).

[5] Cornill, *Einleitung*, 87.

[6] G. von Rad, *Das formgeschichtliche Problem des Hexateuchs* (BWANT 78; Stuttgart, 1938).

Samuel and Kings[7], and to the editing of Deuteronomy and Joshua along with Genesis-Numbers. In the post-*Studien* period, however, most scholars have held quite a different view[8]. It has been generally accepted that Deuteronomy-Kings are to be understood as a self-contained unit which was first composed by a Dtr author, and only subsequently joined to the Tetrateuch. A significant minority, it is true, have dissented from this view[9]. In general, however, their arguments have not been regarded as compelling[10]. As Nelson says,

---

[7]   The view taken by individual scholars of the Dtr contribution to Judges-Kings naturally depended upon the extent to which they believed that he had before him continuous sources. K. Budde's view (*Die Bücher Richter und Samuel, ihre Quellen und ihr Aufbau* (Giessen, 1890)) that J and E could be traced through to the books of Kings was adopted by a few scholars (I. Benzinger, *Jahvist und Elohist in den Königsbüchern* (BWANT 27; Berlin, 1921); R. Smend, Snr., "JE in den geschichtlichen Büchern des AT." *ZAW* 39 (1921) 181-217; G. Hölscher, "Das Buch der Könige, seine Quellen und seine Redaktion" in ΕΥΧΑΡΙΣΤΗΡΙΟΝ: *Studien zur Religion und Literatur des Alten und Neuen Testaments* (FS Gunkel; FRLANT 36; Göttingen, 1923), 1: *Zur Religion und Literatur des Alten Testaments* 158-213), but did not gain widespread acceptance. The majority view with regard to Kings was that these books were a Dtr composition. Most also accepted A. Kuenen's suggestion (*Historisch-kritisch onderzoek naar het ontstaan en de verzameling van de boeken des Ouden Verbonds*, 1: *Het onstaan van de Historischen Boeken des Ouden Verbonds* (Leiden, 1861) 249-282) that they were written before the exile and subsequently edited. There was more agreement that at least two sources existed in Judges and Samuel, although an increasing number of scholars were moving away from this position even before Noth's time, influenced by such studies as those of H. Gressmann (*Die älteste Geschichtsschreibung und Prophetie Israels (von Samuel bis Amos und Hosea)* (SAT 2/1; Göttingen, 1910)), L. Rost (*Die Überlieferung von der Thronnachfolge Davids* (BWANT 42; Stuttgart, 1926)) and I. Hylander (*Der literarische Samuel-Saul-Komplex (1. Sam. 1-15) traditionsgeschichtlich untersucht* (Uppsala, 1932)).

[8]   See the various reviews of research on the DH by N. H. Snaith, "The Historical Books", in H. H. Rowley (ed.), *The Old Testament and Modern Study: A Generation of Discovery and Research* (Oxford, 1951) 84-114; E. Jenni, "Zwei Jahrzehnte Forschung an den Büchern Josua bis Könige", *TRu* N.F. 27 (1961) 1-32, 97-146; A. N. Radjawane, "Das deuteronomistische Geschichtswerk: Ein Forschungsbericht", *TRu* N.F. 38 (1974) 177-216; J. R. Porter, "Old Testament Historiography" in G. W. Anderson (ed.), *Tradition and Interpretation: Essays by Members of the Society for Old Testament Study* (Oxford, 1979) 125-162; and H. Weippert, "Das deuteronomistische Geschichtswerk: Sein Ziel und Ende in der neueren Forschung", *TRu* N.F. 50 (1985) 213-249.

[9]   A few scholars have persisted in the older view that Pentateuchal sources could be found in some or all of the historical books. Perhaps the most notable of these are O. Eissfeldt ("Die Geschichtswerke im Alten Testament", *TLZ* 72 (1947) 71-76; idem, *Geschichtsschreibung im Alten Testament: Ein kritischer Bericht über die neueste Literatur dazu* (Berlin, 1948); idem, "Deuteronomium und Hexateuch" in R. Sellheim and F. Maass (eds.), *Kleine Schriften* (6 vols.; Tübingen, 1962-1979), 4:238-258) and G. Hölscher (*Geschichtsschreibung in Israel: Untersuchungen zum Jahvisten und Elohisten* (SHVL 50; Lund, 1952)), although we may also note the more recent study by H. Schulte (*Die Entstehung der Geschichtsschreibung im Alten Israel* (BZAW 128; Berlin, 1972)). A. Weiser (*Einleitung in das Alte Testament* (6th ed.; Göttingen, 1966) 131-166; *Samuel: Seine geschichtliche Aufgabe und religiöse Bedeutung* (FRLANT 81; Göttingen, 1962)), G. von Rad (*Theologie des Alten Testaments*, 1: *Die Theologie der geschichtlichen Überlieferungen Israels* (EET 1; 2nd ed.; Munich, 1958) 326-344), and G. Fohrer (*Einleitung in das Alte Testament* (10th ed.; Heidelberg, 1965) 212-257) all object to Noth's thesis that the degree and type of Dtr activity in the books varies to such an extent that a single Dtr author is hardly likely. They prefer to see the books as separate compositions. There is a lack of Dtr material in Samuel, while differences in the method of presentation exist between Judges and Kings which suggest that they are from different Dtr hands. There is also no unified Dtr theological perspective to be found in Deuteronomy-Kings.

[10]   Most have felt that the unevenness of the Dtr contribution can be satisfactorily explained on the basis of the different character of the sources used by the Dtr, or the time of crisis in which they were taken up by him (so Porter, *Historiography*, 137-139). It has usually either been denied, on the basis of studies like those of W. Richter (*Traditionsgeschichtliche Untersuchungen zum Richterbuch* (BBB 18; Bonn, 1963); idem, *Die Bearbeitungen des 'Retterbuches' in der deuteronomischen Epoche* (BBB 21; Bonn, 1964)), G. W. Trompf ("Notions of Historical Recurrence in Classical Hebrew Historiography", in J. A. Emerton (ed.), *Studies in the Historical Books of the Old Testament* (VTSup 30; Leiden, 1979) 213-229) and H.-J. Boecker (*Die Beurteilung der Anfänge des Königtums in den deuteronomistischen Abschnitten des I. Samuelbuches: Ein Beitrag zum Problem des 'deuteronomistischen Geschichtswerks'* (WMANT 31; (Neukirchen-Vluyn, 1969)), that the differences in theological perspective within the DH threaten the case for a single author; or such differences have been reinterpreted as demonstrating that a unified and continuous history has undergone further redaction (so T. Veijola, *Das Königtum in der Beurteilung der deuteronomistischen Historiographie: Eine redaktionsgeschichtliche Untersuchung* (AASF B/198; Helsinki, 1977)).

... the majority of scholars now accept the hypothesis of a Deuteronomistic historian in one form or another[11].

The current debate about Deuteronomy and the historical books is not for the most part, then, about whether a DH comprising Deuteronomy-Kings exists, but rather about its precise nature and date. An outline and critique of the developing stages and present state of the debate follows below (1.3, 1.4). It is appropriate first of all, however, briefly to review the arguments presented by Noth which have proved so successful in persuading scholars that his basic case is correct.

---

[11]   R. D. Nelson, *The Double Redaction of the Deuteronomistic History* (JSOTSup 18; Sheffield, 1981) 13.

1.2 Noth and the Deuteronomistic Historian

Noth had already established the basis for the new understanding of Joshua which detached it from the Pentateuch in his commentary on that book which had been published a few years previously[12]. In this commentary, he developed Alt's views[13] regarding the lists of tribal boundaries and cities contained in Joshua 13-19, and the aetiological character of the stories in the earlier part of the book. Joshua 13-21, he maintained, had little to do with P (although chap. 21 and some brief expansions indicated a minor contribution), but were first introduced to the book of Joshua by a secondary Dtr editor. While allowing that Dtr used a pre-Dtr collection of the stories in Joshua 1-12, he questioned whether the collector had any relation to the Pentateuchal authors:

> Es scheint mir allzusehr an positiven Argumenten dafür zu fehlen, um den 'Sammler' mit
> einem der Erzähler des Pentateuch sicher oder auch nur wahrscheinlich zu identifizieren[14].

This denial of the existence of Pentateuchal sources in most of Joshua cleared the way for the thoroughgoing reappraisal of Deuteronomy-Kings which is found in *Studien*. The opening chapters of the book (pp. 3-27) bring together the evidence which to Noth indicated that Joshua-Kings were not merely individual books which had undergone Dtr redaction or redactions, but rather the components of a single and unified work, whose *origin* is to be traced to a Dtr author. The evidence was, first of all, of a linguistic nature (pp. 4-5). The Dtr stratum in the historical books had long been identified by an analysis of its language, and Noth accepted the results of this analysis. He now emphasized the uniformity of style which permeated the books. He did not, however, place too much emphasis on such an argument for the unity of DH, preferring rather to concentrate on the structure of the work as a whole. He pointed, on the one hand, to the presence throughout the books of generalized retrospective and anticipatory passages in Dtr language, which shared a common theology of

---

[12] M. Noth, *Das Buch Josua* (HAT 1/7; Tübingen, 1938).

[13] Alt had suggested ("Judas Gaue unter Josia", *PJ* 21 (1925) 100-116) that the list of towns in Joshua 15 was based on a list of the twelve provinces of Josiah's kingdom, and ("Das System der Stammesgrenzen im Buche Josua", in A. Jirku (ed.), *Sellin-Festschrift: Beiträge zur Religionsgeschichte und Archäologie Palästinas* (Leipzig, 1927) 13-24) that the list of the tribal boundaries in Joshua 13-19 was based on a document from the period before the monarchy. These chapters were not, then, a late idealized composition from P, as the source critics had claimed. He further asserted ("Josua", in P. Volz, F. Stummer and J. Hempel (eds.), *Werden und Wesen des Alten Testaments: Vorträge gehalten auf der internationalen Tagung alttestamentlicher Forscher zu Göttingen vom 4.-10. September 1935*, (BZAW 66; Berlin, 1936) 13-29) that the stories in Joshua 3-9 were best understood as having an aetiological origin.

[14] Noth, *Josua*, xiii.

history (pp. 5-6). These passages bound the books together into one entity, and suggested that one originally coherent narrative had subsequently been disrupted by the division of the material into separate books, and by the addition of secondary material. The overarching chronological framework of the material, which reached from Joshua to Kings and preceded the elaboration of many of the details of the stories, also pointed in the same direction (pp. 18-27). On the other hand, Noth was at pains to point out that the pre-Dtr material had no intrinsic coherence of its own, but was only given such coherence by the Dtr passages which accompanied it. Only in short passages was there any evidence of the pre-Dtr compilation of individual traditions. This being the case, the assumption that extended and continuous sources, whether related to the Pentateuchal sources or not, underlay the Dtr editorial activity, was clearly mistaken (pp. 10-11). Thus Noth was able to argue that Dtr was not merely a redactor, but an author, in the sense that he was the first to provide the traditional materials with a framework and form them into a continuous narrative (pp. 11-12). This narrative was quite different in nature from that of the Pentateuch, which showed no signs of Dtr editing at all. The beginning of the Dtr work was not to be found in Genesis, as had previously been thought, but rather in Deuteronomy 1 (pp. 12-14).

Having established the general arguments for regarding Deuteronomy-Kings as a self-contained whole, distinct from the Tetrateuch, Noth then examined the various sections of the work in more detail (pp. 27-87), which need not be repeated here. The concluding chapters further described the activity of Dtr as author; his historical context; his attitude to the traditions which he used; and his theology (pp. 87-110). Noth's Dtr wrote shortly after 562 B.C. (p. 12), in order to compile and explain the traditions concerning the history of his people (p. 100).

The originality of Noth's thesis lies not in the view that there is a fundamental continuity between the historical books, for this was the common assumption of the source-critics who followed Budde; nor in the view that the traditions in these books had first been organized by a Dtr hand, for Wellhausen[15] had held this to be true for Judges and Kings, and the work of scholars like Alt and Rost had implied such a conclusion for Joshua and Samuel. The originality of the thesis lies in his combination of these two views for the first time, that is, in his claim that the continuity between the historical books derives solely from Dtr, cannot be explained on any other basis, and is of quite a different nature to that found in the Tetrateuch. It is this emphasis on Dtr as the author of a continuous narrative, and the distinction between the DH and the Tetrateuch, which marks Noth off from all his predecessors. His work was therefore radically different to that which had gone before, while at the same time utilizing many of the insights of previous scholarship, and applying them in

---

[15]   Wellhausen, *Prolegomena*, 223-293.

a new way. At several points, his thesis depends only upon a different interpretation of what was commonly accepted to be the evidence which the text afforded as to its origin and history. Most notably, while accepting that differences were to be observed within the Dtr material, Noth did not share the view that these constituted evidence of different and parallel Dtr strands, or of separate Dtr redactions of individual books[16]. Noth thought that the differences could be accounted for on the theory of a unified DH which had subsequently attracted fragmentary additions in Dtr style. His interpretation of the evidence in Kings was also different from most who preceded him. He regarded indications there of a pre-exilic Dtr book, as indeed indications elsewhere of pre-exilic Dtr redaction, as the result of the incorporation of earlier traditions into the exilic work[17]. The survey of research which follows will demonstrate the extent to which Noth's interpretation of the evidence at these and other critical points was accepted, and the extent to which it was modified by his successors.

---

[16] Noth, *Studien*, 6-9. Noth here tackles specifically Eissfeldt, *Einleitung*, 285-286, 301, 316-317, 337-340, on the former issue, and W. Rudolph, *Der "Elohist" von Exodus bis Josua* (BZAW 68; Berlin, 1938) 240-244, on the latter.

[17] Noth, *Studien*, 91, n. 1.

1.3 Modifications of Noth's Thesis

If it may be said with confidence that Noth's basic idea of a self-contained and continuous DH reaching from Deuteronomy to Kings has won general acceptance among scholars, it must at the same time be admitted that his own precise formulation of the theory has by no means gained unqualified approval. Noth's analysis has been called into question both because of the presence within passages assigned to Dtr of various kinds of tensions which are unexpected in the work of a single author, and because of the presence in passages excluded by Noth from his DH of a significant amount of material which is stylistically and linguistically indistinct from material which is included. His own method of dealing with these elements was to attempt to diminish their significance by arguing, on the one hand, that the tensions were a result of the incorporation of source materials of differing perspectives, rather than the result of redaction by different editors, and, on the other, that the material in Dtr style outside the DH represented isolated Dtr and post-Dtr additions. Neither feature thus threatened his belief that only one Dtr author and redactor was to be found within the work. A similar approach may be found in the recent work by Hoffman[18] on the cult-reform theme in the DH. He argues that most of the tensions can be explained by the fact that the differing characteristics of the traditions known to Dtr demanded differing literary adaptation. The few examples of secondary working which do exist cannot overturn the thesis that the DH is fundamentally the work of one author[19]. Most scholars, however, have not been content with this kind of resolution of the problems posed by Noth's analysis of the DH, and have argued that a more sophisticated articulation of his hypothesis is necessary in order to account for all the evidence of Dtr activity in the text. Most would therefore allow for a Dtr "school" which was at work over a longer period of time than Noth envisaged. The degree to which such a position has been worked out in detail varies considerably from scholar to scholar. Many write rather vaguely on the subject, without tackling specific issues. Sometimes it is denied that it is possible to be more than general about the growth of the Dtr literature[20]. More

---

[18] H.-D. Hoffman, *Reform und Reformen: Untersuchungen zu einem Grundthema der deuteronomistischen Geschichtsschreibung* (ATANT 66; Zürich, 1980).

[19] We may also note here the recent commentary by T. R. Hobbs (*2 Kings* (WBC 13; Waco, Texas, 1985)), in which tensions in the narrative are also explained in terms of the craft of the author (cf. especially pp. xxvi-xxx).

[20] M. Weinfeld (*Deuteronomy and the Deuteronomic School* (Oxford, 1972) 8) states clearly what many scholars of the previous two decades imply by their approach when he argues that while it is not improbable that two editorial strands are contained in the DH, we possess no fixed criterion by which to distinguish them. For a similar view, see his recent article, "The Emergence of the Deuteronomic Movement: The Historical Antecedents", in N. Lohfink (ed.), *Das Deuteronomium: Entstehung Gestalt und Botschaft* (BETL 68; Leuven, 1985), 76-98, on p. 93, n. 57.

often, it is assumed that the question of the redactional history of the text is relatively unimportant, since Dtr theology is unified enough to be treated as of one piece[21]. Two groups of scholars, however, have attempted to be more specific, arguing that different layers can be identified within the work, and the narrower historical context in which they were produced established. The first group argue for a pre-exilic compilation of the history, with exilic or post-exilic redaction; while the second accept an exilic date for the work, but argue for further exilic redaction. Since all operate, however, within the framework of a continuous and self-contained DH reaching from Deuteronomy to Kings, it seems justifiable to call both of these newer theories modifications of Noth's thesis rather than objections to it. The extent to which their arguments have succeeded in winning over large numbers of scholars to their respective positions, including some who had previously held a more general view of the development of the DH[22], suggests that their views require close examination.

1.3.1 Pre-Exilic History with Further Redaction

The idea that Noth's DH is fundamentally a pre-exilic rather than an exilic work is found as early as 1949, in an essay by Albright[23]. Albright argued that it was highly improbable that so much older material had survived the catastrophe of the exile, and pointed to the similarity of style between the Dtr material and the Lachish letters as additional evidence that Dtr worked before the fall of Jerusalem. It cannot be said, however, that these arguments have played any great part in persuading other scholars to accept the pre-exilic compilation of the DH. Much more determinative for the development of such a view has been the fact that many scholars after Noth continued to hold to a double Dtr redaction of Kings. In doing so, they rejected Noth's opinion that the tensions to be found within the books are due to the incorporation of sources, while accepting many of his fundamental insights about the nature of the DH as a whole. A synthesis of some kind between the overall theory and this opinion of Kings was therefore required, and it was a natural and logical step, if these books were accepted as the final part of the DH, but to be regarded as primarily a pre-exilic work, to suggest that perhaps the whole DH was to be regarded as pre-exilic also. The first example of this kind of logic being worked out is to be found in Bright's commentary on Joshua[24]. He

---

[21] This assumption is noted and criticized by P. Diepold, *Israels Land* (BWANT 95; Stuttgart, 1972) 25. I shall not discuss these more general positions, since in treating the Dtr material as for all practical purposes a unified whole, they do not represent any serious modification of the Nothian thesis.

[22] We may note, for example, R. E. Clements, "The Isaiah Narrative of 2 Kings 20:12-19 and the Date of the Deuteronomic History", in A. Rofé and Y. Zakovitch (eds.), *Isac Leo Seeligmann Volume: Essays on the Bible and the Ancient World* (3 vols.; Jerusalem, 1983), 3:209-220, when compared with idem, *God and Temple* (Oxford, 1965), passim; and J. A. Soggin, *Judges* (OTL; London, 1981) xi, when compared with idem, *Le livre de Josué* (CAT 5A; Neuchâtel, 1970) 10-13.

[23] W. F. Albright, "The Biblical Period", in L. Finkelstein (ed.), *The Jews: Their History, Culture, and Religion* (2 vols.; New York, 1949), 1:3-69, on pp. 45-46 and 62, n. 108.

[24] J. Bright, "The Book of Joshua: Introduction", *IB* 2:541-550.

says of the DH:

> The date of its composition, and *therefore* [emphasis mine] of the Deuteronomic edition of
> Joshua, will depend partly upon the date assigned for the last part of the work, the book of
> Kings. One is inclined, with the majority of scholars, to date the original edition of Kings in the
> late seventh century, against Noth, who places it in the mid-sixth century[25].

It must be said that explicit statements of this kind are not frequent in the commentaries,
books and articles touching upon the historical books in the period after Noth. Consequently,
it is difficult to assess the extent of the support for this type of theory at that time. Wright
could write in 1953:

> Most scholars ... believe that the history was completed before the fall of Jerusalem, between
> ca. 609 and 598 B.C., though later revised and brought up to date during the Exile ...[26]

This may well have been the case, but we lack documentary evidence which would confirm
that it was. Indeed, the majority of commentaries on Deuteronomy and the historical books
before 1964 either do not mention Noth at all, or mention him only in passing without
interacting with his ideas. Thus Timm[27] could complain that there had been little attempt in
the two decades since Noth to approach individual sections of the books comprising the DH
from the standpoint of their function in the work as a whole. Occasionally, however, there
are hints in the commentaries that some of the authors do tend towards accepting a double
redaction theory for the DH. Of particular importance are the commentaries on Samuel and
Kings by de Vaux. De Vaux accepted the idea of a DH stretching from Deuteronomy to
Kings, and was prepared to allow that it may date from before the exile[28]. Given this fact, his
comments on Kings[29] make interesting reading. He perceives a difference between the
theology of the pre-exilic books and that of the exilic redaction, particularly in their view of
retribution, and he specifically rejects Noth's view that the tension is due to the incorporation
of sources, pointing out that it affects the very structure of the books itself. His belief is that
the books of Kings were originally produced before Josiah's death. The framework, which
has less fixity in the introductory and concluding formulae of the closing chapters than in the
remainder, was extended to the end of the books during the exile. De Vaux does not fully
work through the implications of this difference in theology and framework in Kings for the

---

[25] Ibid., 543.

[26] G. E. Wright, "The Book of Deuteronomy: Introduction", *IB* 2:311-330, on pp. 316-317.

[27] H. Timm, "Die Ladeerzählung (1. Sam. 4-6; 2. Sam. 6) und das Kerygma des deuteronomistischen
       Geschichtswerks", *EvT* 26 (1966) 509-526.

[28] R. de Vaux, *Les livres de Samuel* (SBJ; Paris, 1953) 11-12.

[29] R. de Vaux, *Les livres des Rois* (SBJ; 2nd ed.; Paris, 1958) 15-17.

rest of the DH, but his view of the books suggests an earlier version of the double redaction theory of Cross and Nelson which will be discussed shortly.

A more detailed attempt at a synthesis of Noth's thesis with the critical view of Kings is to be found in the commentaries of Gray[30]. These, says Nelson,

> ... extended the theory of a double redaction to the Deuteronomistic History as a whole, involving a "Deuteronomic compiler" and a "Deuteronomic redactor". Gray believed that the historical break between these two came between the outbreak of Jehoiakim's revolt in 598 and the accession of his successor[31].

Although it is certainly true that Gray was the first to attempt to take Noth's overall thesis seriously in his exegesis within the various books, while giving due weight to older theories about Kings, it is questionable whether his understanding of the growth of the text is as clear as Nelson makes out. Examination of the introduction to the commentary on Kings reveals some confusion. The term "compiler" means for Gray the person who composed the main body of the work, selecting from his sources in accordance with his subject and theology (p. 15). But when did he carry out his work? On the one hand, in accordance with the older view, Gray states that Kings is a pre-exilic compilation with post-exilic redaction (pp. 13-15). The earlier version has no knowledge of Judah's exile, but great confidence in the Davidic promise. On the other hand, in accordance with Noth, Gray affirms that the compiler had experienced the decline and fall of Judah (p. 17), and had selected from his sources in order to illustrate the failure and fall of the monarchy (p. 12). It thus appears that he cannot make up his mind whether the compiler worked before the exile or after it. The root of his difficulty here is not hard to find. Gray does not fully work through the implications of a pre-exilic dating of the DH for our understanding of its message. Thus in his discussion of the theological perspective which determined the compiler's selection and use of his sources, Gray is heavily influenced by Noth's analysis, which of course depended upon a much later date for the compilation. The theological differences which on pp. 13-14 mark out the compilation from the redaction in practice play no part in Gray's discussion of the compiler's theology, and indeed the description of his theology on p. 17 stands in direct conflict to that on p. 14. A more consistent working through of the theory of pre-exilic compilation for the DH would have started from the insights contained on the latter page, and would thus have led to a different understanding of the *kerygma* of the original edition, and a comparison of the theology of the original with that of the exilic edition. It is primarily Gray's

---

[30]   J. Gray, *I and II Kings* (OTL; London, 1964); idem, *Joshua, Judges and Ruth* (NCB; London, 1967). For the purposes of this historical review, the first edition of the commentary on Kings is cited throughout this chapter, although the weaknesses in the introduction are equally apparent in the later editions. In subsequent chapters, however, unless it is otherwise stated, the third edition (London, 1977) will be cited.

[31]   Nelson, *Redaction*, 19.

unwillingness to move towards such a position, because of his concern to stress the unified nature of Dtr theology and his acceptance of Noth's idea of the message of the DH, which leads to the confusion in his description of the development of the work. He is effectively caught between the older and newer theories about the books of Kings, and fails satisfactorily to resolve the tension between them.

If Gray's presentation cannot be judged to be particularly convincing, then it is with justification that more recent supporters of pre-exilic compilation and exilic redaction look to the work of F. M. Cross[32] as the foundation for their work. Cross provided precisely that which Gray's commentaries had shown to be necessary, namely a theological basis for the differentiation of two layers within the DH. Working mainly from Kings, but with an eye to the literary-critical results obtained by previous scholars in the other books which comprise the DH, Cross suggested that the themes of the pre-exilic and exilic editions of DH could be distinguished. The pre-exilic edition had two themes. On the one hand, there were the promises to David, which provided a theme of grace and hope. For the pre-exilic Dtr, the crucial factor in Judah's history was the faithfulness of David, which is persistently referred to or alluded to throughout the books of Kings. This first theme finds its climax in the reform of Josiah, who is portrayed as a second David. On the other hand, there is the theme of judgement associated with Jeroboam, whose sin is regarded by Dtr as the crucial event in the history of the northern kingdom. In this sin Israel's doom was sealed. Dtr has placed these two themes as the core around which his work is built[33]. The work dates from Josiah's reign, and is a propaganda document designed to persuade Israel to return to Judah and the Temple, and to persuade Judah that its restoration to ancient grandeur depends upon the return of the nation to the covenant with Yahweh, and upon the whole-hearted return of her king to the ways of David. The elements of the DH which are in conflict with the thrust of this pre-exilic work are regarded by Cross as belonging to an exilic "sub-theme", which is articulated most clearly in the pericope dealing with Manasseh in 2 Kgs 21:2-15. This passage speaks of the inevitability of Judah's condemnation, and clouds the distinction between Judah and Israel which is fundamental to the earlier edition. While by no means all of the passages which mention the exile must be regarded as exilic, a combination of literary-critical indicators, lack of consistency of some of the passages with the themes of the first edition, and the orientation of particular passages towards the exiles, led Cross to assign

---

[32] F. M. Cross, *Canaanite Myth and Hebrew Epic: Essays in the History of the Religion of Israel* (Cambridge, Massachusetts, 1973) 274-289. An earlier version of this material appeared as "The Structure of the Deuteronomic History", in J. M. Rosenthal (ed.), *Perspectives in Jewish Learning, 3* (Chicago, 1967) 9-24.

[33] For an extensive development of the idea that David and Jeroboam are the two crucial figures of at least Samuel and Kings, with Josiah as the second David, see J. W. D. Holder, *Models of Kingship in the Books of Samuel and Kings: A Literary and Theological Study of Kingship in the Books of Samuel and Kings*, (Ph.D thesis; University of London, 1985). Holder sees David and Jeroboam as prototypes of favour and disfavour, within the framework of which later pairs of kings (Ahab/Josiah; Ahaziah/Hezekiah; Jehu/Manasseh) are discussed and evaluated.

various parts of the DH to the exilic Dtr[34]. In this manner, he was able to integrate in a very plausible way older literary-critical work, particularly on Deuteronomy and Kings, with the concept of a self-contained and continuous DH.

The influence of Cross's work on scholarship has been enormous. Several of the commentaries which have appeared since the publication of *Myth* have taken a double redaction theory as the basis for an explanation of the text, each slightly modifying Cross's understanding of the passages to be attributed to Dtr^2[35]. Numerous articles and two important monographs which accept Cross's analysis have also appeared. Among the articles, we may note in passing those by Ogden, Cortese, Rosenbaum and Kumaki[36]. Of more direct importance in terms of their contribution to the debate about the redactional development of the DH are two by Levenson[37]. In the first of these, Levenson argues that Deuteronomy 4 derives from Cross's Dtr^2, and forms one end of a framework around the Book of the Torah. This being the case, it appears that it was the exilic Dtr who inserted the latter into the history, a conclusion which is supported by the theological conflict which exists between the Book of the Torah and the history. This conflict is seen especially in the key position accorded to the king, and in the importance attached to the Davidic dynasty, in the history. Whereas the Davidic covenant is the central feature of the pre-exilic DH, for the Book of the Torah and its exilic framework the covenant on the plains of Moab is central. In the later article, which presupposes these results, Levenson further modifies Cross's theory, suggesting that in 1 Kings 8 only 8:15-21 are to be assigned to Dtr^1. 8:23-53, and probably also 8:56-61, derive from Dtr^2.

---

[34] Deut 4:27-31; 30:1-10; 2 Kgs 21:2-15; 22:15-20 (in its present form); 23:25b-25:30. Other passages which include short exilic glosses are Deut 28:36-37, 63-68; 29:27; Josh 23:11-13, 15-16; 1 Sam 12:25; 1 Kgs 2:4; 6:11-13; 8:25b, 46-53; 9:4-9; 2 Kgs 17:19; 20:17-18. "Suspect" are Deut 30:11-20; 1 Kgs 3:14.

[35] R. G. Boling, *Judges* (AB 6A; Garden City, 1975) 29-38; P. K. McCarter, Jnr., *I Samuel* (AB 8; Garden City, 1980) 14-17; idem, *II Samuel*, (AB 9; Garden City, 1984) 4-8; R. G. Boling and G. E. Wright, *Joshua* (AB 6; Garden City, 1982) 41-72. A. D. H. Mayes' commentary (*Deuteronomy* (NCB; London, 1979)) must also be mentioned at this point, although he does not actually mention Cross, but rather follows Gray in his dating of the pre-exilic work (cf. p. 89). His analysis of the text of Deuteronomy is nevertheless an important contribution to the debate. The majority of scholars who hold to the view that there was a pre-exilic edition of the DH would, under the influence of Cross, date it in Josiah's reign, although a few (for example, Clements, "Date") have followed older commentators on Kings and have assigned it a later pre-exilic date.

[36] G. S. Ogden, "The Northern Extent of Josiah's Reforms", *AusBR* 26 (1978) 26-34; E. Cortese, "Problemi attuali circa l'opera deuteronomistica", *RivB* 26 (1978) 341-352; J. Rosenbaum, "Hezekiah's Reform and the Deuteronomistic Tradition", *HTR* 72 (1979) 23-43; F. K. Kumaki, "The Deuteronomistic Theology of the Temple - as Crystallized in 2 Sam 7, 1 Kgs 8", *AJBI* 7 (1981) 16-52.

[37] J. D. Levenson, "Who Inserted the Book of the Torah?", *HTR* 68 (1975) 203-233; idem, "From Temple to Synagogue: 1 Kings 8", in B. Halpern and J. D. Levenson (eds.), *Traditions in Transformation: Turning Points in Biblical Faith* (Winona Lake, Indiana, 1981) 143-166. See also his short article "The Last Four Verses in Kings", *JBL* 103 (1984) 353-361.

In an essay contained in the same volume as Levenson's on Deuteronomy 4, Friedman[38] presents his own thoughts about Dtr^1 and Dtr^2 in several of the key passages of the DH. In addition, he makes several observations of a more general nature in favour of the proposal that the first edition of the DH was written in Josiah's reign. Josiah, he notes, is linked with Moses as no other king is linked with him. This implies that we have here the two ends of the framework of the history, with Josiah, as the new Moses, the focal point. The idea that the material on Josiah ends the history gains further support from the fact that the material after 2 Kings 23 lacks any distinctive Dtr themes. There is no trace of the prophecy/fulfilment pattern which is central to the history up until this point, nor any reference to במות; nor are there any reminiscences of David.

A thematic argument similar to Friedman's is also employed by Nelson[39], who maintains that Dtr^1 had Josiah in mind when he composed the book of Joshua, and that Joshua himself is presented as a prototype of the ideal Dtr monarch. This gives support to the idea that the DH was written in Josiah's reign. Further articles which take Cross's general analysis as their basis have come from Boling and Peckham[40]; and most recently, from Cohn, Zevit and Vanoni[41].

The two monographs referred to have come from Nelson and Mayes[42]. In a work appearing in the same year as his article on Joshua and Josiah, Nelson[43] added to Cross's thematic arguments for a pre-exilic DH detailed literary-critical arguments which lead to the same conclusion. He, like Friedman, was concerned to demonstrate that the last chapters of Kings were different from the remainder, and argued that the framework sections showed more fixity of form and different interests to those in the earlier material. In this way, he sought to resolve a major problem afflicting all theories of a pre-exilic Kings: that of finding

---

[38]   R. E. Friedman, "From Egypt to Egypt: Dtr^1 and Dtr^2", in B. Halpern and J. D. Levenson (eds.), *Traditions in Transformation: Turning Points in Biblical Faith* (Winona Lake, Indiana, 1981) 167-192. See also idem, *The Exile and Biblical Narrative: The Formation of the Deuteronomistic and Priestly Works* (HSM 22; Chico, California, 1981) 1-43.

[39]   R. D. Nelson, "Josiah in the Book of Joshua", *JBL* 100 (1981) 531-540.

[40]   R. G. Boling, "Levitical History and the Role of Joshua", in C. L. Meyers and M. O'Connor (eds.), *The Word of the Lord Shall Go Forth: Essays in Honor of David Noel Freedman in Celebration of His Sixtieth Birthday* (ASORSVS 1; Winona Lake, Indiana, 1983) 241-261; B. Peckham, "The Composition of Deuteronomy 5-11", in C. L. Meyers and M. O'Connor (eds.), *The Word of the Lord Shall Go Forth: Essays in Honor of David Noel Freedman in Celebration of His Sixtieth Birthday* (ASORSVS 1; Winona Lake, Indiana, 1983) 217-240.

[41]   R. L. Cohn, "Convention and Creativity in the Book of Kings: The Case of the Dying Monarch", *CBQ* 47 (1985) 603-616; Z. Zevit, "Deuteronomistic Historiography in 1 Kings 12-2 Kings 17 and the Reinvestiture of the Israelian Cult", *JSOT* 32 (1985) 57-73; G. Vanoni, "Beobachtungen zur deuteronomistischen Terminologie in 2 Kön 23,25-25,30", in N. Lohfink (ed.), *Das Deuteronomium: Entstehung, Gestalt und Botschaft* (BETL 68; Leuven, 1985) 357-362. Zevit, however, dates the first Dtr after the death of Josiah.

[42]   In addition, we may note B. Halpern (*The Constitution of the Monarchy in Israel* (HSM 25; Chico, California, 1981), who works within a pre-exilic/exilic framework; S. L. McKenzie (*The Chronicler's Use of the Deuteronomistic History* (HSM 33; Atlanta, 1985)) who presupposes the pre-exilic/exilic distinction in his study of Chronicles and the DH; and G. E. Gerbrandt (*Kingship According to the Deuteronomistic History* (SBLDS 87; Atlanta, 1986)), who thinks that this distinction is probably correct, although he does not believe that the ideology of the second redactor differed significantly from that of the first.

[43]   Nelson, *Redaction*.

a plausible ending for it, given that the framework goes all the way to the end of the books. He then attempted to find a basis for the differentiation of two layers throughout the history, by examining differences in language and style within the Dtr material. He was thus able further to extend the material attributable to Dtr[244], although in respect of 1 Kgs 2:4, 8:25 and 9:4-5, this process is reversed. His chapter on the dynastic oracle argues that these verses refer to the throne of the northern kingdom, and not to the throne of Judah. Since there is therefore no conflict between their conditional promise of kingship, and the unconditional promise of kingship found in Dtr[1]'s work, they may be understood as part of the pre-exilic edition. A final chapter, discussing the theological perspectives of the two Dtrs., is in many ways the end-point of the move away from the unified Dtr theology of Noth and of the adherents of the "Dtr school" theory.

The most comprehensive attempt to deal with the entire DH from the perspective outlined above is that of Mayes[45], who also tries to achieve a detailed synthesis of the more recent literary-critical studies in the books comprising the DH and the general double redaction theory of Cross. Mayes finds two Dtr redactions throughout the DH, with the exception of the books of Kings, where he incorporates into his analysis the work of H. Weippert[46] on the "judgement formulae". He accepts her claim that the framework of Kings developed in three stages, arguing that the Josianic historian used an early Dtr Kings as a major source for his account of the monarchy[47]. The exilic Dtr later brought the history down to the exile.

The theory of a pre-exilic compilation of the DH with exilic redaction has thus won widespread acceptance in the scholarly world, and continues to provide a starting point for much of the research which is presently being done on Deuteronomy and the historical books.

[44]   According to Nelson (p. 120), the following passages or verses betray the hand of the second Dtr: Deut 4:19-20; Josh 23:4, 7, 12-13; 24:1-24; Judg 1:1-2:5; 6:7-10; 1 Kgs 8:44-51; 9:6-9; 2 Kgs 17:7-20, 23b-40; 21:3bβ-15; 22:16-17, 20b; 23:4b-5, 19-20, 24; 23:25b-25:30. It should be noted, however, that this list is not entirely consistent with the detailed discussion of exilic additions on pp. 43-98.

[45]   A. D. H. Mayes, *The Story of Israel between Settlement and Exile: A Redactional Study of the Deuteronomistic History* (London, 1983).

[46]   H. Weippert, "Die 'deuteronomistischen' Beurteilungen der Könige von Israel und Juda und das Problem der Redaktion der Königsbücher", *Bib* 53 (1972) 301-339. For a detailed discussion of Weippert's views, see 2.2 below.

[47]   M. Weippert ("Fragen des israelitischen Geschichtsbewusstseins", *VT* 23 (1973) 415-442) had already developed her thesis in a way analogous to that of Mayes, arguing that her second redactor, who looks back to the ideal king, was the editor who joined the Samuel-Saul-David complex and the history of Solomon to the history of the divided kingdom. H. Weippert ("Die Ätiologie des Nordreiches und seines Königshauses (I Reg 11,29-40)", *ZAW* 95 (1983) 344-375) has now taken on this suggestion, understanding the second editor as working in both Samuel and Kings.

1.3.2 Exilic History with Further Redaction

As the theory of a pre-exilic DH with exilic redaction has come to be associated predominantly with the name of Cross, so among the scholars who accept the idea of an exilic work with further exilic redactions the work of R. Smend is acknowledged as foundational. In this case too, however, the roots of the theory lie further back. Smend himself[48] views the work of the newer "school" as confirming in particular the original insights of Jepsen, albeit in a modified form. Jepsen[49] found two main redactions in the books of Kings, which he argued could be associated with two stages in the growth of the books which comprise the DH. The first of these, termed R^I, was carried out by a priest connected with the Jerusalem Temple between 586 and 566 B.C. This redactor gave the books of Kings their basic shape, combining a synchronic chronicle of the kings of Israel and Judah (S) and an annalistic source (A) with his own material, in order to produce a cult-history of Israel. Given the frequent reference back to David which takes place in it, this history must also have contained the greater part of the books of Samuel, and it may also have included the older part of Judges 1 and 17-21, whose pro-monarchical theme fits well with the concerns of R^I. The first redactor wrote his work in order to explain within a theological framework the disaster which had befallen Israel, and to encourage Judah to return to her God and Temple. His standpoint, however, was not that of Deuteronomy, but rather that of the Temple, so that this initial historical work is not to be described as Dtr. This description Jepsen reserved for his second, "nebiistische" redactor, R^{II}, whom he regarded as equivalent to Noth's Dtr, and who can be differentiated from R^I by his language, style, and theological concerns. It was this redactor who extended the history back to Deuteronomy, and introduced the "book of the law" as the standard by which everything was now to be judged. He also introduced the prophetic stories and comments which mark our present books of Kings. The difference which Jepsen noted between the theological perspectives of his two redactors may perhaps most clearly be seen in his analysis of their view of Israel's major fault. For R^I, according to Jepsen, worship at the Temple is the most important thing, and the chief sin of the people is worship at the high places. For R^{II}, however, whose perspective is that of Deuteronomy, worship of "other gods" is the chief sin, and he reinterprets the history accordingly, seeing the worship at the במות in that context:

---

[48]   R. Smend, *Die Entstehung des Alten Testaments* (TW 1; Stuttgart, 1978) 123.

[49]   A. Jepsen, *Die Quellen des Königsbuches* (2nd ed.; Halle, 1956).

Was bei R^I zunächst falscher Jahwedienst war, ist bei R^{II} nichts anderes als Götzendienst, Verehrung fremder Götter ...[50]

Even from this extremely brief account of Jepsen's work, its influence on Smend and his followers may immediately be seen. Fundamental to their position is the distinction made by Jepsen between the cultic history and the later prophetic and legal materials on formal, linguistic and theological grounds[51]. Earlier adumbrations of the later position may also be found in other articles and monographs which pre-date Smend, and which are particularly concerned with the themes of the DH. Thus Wolff[52], who demonstrated the importance of the "return" theme to the DH, over against Noth's fundamentally negative assessment of the message of the work, also found a "second Dtr hand" in Deuteronomy 4 and 28-30. A second Dtr carried the "return" theme back into Moses time, in order to mesh Deuteronomy with the DH and to ensure that the entire work would be read and taken to heart in his own day. The monograph of Steck[53] carried these ideas still further. Steck accepted three levels of Dtr material dating from the exile. Following Jepsen, he viewed the basic history as excluding Deuteronomy, Joshua, and the Dtr Judges, and he accepted Noth's view of the history as a doxology of judgement for this level. A second stage is represented by the addition of these books and by redactional material such as 1 Kgs 8:46-53, which gives the hope that repentance will lead to forgiveness from Yahweh and pity from Israel's enemies. Deut 30:1-10 is illustrative of the third stage, in which homecoming and restitution are explicitly promised. Braulik[54], who based his work not only on these scholars, but also on the modifications which Noth himself later made to his literary-critical analysis of Kings in his unfinished commentary[55], argued that the same author wrote Deut 4:1-40 as is responsible for 1 Kgs 8:52-53, 59-60. These verses are theologically distinct from 1 Kgs 8:44-51, and later than them. This later author is, for Braulik, critical of the Dtr Temple theology, and puts the people rather than the king in the foreground of his work.

The new framework which was to become the one adopted by most of those who now advocate an exilic DH with further exilic redaction was first introduced by Smend in an

---

[50] *Quellen*, 81.

[51] The influence of Jepsen's monograph may also be seen in a more direct way in K.-D. Schunck, *Benjamin: Untersuchungen zur Entstehung und Geschichte eines israelitischen Stammes* (BZAW 86; Berlin, 1963), who finds both priestly and prophetic editors in Samuel.

[52] H. W. Wolff, "Das Kerygma des deuteronomistischen Geschichtswerks", *ZAW* 73 (1961) 171-186.

[53] O. H. Steck, *Israel und das gewaltsame Geschick der Propheten: Untersuchungen zur Überlieferung des deuteronomistischen Geschichtsbildes im Alten Testament, Spätjudentum und Urchristentum* (WMANT 23; Neukirchen-Vluyn, 1967), especially p. 66, n. 3, and pp. 137-143.

[54] G. Braulik, "Spuren einer Neubearbeitung des deuteronomistischen Geschichtswerkes in I Kön 8,52-53.59-60", *Bib* 52 (1971) 20-33.

[55] M. Noth, *Könige* (BKAT 9/1: Neukirchen-Vluyn, 1968).

article in the von Rad *Festschrift*[56]. The article first examined three verses of Dtr character which Noth himself, in his commentary on Joshua and in *Studien*, had described as secondary: Josh 1:7-9. Smend maintained that 1:7-9aα were indeed secondary, interrupting the formula of institution found in 1:1-6, 9aβ, b. Josh 1:7-9aα was thus the work of a later Dtr editor, named DtrN by Smend because of the interest shown in these verses in obedience to the book of the law. Turning next to Joshua 13-21, Smend noted that a similar interruption of form takes place in 13:1-7. The literary construction of 13:1a, bα parallels that of Josh 1:1, 2a, an introductory sentence setting the scene and giving the presupposition for what follows, while the divine speech begins by repeating this presupposition. While Josh 1:2b, however, immediately continues with a divine command, this command is not found in Joshua 13 until v 7. The consequent possibility that 13:1bβ-6 are secondary is supported by three other points. In the first place, 13:1bβ-6 is unlikely as a divine speech. Secondly, the command of v 6 is an unlikely prelude to v 7. Finally, the subject matter of the intruding verses is not that of the surrounding context. In 13:1bβ-6, in fact, the land has not yet been completely conquered, whereas in DtrG, the basic history[57], it has (10:40-43, 11:16-20, 23), and it is thus possible to divide it up among the tribes. Smend therefore argued, against Noth, that Joshua 13-21 as a whole is a part of DtrG, and that it is Joshua 23, which shares the perspective of 13:1bβ-6 as to the incompleteness of the conquest, and is linked to it by the references to those who remain in the land, which is the secondary Dtr material. The link between all the passages thus described as secondary is confirmed by the close connection between Josh 1:7-9 and 23:6. All of this material may be attributed to DtrN, a redactor who has made the conquest of the land dependent on obedience to the book of the law, and who sees the continued presence of foreign peoples in the land as evidence that the law has not been kept. To his hand may also be attributed Judg 1:1-2:9; 2:17, 20-21, 23. In this way, Smend was able to resolve within a Dtr framework a tension which had long been discussed in OT scholarship, between the two contradictory pictures of the conquest, as well as resolving a major problem created by Noth himself, in his attribution of so much material to secondary Dtr editing without allowing for a second Dtr editor. Smend's belief, expressed at the end of the article, was that further study throughout the DH would reveal that DtrN could be found in all its parts. It is in this context that he refers to the dissertation of Dietrich on the subject of the redactional history of Kings.

---

[56] R. Smend, "Das Gesetz und die Völker: Ein Beitrag zur deuteronomistischen Redaktionsgeschichte", in H. W. Wolff (ed.), *Probleme biblischer Theologie: Gerhard von Rad zum 70. Geburtstag* (Munich, 1971) 494-509.

[57] It should be noted here that in the later writings of scholars of this group the symbol DtrG is replaced by DtrH, without any change in reference being intended.

Dietrich's dissertation, published in 1972[58], takes as its starting point four prophetic speeches in Kings which have a similar form, and have so much in common that it is probable that one hand is responsible for them all. Other texts which are linked to these speeches by theme and form, as well as the fulfilment notices which refer back to them, are then studied, and it is surmised that there is probably one redactor at work in all of this material, "Red P". This redactor, as the Huldah oracle of 2 Kings 22 shows, is not to be placed before 587 B.C. In the course of the analysis of 1 Kings 11 and 21 respectively, Dietrich also finds a Dtr redactor who is later than Red P and whose interest is in the law (DtrN), and a Dtr earlier than DtrN, who is the historian himself (DtrG). At this initial stage of the discussion of form, the question is left open whether DtrG and Red P are the same person, but the remainder of the dissertation is devoted to the attempt to demonstrate that they are not. Dietrich argues that Red P develops the language of DtrG, and also draws out and makes explicit the link between religious deterioration and political decline which is only implicit in DtrG. Red P may thus be differentiated from DtrG linguistically and theologically, and may be understood to be a separate redactor, DtrP. Dietrich further argues that a close study of the text reveals that there are factual contradictions and examples of disturbance in the text which support this distinction. He dates the three Dtr redactors as follows: DtrG around 580 B.C., DtrN around 560, and DtrP at some point in between.

Further important work within this general context has been carried out by Veijola, who has produced two major monographs with a direct bearing on our understanding of the books which comprise the DH[59]. Both of these start from problems with the themes of the DH which arise from Noth's treatment of the work, and seek to resolve them with the help of the theory of three Dtr redactors. The first of these problems has to do with the Dtr view of the Davidic dynasty. It has long been argued by various scholars[60] that, far from containing a message of unrelieved gloom, DH has a message of hope based on the future of the Davidic dynasty. Veijola maintains that the lack of agreement on this point derives in part from the fact that only the Davidic material in Kings has been considered as relevant to the understanding of Dtr's message, due to the general acceptance that in Samuel, Dtr had incorporated already existing complexes of tradition without commenting on them to any

---

[58]   W.   Dietrich,   *Prophetie   und   Geschichte: Eine   redaktionsgeschichtliche   Untersuchung   zum deuteronomistischen Geschichtswerk* (FRLANT 108; Göttingen, 1972).

[59]   T. Veijola, *Die ewige Dynastie: David und die Entstehung seiner Dynastie nach der deuteronomistischen Darstellung* (AASF B/193; Helsinki, 1975); idem, *Königtum.* A third monograph, *Verheissung in der Krise: Studien zur Literatur und Theologie der Exilszeit anhand des 89. Psalms* (AASF B/220; Helsinki, 1982), is a more general study which centres on Ps 89, but ranges widely over the literature considered by Veijola to be exilic. It has no direct bearing on the analysis of the DH, although it is helpful in filling out the picture of Veijola's views on the Dtr redaction of Kings.

[60]   So G. von Rad, *Deuteronomium-Studien* (FRLANT 58; Göttingen, 1947) 52-64; and, among others, S. Amsler, *David, roi et messie: La tradition davidique dans l'Ancien Testament,* (CT 49; Neuchâtel, 1963) 61-64; and E. Zenger, "Die deuteronomistische Interpretation der Rehabilitierung Jojachins", *BZ* N.F. 12 (1968) 16-30.

great extent. Only Carlson[61] in the period before Veijola had argued that substantial parts of Samuel should be attributed to Dtr influence, and Veijola rejects his understanding of the text because of his failure to engage in literary-critical analysis of the Dtr material of the kind carried out by Smend and Dietrich[62]. The application of the latter approach to the books of Samuel, particularly to 1 Sam 20:12-17, 42b; 1 Samuel 25; 2 Samuel 21-24; and to 1 Kings 1-2, demonstrates that this material is indeed the result of Dtr editing, and that there is a threefold picture of David contained in it, corresponding to the three redactional levels found in Kings by Dietrich. DtrG has a positive view of David, idealizing him and his dynasty: he is exemplary in his piety and justice, and his house is the legitimate and enduring dynasty. David is both נגיד and servant of Yahweh. For DtrP, however, David is never servant of Yahweh, a title which is reserved for prophets, and the king is not so idealized, being in this portrayal sinful, but willing to repent. A future for the royal house is not envisaged by DtrP. Finally, DtrN, like DtrG, does see a place and a future for David's house, but only in so far as its members are obedient to the law[63].

Veijola's second monograph, which builds on his earlier work, is an attempt to apply the new insights to another problem area of OT scholarship, the account of the rise of the monarchy in the DH. Noth's view, which was itself based on the work of earlier scholars such as Wellhausen, was that the antimonarchical strand of the account represented Dtr's authentic view, while the pro-monarchical strand represented the perspective of the earlier material which he had used. Such a position had long been felt to be unsatisfactory, and had called forth several articles and monographs which attempted to give the pro-monarchical strand more weight in the Dtr presentation, while preserving the essential unity of the DH[64]. Noting the tensions even within these attempts, however, Veijola argues rather that the best solution is to see two Dtr redactional layers in the material. DtrG used older traditions which had a similar outlook to his own, and he described the rise and role of the monarchy in a way consistent with Deut 17:14-20. Insofar as kings ruled according to this law, they were, like the judges, divinely called and legitimated. DtrN, however, had a more negative view of

---

[61] R. A. Carlson, *David, the Chosen King: A Traditio-Historical Approach to the Second Book of Samuel* (trans. E. J. Sharpe and S. Rudman; Uppsala, 1964).

[62] See further T. Veijola, "Remarks of an Outsider Concerning Scandinavian Tradition History with Emphasis on the Davidic Traditions", in K. Jeppesen and B. Otzen (eds.), *The Productions of Time: Tradition History in Old Testament Scholarship* (trans. F. H. Cryer; Sheffield, 1984) 29-51.

[63] F. Langlamet ("Pour ou contre Salomon? La rédaction prosalomonienne de I Rois, I-II", *RB* 83 (1976) 321-379, 481-528) agrees with Veijola and his predecessor E. Würthwein (*Die Erzählung von der Thronfolge Davids - theologische oder politische Geschichtsschreibung?*, (ThS 115; Zürich, 1974)), that a pro-Solomonic edition of 1 Kings 1-2 overlies an earlier narrative, but does not agree that the editor is DtrG.

[64] So, for example, Boecker, *Beurteilung*; D. J. McCarthy, "The Inauguration of Monarchy in Israel: A Form-Critical Study of I Samuel 8-12", *Int* 27 (1973) 401-412; R. E. Clements, "The Deuteronomistic Interpretation of the Founding of the Monarchy in I Sam. viii", *VT* 24 (1974) 398-410. A more recent article of similar tenor has been contributed by A. D. H. Mayes ("The Rise of the Israelite Monarchy", *ZAW* 90 (1978) 1-19).

kingship, condemning it as the result of the people's disobedience, and as the rejection of Yahweh's kingship, his positive estimate of David notwithstanding.

The major monographs just described, which have extended the theory across all the books of the DH, have in turn precipitated a whole series of articles and monographs written from this point of view, and the influence of the theory has now been felt in the introductions and commentaries. Dietrich himself has contributed further on the subject[65], arguing that three redactors may be identified in 2 Kings 22, while Roth has differentiated two theologies of rest within the Dtr material of the DH[66]. Bickert[67], while differing with Veijola in the detail, also adopts the tripartite division of the DH in his discussion of Yahweh's action in history. He is mainly interested in the extent and perspective of DtrP in the books of Samuel. Hoppe[68] accepts the theory as the background for his discussion of the meaning of the book of Deuteronomy. Spieckermann[69] also accepts the theory as the basis for his own work, and Levin[70] is influenced by it, although using different terminology, and dating DH and its redactions much later. Foresti[71] finds DtrH[72], DtrP and DtrN in 1 Samuel 15 and other passages in 1 Samuel. The theory also finds a place in the recent important commentaries of Soggin, Würthwein, and Jones[73] and in Soggin's *Introduction*[74].

We must finally in this section consider a recent article by Lohfink[75], which attempts to take the discussion of the DH forward by combining some of the insights of scholars from

---

[65]   W. Dietrich, "Josia und das Gesetzbuch (2 Reg. xxii)", *VT* 27 (1977) 13-35.

[66]   W. Roth, "The Deuteronomic Rest Theology: A Redaction-Critical Study", *BR* 21 (1976) 5-14. For a more comprehensive account of Roth's views on the DH, see his article "Deuteronomium / Deuteronomistisches Geschichtswerk / Deuteronomistische Schule", *TRE* 8:530-552.

[67]   R. Bickert, "Die Geschichte und das Handeln Jahwes: Zur Eigenart einer deuteronomistischen Offenbarungsauffassung in den Samuelbüchern", in A. H. J. Gunneweg and O. Kaiser (eds.), *Textgemäss: Aufsätze und Beiträge zur Hermeneutik des Alten Testaments* (FS Würthwein; Göttingen, 1979) 9-27. The impression given here of Bickert's position with regard to the Dtr editors, however, must be be balanced against that given by his "Die List Joabs und der Sinneswandel Davids: Eine dtr bearbeitete Einschaltung in die Thronfolgeerzählung - 2 Sam. xiv 2-22", in J. A. Emerton (ed.), *Studies in the Historical Books of the Old Testament* (VTSup 30; Leiden, 1979) 30-51, where he argues that Veijola's DtrG is actually the latest Dtr layer in Samuel, coming after DtrM (=Midrasch) and DtrN. It is not to be identified with the DtrG of Kings.

[68]   L. J. Hoppe, "The Meaning of Deuteronomy", *BTB* 10 (1980) 111-117.

[69]   H. Spieckermann, *Juda unter Assur in der Sargonidenzeit* (FRLANT 129; Göttingen, 1982).

[70]   C. Levin, *Der Sturz der Königin Atalja: Ein Kapitel zur Geschichte Judas im 9. Jahrhundert v. Chr.* (SBS 105; Stuttgart, 1982).

[71]   F. Foresti, *The Rejection of Saul in the Perspective of the Deuteronomistic School: A Study of 1 Sm 15 and Related Texts* (SThT 5; Rome, 1984).

[72]   See n. 57 above.

[73]   Soggin, *Judges*; E. Würthwein, *Die Bücher der Könige: Das erste Buch der Könige, Kapitel 1-16* (ATD 11/1; Göttingen, 1977); idem, *Die Bücher der Könige: 1. Kön. 17-2. Kön. 25* (ATD 11/2; Göttingen, 1984); G. H. Jones, *1 and 2 Kings* (NCB; 2 vols.; Grand Rapids and London, 1984).

[74]   J. A. Soggin, *Introduction to the Old Testament* (revd. ed.; London, 1980). It should be noted, however, that in a later article ("Problemi di storia e di storiografia nell'antico Israele", *Hen* 4 (1982) 1-16), although he retains the tripartite division DtrH, DtrP and DtrN, he dates H and P to the pre-exilic, and N to the post-exilic period.

[75]   N. Lohfink, "Kerygmata des deuteronomistischen Geschichtswerks", in J. Jeremias and L. Perlitt (eds.), *Die Botschaft und die Boten: Festschrift für Hans Walter Wolff zum 70. Geburtstag* (Neukirchen-Vluyn, 1981) 87-100.

both the Cross and Smend camps, while remaining firmly on the side of those who talk of an exilic work. The article is based on much of the author's previous research, especially in Deuteronomy, and is fundamentally an attempt to plot the growth of the DH by identifying different *kerygmata* within it and suggesting plausible settings for them. It is particularly noteworthy because Lohfink is prepared to accept far more pre-exilic Dtr activity than any of the other scholars who hold to an exilic work. Thus he accepts that the arguments for a Josianic edition of Kings are sound, and in addition argues that a further pre-exilic Dtr work may be found in Deuteronomy 1-Joshua 22. This is marked off from the Pentateuch and from the rest of DtrG by its specific language and ideology. It is not to be seen, therefore, as of one piece with the pre-exilic Kings, and as forming the beginning of a pre-exilic DH. Both the message of the work, however (that Yahweh gives all peoples their lands for all time), and the ideology which provides the social background to the narrative (that of royal land-allocation to vassals), lead Lohfink to the conclusion that it, too, dates from Josiah's reign. Its purpose was to provide the king with the necessary propaganda material to persuade his subjects that the expansion into the northern kingdom was justified. At the same time, it also served to legitimate the introduction in Josiah's time of the law of Deuteronomy. To this work Lohfink gives the symbol DtrL (=*Landeroberungserzählung*). The two Josianic documents were then at a later, exilic date combined with other material to form Noth's DtrG, whose *kerygma* concerned Israel's guilt and downfall. In addition to these three *kerygmata*, Lohfink identifies at least two more. First of all, he accepts the existence of DtrN in Joshua-Judges, as presented by Smend. The *kerygma* of DtrN differs from what has gone before, in that now the possession of the land is dependent on, and the result of keeping the law. Against the Smend school, however, and particularly against Dietrich, he does not believe that this DtrN can be identified with the DtrN at work in Kings. Secondly, he argues that another Dtr editor, whom he calls DtrÜ (=*Überarbeiter*), can be found at work in the final form of Deuteronomy 7-9. The author's message stands in conflict with that of DtrN, in that he questions Israel's ability ever to keep the law, and stresses the priority of Yahweh's grace in her relationship with him. It is to this editor that Wolff's "second hand" most clearly corresponds.

As with the theory of pre-exilic compilation and exilic redaction, then, the theory of exilic compilation and redaction has had a widespread influence on the scholarly world, and continues to provide the stimulation for further refinements to Noth's original thesis.

1.4 The Current Debate: A Critique

None of the positions which have been adopted in the current debate on the DH are, in my view, entirely satisfactory. Perhaps the least satisfactory is that of the advocates of unity of authorship. The presence of theological tensions within the work, as well as the significant amount of literary-critical evidence that the Dtr material is from more than one hand, remain as problems for this position, in spite of Hoffman's recent attempt to defend it. Noth's explanation of the secondary material as unconnected Dtr and post-Dtr additions seems very weak in view of two facts. In the first place, many of his post-Dtr additions are indistinguishable in language and style from his Dtr material. Secondly, the proponents of the various redactional theories have had considerable success in connecting much of this material and forming redactional layers. It is notable, then, that in Hoffman's renewed defence of the position he abandons completely the attempt to argue the case on the basis of a literary-critical approach, and instead invites a complete reappraisal of the evidence adduced in favour of the view that DH is not unified. So far as he is concerned, Noth's great mistake was that he did not carry through consistently the view expressed in *Studien* that Dtr was an "author" and not a "redactor". In practice, he allowed that Dtr was both author and redactor, and accepted the validity of both literary and redaction-criticism. This opened the door to the later redactional studies in which the new idea expressed by Noth has receded into the background, and the stress has been on the redactional complexity of the work. For Hoffman, however, such methods of textual analysis are outdated, and the evidence which has usually been regarded as indicating sources or redactional layers is rather to be understood in terms of the literary method and style of the Dtr author[76]. Consequently, much of the Dtr material which has been regarded by scholars since Noth as secondary (for example, Joshua 24[77]) need no longer be regarded as such, but may be absorbed into the unified DH, and its threat to the theory of unity of authorship thereby removed.

Such an approach will obviously appeal to those who agree with Hoffman's assertions about literary and redaction-criticism, and about Dtr method and style. Since they are merely assertions, however, and no evidence is presented as to why one should reject the older critical methods, or view the many textual inconcinnities as various aspects of Dtr method

---

[76] Hoffman, *Reform*, 15-21. For an even more radical application of this type of approach, see R. Polzin, *Moses and the Deuteronomist: A Literary Study of the Deuteronomic History*, 1: *Deuteronomy, Joshua, Judges* (New York, 1980), who consciously ignores all previous work on the DH, and all historical questions, and attempts an entirely fresh analysis of it as a unified work.

[77] Hoffman, *Reform*, 300-306.

and style, it is unclear what persuasive power his views could ever have. His handling of many of the individual passages within Kings where sources and redaction have long been suspected will certainly do nothing to convince the scholar who is prepared to allow even the possibility that the present form of the text is the result of the editing of sources[78]. A prior commitment to his general position is essential for his explanation of the text in these specific places to sound at all plausible, precisely because "Dtr style and method" is not the most obvious explanation[79]. This is particularly so in books which themselves claim to have incorporated sources, and thus predispose one to reckon with their existence. The question is, why should such a prior commitment be made? Why should we decide in advance the way in which the text is to be interpreted in every case, and exclude all other possibilities *a priori*? It is certainly reasonable to assume that the present form of the text, in spite of all its unevenness and its "odd" features, is a coherent entity with a meaning of its own, and that we may read it as such. The attempt to understand what a given text means in its present form is clearly a legitimate part of the work of the biblical scholar, and a part which has until recently been much neglected. Is it reasonable to assume, however, as Hoffman does, that the theory of single authorship will virtually always provide a sufficient explanation of *why* the text is as it is? I say "virtually always", because even Hoffman cannot bring himself to believe that absolutely all the data can be explained in this way, as will be seen in a moment. There is thus a certain inconsistency in his method. Generally, however, he rejects out of hand all other attempts to understand why the text has the form it does, and insists on single authorship as a sufficient explanation. It is this refusal to allow the validity of other approaches at the level of the discussion concerning how the text came into being which is difficult to accept. Many scholars will rather agree with Lohfink[80] that the synchronic and diachronic approaches do not exclude each other. If one does accept that literary and redaction-criticism still have an important role to play in understanding texts, then the literary-critical evidence that the Dtr material in the DH is from more than one hand remains a serious problem for the hypothesis of unity of authorship.

No less serious is the presence of theological tensions within the work. It is certainly possible that some of these tensions are, as has been suggested, the result of the incorporation of different sources (Noth) or traditions (Hoffman), and are not therefore to be taken as evidence against the theory. Such an explanation is particularly plausible where there is evidence that older traditions have been taken over wholesale. It is more difficult to

---

[78] This is particularly true of his treatment of 2 Kings 22-23, which are central to Hoffman's case, and to which 102 pages are devoted (pp. 169-270). Thus Mayes (*Story*, 14) says that "... his argument for the unity of II Kings 22f. (as indeed of other passages) can hardly withstand examination ...".

[79] Indeed, Spieckermann (*Juda*, 119) points out that Hoffman's whole case is only possible because he works with a *Deuteronomismusdefinition* which is far more extensive than any of his predecessors.

[80] Lohfink, N., "Zur neueren Diskussion über 2 Kön 22-23", in N. Lohfink (ed.), *Das Deuteronomium: Entstehung, Gestalt und Botschaft* (BETL 68; Leuven, 1985) 24-48.

accept this explanation, however, when it comes to material which is thoroughly Dtr, and which forms part of the structure of the work into which the sources or traditions have been received. Even Hoffman is compelled to allow for a certain degree of disunity at the redactional level as opposed to the source level in the case of 2 Kgs 17:34-41[81]. He attributes this passage to a second Dtr hand because of tensions between the cult-reform theme here and the same theme elsewhere in Kings. Given his acceptance of the possibility that some thematic tensions are best understood in this way, indeed, it must be adjudged a serious flaw of his book that, following Noth, he simply assumes the unified nature of the structure of Kings generally, and completely ignores studies like those of Cross and Weippert[82] which suggest that it is not unified. The tensions noted by Cross with regard to the themes of the books cannot easily be explained at the source or tradition level, since it is universally accepted that the framework of the books, with its theological evaluations of the various kings and its explanation of the history of each kingdom, is a Dtr composition. It seems far more satisfactory to explain tensions like these as the result of editing by different Dtr redactors, as Cross has attempted to do, and thus to accept that the secondary Dtr activity in the text is far greater than the advocates of unity of authorship would allow. Theological tensions and Dtr additions taken together, then, encourage one to believe that the redactional theories about the way in which the DH came into existence are closer to the mark than the theory of unified authorship.

Of the two main redactional approaches to the DH, that of the Göttingen school seems the weaker. The weakest aspect of the theory, in spite of the detailed work of Dietrich which provides its foundation, is undoubtedly the separation of DtrP from DtrG. Even Smend differentiates the *certainty* with which DtrG and DtrN may be identified, and the *probability* of the existence of DtrP[83]. The problem with Dietrich's book lies in the fact that what begins as a distinction between materials on the basis of form[84] ends up becoming a distinction between the redactors who introduced the materials, without sufficient justification being given for this development. In leaving open, in his first chapter, the question of whether Red P is the same person as DtrG (p. 46), he appears to accept that formal analysis by itself tells us little about the redactional process. His third and fourth chapters then proceed to attempt to differentiate the language and theology of the two kinds of material. These differences are few in number, however, and of a minor nature. Dietrich has to admit that Red P is dependent to a great extent on DtrG for his language and thought, and that his theological perspective is only different from DtrG in that it makes explicit what is already implicit

---

[81]   Hoffman, *Reform*, 137-139.

[82]   Cross, *Myth*; Weippert, "Beurteilungen".

[83]   Smend, *Entstehung*, 123.

[84]   It may be noted that even this formal analysis has been questioned, many scholars seeing more complexity in the prophetic material than Dietrich does. See, for example, the reviews by H. J. Stoebe, *TLZ* 99 (1974) 181-183, and F. Langlamet, *RB* 81 (1974) 601-606, and the comments of Mayes, *Story*, 116-120.

there. Given that we are dealing with different types of material, historical and prophetic, some variation of the type noted by Dietrich is to be expected in any case, and it is therefore doubtful whether his explanation of such minor differences as exist in terms of different redactors can really be sustained. Indeed, the *similarity* between the language of DtrG and Red P is itself appealed to in chap. 5 as the reason why it is difficult to prove whether DtrP introduced older narratives to the DH (p. 110). Chap. 5 also attempts to find literary-critical indications that Red P is different from DtrG, but again, the number of clear indications is not great. Dietrich explains this by saying that

> ... offenbar ist DtrP ein äusserst geschickter Redaktor gewesen, der es verstand, in das Werk von DtrG sehr behutsam und für den unbefangenen Leser kaum merklich prophetische Akzente hineinzusetzen[85].

This looks suspiciously like special pleading. The fact is that there are very few indications indeed, either from study of the language, or from study of the theology, or from literary-critical analysis, that Red P is a separate redactor from DtrG. The few indications which do exist, if they are not simply evidence of the incorporation of older prophetic narratives by DtrG, as Mayes[86] has argued against Dietrich in the case of 1 Kgs 11:29-39, are certainly not sufficient to support a thoroughgoing distinction between an historian and a prophetic redactor. History and prophecy, after all, are subjects in which a single author could have been interested. All that such evidence suggests is that *some* prophetic material has been added to DH by a later redactor. It does not suggest either that all the rest of the prophetic material comes from the same hand, or that this redactor could not also have added historical or legal material. The difficulty of holding all the prophetic material together as a unified redactional layer is, indeed, acknowledged by Würthwein in his commentary on Kings[87], although it does not in his case lead to the abandonment of DtrP. He rather divides it into DtrP^1 and DtrP^2, both of which are circles of authors rather than individuals. These are, it seems to me, desperate measures to defend a distinction for which there is little evidence in the first place. The existence of DtrP in Kings must be regarded as extremely doubtful, and if this is the case, then it must also be regarded as such in Samuel, where the material attributed to him is much more sparse.

An assessment of DtrN is rather more difficult. On the one hand, some of the literary-critical evidence presented for the distinction between DtrN and DtrG in the earlier books of the DH, such as that adduced by Smend in Joshua, seems quite strong. On the other hand, much of the case for DtrN in Kings is extremely weak. In the first place, the distinction here

---

[85] Dietrich, *Prophetie*, 139.
[86] *Story*, 116-118.
[87] Würthwein, 496-498.

often depends for its plausibility upon the acceptance that DtrP is later than DtrG, and therefore that any Dtr editing of DtrP must be later than DtrG. If DtrP and DtrG are not different authors, however, much of the DtrN material may be explained simply as the editing which took place when the Dtr author incorporated the older material into the books of Kings. Secondly, and following on from this, the literary-critical basis for a distinction between DtrG and DtrN in parts of Kings where DtrP does *not* appear is often so weak that if one does not already have such a distinction in mind because of the DtrP passages, then the presence of two redactors is by no means obvious[88]. It seems far more likely in these cases that the DtrN and DtrG material is from the same hand. It is unfortunate, indeed, that the implication of such passages, that the original history contained at least some of the "nomistic" material attributed to DtrN, has not been followed through by the Göttingen scholars, since it is accepted by all that DtrN is itself not a unity, but has been added to in the same style. On the basis of the Göttingen theory, it must therefore be supposed that DtrN, like DtrP, is not simply an individual, but a school or a circle of authors, progressively expanding the DtrN contribution. Thus in 1 Kgs 8:14-61, for example, Dietrich[89] finds DtrN and two further expansions; Würthwein[90], DtrN and three expansions; Veijola[91], DtrH, DtrN and one further expansion; and Stahl, in a recent unpublished dissertation[92], DtrN, a further DtrN expansion, and a fourth redactional school, DtrTh, which is apparently responsible for no less than four other redactional layers in the chapter. The very complexity of the Göttingen thesis at this point, even in its milder forms, prompts one to ask whether there is not something seriously wrong with the basic assumptions which lie behind it. The evidence can be much more simply explained if it is supposed that only the later DtrN material is to be associated with the DtrN who has edited DtrG, and that the primary DtrN material is from the hand of DtrG himself.

Another feature of the theory adds to one's sense of doubt. As the redactional reconstruction stands, it singularly fails to resolve two of the major problems connected with Noth's view of Kings. These are, firstly, that it did not take seriously enough the evidence which exists that the books had a pre-exilic as well as an exilic form; and, secondly, that it failed to resolve the tension which exists in Kings between the conditional and unconditional understandings of the Davidic covenant. The Göttingen approach leaves the first problem unresolved on the level of DtrG, which is simply assumed to be an exilic work, and it

---

[88]   Thus 1 Kgs 15:4 and 2 Kgs 8:19 are attributed to DtrN, although there is no evidence that they are secondary insertions.

[89]   Dietrich, *Prophetie*, 74, n. 39.

[90]   Würthwein, 91-103.

[91]   Veijola, *Verheissung*, 150-158.

[92]   R. Stahl, *Aspekte der Geschichte deuteronomistischer Theologie: Zur Traditionsgeschichte der Terminologie und zur Redaktionsgeschichte der Redekompositionen* (Diss. B; Jena, 1982) 96-99. I have not seen this dissertation, but depend here upon the author's own summary of his work in *TLZ* 108 (1983) 74-76.

merely moves the second on to the level of DtrN. DtrN supposedly held to both views of the Davidic promise, while at the same time stressing that obedience to Dtn law is essential if blessing is to follow, and that disobedience inevitably leads to Yahweh's wrath. The alternatives are not discussed. The work of Cross[93], however, with which the Göttingen scholars never interact, provides a plausible resolution of these problems, using a redactional model which cuts across the distinction between DtrG and DtrN in Kings. Even more significantly, Mayes[94] has recently demonstrated how it is possible to combine the Cross analysis with the better evidence for DtrN in the earlier books of the DH so as to provide a simple and plausible double redaction theory for the whole work which avoids the criticisms which have been made here of the Göttingen thesis. That this is so is confirmatory evidence that, however valid some of the literary-critical conclusions which lie behind it may be, the general thesis concerning DtrG and DtrN is seriously flawed. It fails on all points, as did Hoffman's work, satisfactorily to account for the nature of the books of Kings.

Finally, the theory of a pre-exilic DH with exilic redaction must be considered in more detail. My comments already in this section will have betrayed my conviction that this position deserves very serious consideration. Its great strength is that it attempts to do full justice to the evidence, which many scholars over the years have found compelling, that the original Kings was a pre-exilic work. This is not to say, however, that Cross's particular position on Kings, or on the DH as a whole, is free of problems. With regard to the DH, it must be noted that Cross simply assumes, as indeed do many of those who have accepted his analysis of Kings, that a pre-exilic Kings entails a pre-exilic DH. This is clearly not the case. Lohfink's article[95] is a welcome reminder that it is possible to accept a significant amount of pre-exilic Dtr literary activity without accepting a pre-exilic DH, and therefore that any extrapolation from Kings to the remaining books of the DH must be argued rather than assumed. Nor is it clear that we may simply adopt Cross's precise analysis of Kings as our starting point in such an exercise, as the majority of scholars who hold to the idea of a pre-exilic history have done. Although they seem to have gone unnoticed by other scholars, there are very real problems with the understanding of the themes of the books which is advanced in *Myth*.

Cross maintains, it will be recalled, that the two central assertions of the pre-exilic books are, first of all, that the crucial event in the history of the northern kingdom was the sin of Jeroboam (p. 279), in which Israel's doom was sealed (p. 281), and secondly, that the crucial event in the history of Judah was the faithfulness of David (p. 282). The theme connected to the first of these assertions is completed in 2 Kgs 17:1-23, while the climax of the second is

---

[93]   Cross, *Myth*.
[94]   Mayes, *Story*.
[95]   Lohfink, "Kerygmata".

found in the account of the reform of Josiah in 2 Kings 22-23. Analysis of 2 Kgs 17:20-23, however, suggests that the way in which Cross puts these two themes together is misleading. It seems clear from this passage that Jeroboam's sin is not crucial for Israel in the same way that David's faithfulness is crucial for Judah. Israel is exiled in these verses, not because Jeroboam sinned, but rather because the people persisted in imitating Jeroboam's sins. The punishment of the exile thus fell upon them because of their own faults, not because of those of Jeroboam. With David and Judah, on the other hand, the situation is completely different. David's faithfulness protects Judah from Yahweh's rejection *in spite of* their personal faults and those of their kings. Yahweh's benevolence is extended to them irrespective of their conduct. The two themes taken together, then, do not just tell us that Israel was unfortunate in the choice of her first king. They tell us something about the historian's theology of retribution. It is the Davidic dynasty, and the presence of Yahweh in the Jerusalem Temple, which in his view makes the difference between the two states. While it is certainly true, therefore, that a pre-exilic Kings containing these themes might have functioned as a propaganda document for that dynasty, intent on re-establishing suzerainty over the north after the events of 722-721 B.C., it is very difficult to see how it could at the same time have functioned as a call to obedience to the law. According to Cross, the historian wished to communicate to Judah that:

> Its restoration to ancient grandeur depends on the return of the nation to the covenant of Yahweh and on the whole-hearted return of her king to the ways of David, the servant of Yahweh[96].

If the person who formulated the themes under discussion had intended such a message, however, it is doubtful that he would have so presented his message as to suggest that Yahweh's judgement only takes place outside of the covenant with David, and that the breaking of the law within Judah is therefore of no ultimate importance. The fact of the matter is that there is a strong element of discontinuity between the themes identified by Cross, on the one hand, and his suggested climax for the major of them, on the other. In 2 Kings 22-23 there is, in fact, no mention of the unconditional and eternal promises to David. The stress is rather upon the importance of keeping the law as a means of avoiding wrath (22:11-13). Josiah in particular avoids the wrath of Yahweh because of his own obedience, and not because of David (22:14-20). David's role in these chapters is only as a model of righteousness to be imitated (22:2), and even then, as Friedman's observations[97] about the parallelism between Moses and Josiah imply, he is not the primary model. This discontinuity between themes and climax presents a serious problem for Cross's understanding of the

---

[96]   Cross, *Myth*, 284.

[97]   Friedman, "Egypt", 171-173.

redactional development of Kings, and suggests that a re-examination of the whole issue is required.

Such a re-examination is particularly necessary because of recent suggestions that the first Dtr edition of Kings does not derive from Josiah's reign at all, but was rather published during or shortly after Hezekiah's reign. Such an origin for some of the material in Kings was, indeed, accepted long ago by Jepsen[98]. He thought that the sources S (synchronistic chronicle) and A (annals of the kings of Israel and Judah), which provide our present books of Kings with most of their accession and burial formulae, and many other historical details, ended in 2 Kings 18 and did not include the notice of Hezekiah's death in 18:20-21. The unpublished dissertation of Schüpphaus[99] went further, arguing that the material designated S and A by Jepsen was actually part of an historical work which extended from Judges to the reign of Hezekiah in Kings, and included many of the stories about judges and prophets, as well as the various narrative-complexes in Samuel. Both of these scholars thought that this early material in Kings and elsewhere was pre-Dtr[100]. The new interest in *Dtr* material from this period seems to stem from two pieces of recent work from different perspectives. The first of these is the article by H. Weippert[101] which was mentioned in 1.3.1 above. Weippert has been followed in her view of a Dtr Kings written in Hezekiah's reign by M. Weippert[102], and, with a few modifications, by Barrick, Mayes and Lemaire[103]. The second piece of influential work is an unpublished Harvard dissertation by Macy[104] on the sources of the books of Chronicles. On the basis of an analysis of the accession and judgement formulae, the death and burial notices, and the source citations in both Kings and Chronicles, Macy suggests that Chr depended in part upon an earlier Dtr edition of Samuel-Kings than our present edition. He also possessed other Dtr sources which dealt with the period from Hezekiah to the end of the kingdom of Judah[105]. Macy's insights have been accepted by

---

[98]   Jepsen, *Quellen*, 30-60; appendices.

[99]   J. Schüpphaus, *Richter- und Prophetengeschichten als Glieder der Geschichtsdarstellung der Richter- und Königszeit* (Diss. theol.; University of Bonn, 1967).

[100] We may note here a recent article by G. Garbini ("Le fonti citate nel 'Libro dei Re' (a proposito degli 'Atti de Salomone', degli 'Annali dei re di Guida' e degli 'Annali dei re d'Israele')", *Hen* 3 (1981) 26-46), who thinks that the Dtr redactor used a pre-existing annalistic work reaching from David to Hezekiah, and published during the latter's reign, as a major source.

[101] Weippert, "Beurteilungen".

[102] M. Weippert, "Fragen".

[103] W. B. Barrick, "On the 'Removal of the High Places' in 1-2 Kings", *Bib* 55 (1974) 257-259; Mayes, *Story*, 120-124; A. Lemaire, "Vers l'histoire de la rédaction des livres de Rois", *ZAW* 98 (1986) 221-236.

[104] H. R. Macy, *The Sources of the Books of Chronicles: A Reassessment* (Ph.D. thesis; Harvard University, 1975).

[105] Ibid., 115-165, 169-172, 184.

[106] McKenzie, *Use*, 174-176. McKenzie (p. 175, n. 29) in addition cites E. W. Nicholson, *Deuteronomy and Tradition* (Oxford, 1967), as holding the view that the DH had an earlier, pre-Josianic form. In fact, however, Nicholson clearly did not hold to this view (cf. his pp. 113-114, for example).

McKenzie[106] and developed by Halpern[107]. Both of these scholars tentatively suggest that the earliest DH ended with Hezekiah. This full-blown theory of a DH which pre-dates Josiah's reign is also hinted at by Wilson and Heider[108], and one detailed version of what it might have looked like has been provided by Peckham[109].

A quote from Heider will make clear the question which arises from all this new research. Writing of the possibility of an edition of the DH which ended with Hezekiah, he notes:

> If this was the case, Cross's "two grand themes" in his Dtr^1 may fit the "Hezekiah redaction" as well ...[110]

In view of the discussion above, we may go further than this and suggest the possibility that they may well fit such a redaction even better than they fit a Josianic one. This remains to be seen. At any rate, it must be said that Cross's view of Kings, although it is more satisfactory than that of Hoffman or that of the Göttingen scholars, cannot be assumed as the starting point for further study of the DH as a whole. In consequence, the more recent work on the DH which is based on it also requires re-evaluation.

It thus appears that any study of the DH in the context of the present debate cannot take very much for granted. Each of the major positions maintained in that debate seems to have serious weaknesses, and to be unable to provide a completely safe platform upon which to build further research. Critical analysis of the current debate has, however, at least made clear the important position of the books of Kings in the discussion, and has suggested that a more accurate analysis of these books would be useful as a starting point for a re-examination of the whole question. This monograph will attempt to make a contribution in this area. It takes its lead from recent discussion of the books which has recognized the

---

[107] B. Halpern, "Sacred History and Ideology: Chronicles' Thematic Structure - Indications of an Earlier Source", in R. E. Friedman (ed.), *The Creation of Sacred Literature: Composition and Redaction of the Biblical Text* (UCNES 22; Berkeley, 1981) 35-54.

[108] R. R. Wilson, *Prophecy and Society in Ancient Israel* (Philadelphia, 1980) 157; G. C. Heider, *The Cult of Molek: A Reassessment* (JSOTSup 43; Sheffield, 1985) 286-288. We may also note that both T. E. Fretheim (*Deuteronomic History* (IBT; Nashville, 1983) 18) and Weinfeld ("Emergence", 93 n. 57) are prepared to allow that the Dtr school began their work in Hezekiah's reign.

[109] B. Peckham, *The Composition of the Deuteronomistic History* (HSM 35; Atlanta, 1985). This monograph represents a significant shift away from the Cross position which was supported in his earlier "Deuteronomy". It is for this reason that his other work on the double redaction of the DH was not mentioned above, since it is not clear in this whether he still takes the Cross line, or has already moved toward his present position. For the record, he has contributed two other important pieces of work to the debate. In "The Composition of Joshua 3-4", *CBQ* 46 (1984) 413-431, he maintains that a double redaction theory can resolve the well-known problems of Joshua 3-4, and that two editors can be identified throughout the remainder of the book. The second composed the book of Joshua as a commentary on the first's narrative of the conquest (1:1-11:23), and added another part to it as its interpretation (12:1-24:33). A similar approach is employed in his more recent study of 1 Samuel ("The Deuteronomistic History of Saul and David", *ZAW* 97 (1985) 190-209), where to the first editor is ascribed a basic "national epic" dealing with Saul and David. The redactional Dtr layer is a commentary on this, which incorporates the epic into a chronicle of the nation's history by retelling it in such a way as to rationalize the origins of the kingship, and explain the succession from Saul to David.

[110] Heider, *Molek*, 286-287.

importance of their formulaic statements, and particularly of the Dtr "judgement formulae", for any discussion of their redactional development. The review of this work in chap. 2 will prepare the way for the analysis of the judgement formulae which follows in chaps. 3 and 4.

2. THE JUDGEMENT FORMULAE OF THE BOOKS OF KINGS

2.1 Introduction

The judgement formulae of the books of Kings form part of the framework around which the books are constructed. This framework is generally accepted as consisting of the following elements:

A/ Introduction,	comprising	a synchronism
		the age of the king at his accession (Judah only)
		the length of his reign
		his capital city
		the name of the queen mother (Judah only)
B/ Evaluation of the king,	utilizing	the judgement formulae
C/ Conclusion,	comprising	a source citation
		information about the king's death and burial
		a notice about the succession

The individual elements which thus make up the framework, the "regnal formulae", have a general regularity of expression throughout Kings which has traditionally been taken to be good evidence that they derive from one hand[1], and thus that the first edition of Kings ran at least as far as Zedekiah. This point has usually been conceded even by those who, because

---

[1]   The case which the regularity of the formulae makes for the activity of a single author in Kings was recognized as far back as J. G. Eichhorn, *Einleitung in das Alte Testament* (3rd ed.; 3 vols.; Leipzig, 1803), 2:548-579.

of certain other features of the books, have argued for an earlier date. These scholars have simply maintained that the similarity between later and earlier formulae is to be explained in terms of the imitation of an original author by a later editor. The *variations* within the formulae have not, until recently, played much part in their case for a pre-exilic Kings. Where attention has been drawn to these, they have generally been explained on all sides as the result of the incorporation of different sources by the author(s)[2]. Variations within the judgement formulae, which, since these have usually been taken as entirely the work of the author(s) and unrelated to any source, could not be explained in this way, have in the main been ignored.

Four recent studies, however, have examined these latter variations more closely, and have suggested that they are of immense significance for the understanding of the compositional history of Kings.

---

[2]   The sources for the regnal formulae have usually been regarded as either the annals of the kings of Israel and Judah themselves (so B. Maisler, "Ancient Israelite Historiography", *IEJ* 2 (1952) 82-88; and S. R. Bin-Nun, "Formulas from Royal Records of Israel and of Judah", *VT* 18 (1968) 414-432); or some intermediate source which was ultimately derived from them. Thus Wellhausen (*Prolegomena*, 270-291) thought that the redactor's source was either a composition based on the "books of the chronicles", or those books themselves, which were in turn based on the annals. Hölscher ("Könige") also found a single source, which he took to be E. J. Begrich (*Die Chronologie der Könige von Israel und Juda und die Quellen des Rahmens der Königsbücher* (BHT 3; Tübingen, 1929)) and Jepsen (*Quellen*, 30-40) thought that a synchronistic history lay behind the present Kings. Noth (*Studien*, 72-87) found the sources to be unofficial adaptations of the history of the kings, diaries based on the official annals.

2.2 H. Weippert's View of the Judgement Formulae

Weippert's article[3] is presented as a response to Jenni's suggestion[4] that the question of the unity of the DH may be helped towards a resolution by the analysis of its style and language. Using such criteria, she attempts to differentiate various schemes within the judgement formulae which may be linked together and attributed to different redactors. Six different schemes may be identified, referred to by Weippert as IS1; IS2; IN; IIS; IIN; and IIIS, where S refers to formulae for Judaean kings and N to those for Israelite kings. IS1 has the following elements:

1/ the phrase עשה הישר בעיני יהוה.

2/ the comparison of the king with his immediate predecessor.

3/ the observation הבמות לא סרו, followed by a statement that the people sacrificed at them, typically expressed by זבח and קטר, both in the Piel, with בבמות.

IS2 has the following elements:

1/ the phrase הלך בדרך with בית אחאב or מלכי ישראל.

2/ the phrase עשה הרע בעיני יהוה.

Definitive for IN are:

1/ the phrase עשה הרע בעיני יהוה.

2/ the use of לא סר with מן referring to חטאות ירבעם בן נבט, more closely defined as אשר־החטיא את־ישראל.

IIS contains, like IS1, the phrase עשה הישר בעיני יהוה but is differentiated from it by an additional reference to David as אב or עבד. The expression הלך with בדרך or אחר can expand this basic structure.

---

3 Weippert, "Beurteilungen".
4 Jenni, "Forschung", 118.

IIN is much more difficult to define, since it is greatly dependent upon IN. Three elements appear in IIN, however, which do not appear in IN:

1/ הלך with בדרך.

2/ the expansion of החטיא and חטא in the Hiphil by חטא (Qal) or עשה (Qal).

3/ the use of the root כעס in nominal or verbal form.

All the formulae from IIN contain one or two of these elements, although none of them contains all three. In addition, there is no speech form in IIN analogous to IN's use of לא סר referring to the sin of Jeroboam.

IIIS comprises the following elements:

1/ the phrase עשה הרע בעיני יהוה.

2/ a comparison with the predecessors of the king, using ככל אשר־עשה and אב.

The three schemes IS1, IS2, and IN are found in the central section of Kings, in formulae for kings from Jehoshaphat to Pekah, while the two schemes IIS and IIN are found for kings both before 1 Kings 22 and between 2 Kings 18 and 23. IIIS covers the reigns of the last four kings of Judah. Weippert's argument is not only that the language and style of the formulae differ from section to section of the books, but also that, whereas the formulae contained in each of the different parts present a coherent ideology when taken together, this is not the case when the different parts are compared to each other. For this reason, the presence of three different redactors is to be supposed. The existence of R^{III}, a redactor working in the exile, for example, is to be deduced from the fact that the perspective of IIIS concerning the past is so different from that of the other formulae. Its wholly negative assessment of all the kings of Judah is in stark contrast to the positive judgements for at least some of the kings in the earlier sections. Likewise, the existence of redactors I and II may be inferred from the ideological differences which are reflected by the different use of language in the sections of Kings covered by IS1/IS2/IN and IIS/IIN respectively. These differences may be summarized as follows:

1/ There is a tendency in the material in the central part of Kings (R^I) to make a sharp distinction between the kings of north and south, the contrasting use of עשה הרע בעיני יהוה and עשה הישר בעיני יהוה drawing attention to their fundamentally different classification. Even in the case of Ahaz (2 Kings 16), רע is not used, but rather the negative לא־עשה הישר. No such distinction exists in R^{II}, who uses רע of four Judaean kings, and even uses ישר in relation to Jeroboam I (1 Kgs 11:38; 14:8).

2/ R^I has a tendency to exonerate the individual kings of both kingdoms from direct blame for their sins. This tendency is seen in the use of the impersonal הבמות לא־סרו followed by a reference to the people (עם), in the case of the southern kings; and by the statement that the northern kings did not turn away (לא סר) from Jeroboam's sin, the emphasis being placed on Jeroboam, and not on the individual king concerned. R^{II}, on the other hand, does not employ לא סר at all when making an accusation, but the more positive הלך בדרך with חטא or עשה. He thus places the blame directly on the king concerned.

3/ R^I's interest with regard to the cult is that of centralization, the abolition of worship at the high places. The use of עשה הישר בעיני יהוה in relation to kings who tolerated the במות suggests that these are to be understood in terms of an illegitimate form of Yahweh-worship. The disappearance of R^I's criteria for the criticism of the cult after the reign of Ahaz, however, together with R^{II}'s use of כעס, suggests that it was the worship of foreign gods, and not cult centralization, which was the focus of R^{II}'s concern.

4/ R^I compares the king under consideration with his immediate predecessor. R^{II}, on the other hand, compares southern kings with David, the ideal predecessor, and while retaining R^I's pattern with regard to northern kings, names the precursor here on only one occasion. This implies a lack of interest in the concrete details of history.

5/ A lack of interest in history on the part of R^{II} is evidenced in two further ways. First of all, the term חטא is no longer associated in R^{II}'s usage exclusively with the sin of Jeroboam. The juxtaposition of דרך and חטא demonstrates that the latter refers to a more indefinite manner of behaviour. Secondly, R^{II} writes his history in "black and white" terms, giving either unqualified praise or unqualified criticism to each king. For R^I, however, the application of the judgement ישר to a king does not mean that there is nothing in his reign which may be criticized. Nor does the use of רע mean that there is nothing positive to be found. R^I thus backs away from sweeping judgements, being interested in an accurate portrayal of history. R^{II} generalizes, being more interested in the reading of the problems of the present, particularly that of the worship of foreign gods, into the past.

On the basis of these similarities, on the one hand, and differences, on the other, between the various judgement formulae, Weippert postulates two redactors. R^I, whose work reached from Jehoshaphat to Hoshea, was a northerner working in Judah under the influence of Hezekiah's reform, and during his reign. His northern origin explains his unwillingness to attack the individual northern kings, while his southern provenance in Hezekiah's reign explains his interest in the cult connected with the במה, and the standard (its eradication) which he uses to assess the Judaean kings. R^{II}, whose work reached from Jeroboam to Josiah and incorporated R^I, began his work during the reign of Josiah, and finished it during that of Jehoahaz. His interest in the worship of foreign gods and its eradication is the child of the Josian reform, which was principally directed against the gods of Assyria.

2.3 Responses to Weippert

Detailed responses to Weippert have come from Barrick[5], who is fundamentally in agreement with her analysis, and Cortese[6], who is not. Barrick is particularly interested in the phrase הבמות לא־סרו עד העם מזבחים ומקטרים בבמות, which in his estimation is correctly attributed by Weippert to the first of three redactors. However, Weippert has not given enough attention to two other verses where הבמות is combined with the verb סור, namely 1 Kgs 15:14 and 2 Kgs 18:4. In the former case we find הבמות לא־סרו alone, without the comment about the people. However, as Barrick says:

> In terms of vocabulary and syntax this phrase cannot easily be disassociated from the more expansive version found in the subsequent regnal accounts[7].

He is therefore inclined to the view that the reign of Asa must have been included in the work of R^I. Further evidence that this is so is the progression which may be detected throughout the material in which this phrase is used. This is indicated by the use before הבמות of ו (1 Kgs 15:14), then אך (1 Kgs 22:44), and finally רק (2 Kgs 12:4; 14:4; 15:4, 35), which represents a conscious attempt by the redactor to portray a steadily worsening situation leading up to Ahaz, who is the first Judaean king of the series to receive a categorically unfavourable evaluation (ולא־עשה הישר בעיני יהוה אלהיו כדוד אביו, 2 Kgs 16:2b). The end of this series is to be found in 2 Kgs 18:4, another verse in which הבמות is combined with סור : הוא הסיר את־הבמות (18:4aα). The personal pronoun here emphasizes that it was Hezekiah who, unlike all his predecessors, put an end to these sanctuaries. Barrick therefore argues that R^I's work extended from Asa to Hezekiah, rather than from Jehoshaphat to Hoshea, a position supported further by 2 Kgs 18:5b, which is unlikely to have been written by the Josianic R^{II}. The presence of R^{II} in 2 Kings 18, and in 1 Kings 15, need not be totally denied, however, since it is quite likely that a later editor incorporating a pre-existing historical work into his composition would have spliced the two together by adding something of his own at strategic points. Barrick therefore wishes to modify Weippert's scheme "IS1" without denying that she is fundamentally correct in her understanding of the redactional layers.

---

[5] Barrick, "Removal".

[6] E. Cortese, "Lo schema deuteronomistico per i re di Guida e d'Israele", *Bib* 56 (1975) 37-52.

[7] Barrick, "Removal", 258.

An even more detailed response to Weippert may be found in Cortese's article. Cortese is mainly interested in her distinction between R^I and R^{II}. This distinction he does not accept, arguing that such variations in the formulae as exist do not support her case, and may be explained satisfactorily on the basis of a single author. Dealing first of all with the supposed differences between IS and IIS, Cortese points out that the expressions עשה הישר בעיני יהוה ,הלך בדרך, and הלך אחר are common to both schemes. In addition, the distinction which Weippert draws between these layers on the basis of the David material cannot be sustained. While it is true that only Asa, Hezekiah and Josiah are compared positively to David, it is equally true that only these three kings attempted reformation. This feature, then, can be explained in terms of the content of the passages concerned. Furthermore, references to David *can* be found in IS, if we include the negative statements in 2 Kgs 14:3 and 16:2, which are similar to the one found in the assessment of Solomon in 1 Kgs 11:33 (Weippert's R^{II}), and the references to the Davidic promise (1 Kgs 15:4; 2 Kgs 8:19). Cortese therefore concludes that the evidence cannot support Weippert's case. Rather,

> ... non si può fare a meno concludere che le formule IIS e IS sono del medesimo autore, il quale traccia un preciso ed ordinato disegno appunto attraverso le variazioni delle formule le quali perciò non si devono assolutamente dividere in gruppi di origine diversa[8].

Turning next to the differences between IN and IIN, Cortese points to Weippert's own admission that IIN is very similar to IN. Indeed, he argues, the differences between two cases of the same formula in IIN are often greater than those between IN and IIN. Certainly no case can be built upon the three features which she identifies as unique to IIN. הלך ב (though not הלך בדרך) *is* found in IN (2 Kgs 13:11), while the amplifications of the references to Jeroboam's sin, as well as the verses where כעס is used, occur mainly outside the scheme altogether. In fact, the use of לא סר and הלך בדרך actually allow us to draw a homogeneous picture of the northern kings, indicating unity of composition. Only Omri, Ahab and Ahaziah, three kings who involved themselves with foreigners and who made the idolatry of Israel much worse, properly "vex" (כעס) Yahweh. After these three, there are the partial reformations of Joram and Jehu, which restore the situation to what it was before Omri. It is only from the reign of Jehoahaz onwards that לא סר is used alone (2 Kgs 13:2), indicating, Cortese argues, that the kings after Jehu did nothing particularly sinful, nor anything particularly good. They simply accepted passively the situation created by the sin of Jeroboam. The use of הלך ב up until Jehoahaz (with the exceptions of Joram and Jehu) should conversely be taken to indicate a greater obstinacy in sin than does לא סר. The difference in vocabulary, then, rather than being evidence of different redactors, is

---

8   Cortese, "Schema", 45.

sufficiently explained as a device of the author which is intended to draw attention to different phases within the history of the northern kingdom.

Cortese therefore accepts one author for the bulk of the books of Kings, accepting Weippert's arguments for the identity of IIS and IIN, but rejecting those for a distinction between R^I and R^{II}. He leaves open the question of the existence of another redactor, responsible for the formulae for the last four kings of Judah, while appearing to favour such an idea.

2.4 R. Nelson's View of the Judgement Formulae

The second major piece of work on the judgement formulae which must be considered here is that of Nelson[9]. He also rejects Weippert's thesis as to the distinction between R^I and R^{II}, but supports her separation of the last four kings from the rest. Nelson argues that the regnal formulae up until the reign of Jehoahaz of Judah display

... a fascinating diversity within an overall unity of expression[10].

By far the majority of variations within them can be seen to be quite random, and are best explained by positing a single author who, while dependent upon sources which themselves sometimes changed, wrote his own prose freely. The variations in the judgement formulae, too, are best seen as the work of such an author, although Nelson accepts that in their case a purpose can on occasion be perceived. In the judgements on the Israelite kings, for example, Nelson sees an intention to create the impression of the growing weight of constantly repeated sin. This is achieved through the rigidification of the formulae into a more static pattern towards the end of the history of the north (2 Kgs 13:11; 14:24; 15:9, 18, 24, 28). The repetition, particularly in 2 Kings 15, expresses the stubbornness of the disobedience. In general, however, Nelson's view is that most of the material is freely composed to no particular pattern.

The account of the last four kings of Judah is quite different, however. Whereas in the earlier formulae no two verdicts are alike, and on every occasion there is supplementary information, the formulae for the last four kings are all virtually the same, are shorter than their predecessors, and are not supplemented by any additional information. Another difference may be found in the vague use of אבתיו in 2 Kgs 23:32, 37, which does not occur in the earlier formulae, and which is extremely inappropriate in view of the fact that about half of the ancestors referred to "did what was right". These different features in the formulae, and the rigidity with which the last form is used, lead Nelson to the supposition that a second author is at work at the end of Kings. This author, influenced by the last negative judgement available to him (2 Kgs 21:20), had the idea firmly fixed in his mind that a king's father should be cited as a forerunner in his sin, and rigidly adhered to this

---

9   Nelson, *Redaction*, chap. 2 (pp. 29-42).
10   Ibid., 32.

principle, in spite of its inappropriateness in the case of Josiah's sons, Jehoahaz and Jehoiakim. Indeed, it was his unwillingness to attribute blame to Josiah himself which led to the use of אמה in their case, thus generalizing the condemnation. The author of this material may thus be seen to be but an imitator of the original author, and to lack his creative flair. This confirms the older view of the double redaction of Kings, where such imitation was suspected but never proved. A further feature of the last few chapters of Kings which is consistent with the conclusion which Nelson draws from the style of the formulae is their view of the עמהארץ. On no occasion except 2 Kgs 23:31-32 does a king who has been enthroned by this group (23:30), or had positive dealings with them, receive a negative judgement. Nelson takes this to signify that a second author, for whom the political opinions of the עמהארץ were unimportant in his assessment of the king, is at work in 23:31-32.

2.5 A. F. Campbell's View of the Judgement Formulae

Campbell's view of the judgement formulae[11] is deeply influenced by that of Weippert, while diverging from it at significant points. Broadly speaking, it may be said that while he basically accepts Weippert's distinction between IN and IIN, and between both of these and IS, he rejects the division of IS1 from IS2, and of IS from IIS, and is little interested in IIIS. His view of the redactional development of Kings in general is also quite different. For Campbell, the foundational text lying behind Samuel-Kings is a "Prophetic Record" which extends from 1 Samuel 1 to 2 Kings 10. This work was written in the northern kingdom in the 9th century B.C., and dealt with the history of the monarchy from its inauguration to the reign of Jehu. It ended in 2 Kgs 10:28 with the notice that Jehu eradicated Baal-worship in Israel, and it contained no judgement formulae. These were first found in a pre-Dtr northern expansion of the document, which brought the history down to 722 B.C., and is to be dated in the decades after the fall of Samaria in that year. The formulae occurring here are constructed according to what Campbell calls "pattern A", which is virtually equivalent to Weippert's IN (excluding Joram, but including Hoshea), and whose principal component elements are four:

1/ He did what was evil in the sight of Yahweh

2/ Which he made Israel to sin

3/ The sins of X

4/ He did not depart from

Pattern A combines all four elements with a regularity not shared by any other pattern. It is to be distinguished from pattern B, which is found for the Judaean kings from Rehoboam to Hezekiah, and has five principal component elements:

1/ He did what was evil/right in the sight of Yahweh

---

[11] A. F. Campbell, *Of Prophets and Kings: A Late Ninth-Century Document (1 Samuel 1-2 Kings 10)* (CBQMS 17; Washington, 1986) 139-202.

2/ Comparison -   type a: with X his father, with David his father

type b: with others (= the house of Ahab)

3/ He walked in the way of X

4/ He walked in the sins of X

5/ The high places were not taken away, the people sacrificed and burnt incense

Pattern B thus represents Weippert's IS, with the addition of the formulae for Rehoboam, Abijam, Asa and Hezekiah. Unlike Weippert, however, Campbell takes the differences between northern and southern formulae as evidence that they derive from different hands. He notes in particular the lack of interest of the "A" formulae in the במות, and the difference in perspective between "A" and "B" formulae with regard to "the kings of Israel"[12]. He believes that pattern B is to be explained in terms of a pre-Dtr southern document, influenced by the Prophetic Record and its northern expansion, but independent of them. It was composed later than Hezekiah's reform, possibly as a subtle counter-attack against the policies of Manasseh, and it probably ended with one or other of the Isaiah legends.

Finally, pattern C (representing Weippert's IIN, with modifications) is to be distinguished from both A and B. It covers the northern kings from Jeroboam to Joram, and has eight principal component elements:

1/ He did what was evil in the sight of Yahweh

2/ Which he made Israel to sin

3/ Comparison -   type a: with his father (and mother)

type c: degree (i.e. more than X)

4/ The sins of X

5/ He walked in the way of X

---

[12]   Campbell, *Prophets*, 178. He argues that since pattern A begins with Jehu, and it accuses none of the kings of Israel who follow him of reverting to Baalism, the generalized reference to "the way of the kings of Israel" in 2 Kgs 16:3 (pattern B) could hardly have been written by the author of A. A and B must therefore derive from different hands.

6/ He walked in the sins of X

7/ Which he sinned/and in his sin

8/ Provoking Yahweh (God of Israel) to anger

C is different from A in that the idea of "not departing from" is replaced by that of "walking in the way of" where the sin of Jeroboam is concerned. In addition, the blame is placed solely on Jeroboam in A, while in C it has become stereotyped enough to be applied to Baasha and Elah as well. C also has two characteristics not shared by A, namely the emphasis on the sinfulness involved, which is expressed by "which he sinned/and in his sin"; and the phrase "provoking Yahweh to anger". Furthermore, the second type of comparative statement found in C (cf. 3c) is not reflected in A. So far as B's relationship to C is concerned, Campbell notes the simplicity of B over against the complexity of C; the fact that four elements of C do not appear in B (3c, 4, 7, 8 above); and various differences in emphasis between B and C. The formulae constructed according to pattern C, he concludes, are from the hand of Dtr, and were introduced to the Prophetic Record when Dtr first combined this with the northern and southern documents and edited the whole so as to bring the history down to Josiah's reign.

For Campbell, then, analysis of the judgement formulae leads to a very different view of the composition of the books of Kings to that which is normally taken. The formulae derive from two different pre-Dtr sources as well as from the Dtr redactor.

2.6 A. Lemaire's View of the Judgement Formulae

Lemaire's view of the judgement formulae[13] is, like Campbell's, influenced by that of Weippert. He accepts the existence of her R^{III} without much discussion, and modifies R^{I} only by extending the redactor's contribution, with Barrick, to include Hezekiah. His real interest is in R^{II}. Here Lemaire suggests that there are two editors at work rather than Weippert's one. The contribution of the later of the two is to be found in the formulae from Manasseh to Josiah. A characteristic feature here is the reference to "all the host of heaven" (כל־צבא השמים: 2 Kgs 21:3, 5; 23;4, 5), a cult which is never mentioned in relation to Judaean kings before Manasseh. The redactor who is responsible for this part of Kings worked during Josiah's reign. The contribution of an earlier editor is to be found in the formulae for the Judaean kings from Rehoboam to Jehoshaphat, and the Israelite kings from Nadab to Ahaziah. The Judaean formulae have in common a reference to cult-prostitutes (1 Kgs 14:24; 15:3 (implied), 12; 22:47), which are never mentioned again except in 2 Kgs 23:7. Of the northern kings it is said: וילך/ללכת ב(כל־)דרך ירבעם (בן־נבט) ובחטאתו אשר החטיא/עשה להחטיא את־ישראל (1 Kgs 15:26 (implied), 34 (cf. 16:2); 16:19, 26; 22:53), and the phrase בדרך ירבעם is never found again in Kings. The reference in 1 Kgs 13:33 to Jeroboam's "evil way" confirms that this series begins with Jeroboam. Thus, argues Lemaire, we have to reckon with a redaction of the books of Kings around 850 B.C. which first combined the history of the two kingdoms in a single volume. The middle of the ninth century B.C. provides a plausible setting for such a venture, since it was a time of reconciliation and political alliance between Israel and Judah. This edition of Kings, like the earlier editions of the history of David and Solomon and the later revisions of the whole history under Hezekiah, Josiah and the exiled Jehoiachin, is to be understood as the work of scribes at the Judaean royal court, who produced it as propaganda for the various religious reforms and political enterprises undertaken by the king whom they served.

The extent to which this position on the judgement formulae, and indeed the positions of Weippert, Nelson and Campbell, can satisfactorily be maintained, will be the subject of the final section of this chapter.

---

[13] Lemaire, "Rédaction".

2.7 Critique

None of the recent work on the judgement formulae can be said to be entirely convincing, although all of it identifies some features of the formulae which require explanation. Nelson's point about the use of אבחיו in 2 Kgs 23:32, 37, for example, is certainly a strong one[14]. It is indeed strange that these formulae seem to regard the kings of Judah as a group as having "done what was evil", when more than half of them are described in the text as having "done what was right". It may well be the case, then, that 23:32, 37 do derive from a different hand to most of the judgement formulae. This does not prove, however, that the redactional break in the text occurs after the account of Josiah's reign. A negative judgement on the kings in general is not inconsistent with a positive one on a particular king. There is no reason to suppose, then, that a single author could not have written both 2 Kgs 23:25 and 23:32, 37. Nor is it at all clear that such a redactional break is indicated by the language and style of the judgement formulae in general. Close examination of Nelson's case demonstrates, on the contrary, that the prior acceptance of a Josianic date for Kings is essential if it is to have any plausibility. His argument, it will be recalled, is that the formulae for the last four kings of Judah are different from those which precede them. These formulae run as follows:

2 Kgs 23:32   ויעש הרע בעיני יהוה ככל אשר־עשו אבחיו

2 Kgs 23:37   ויעש הרע בעיני יהוה ככל אשר־עשו אבחיו

2 Kgs 24:9   ויעש הרע בעיני יהוה ככל אשר־עשה אביו

2 Kgs 24:19   ויעש הרע בעיני יהוה ככל אשר־עשה יהויקים

What we find here, according to Nelson (p. 38), is a

> ... rigid, rubber-stamp adherence to formula that is unlike anything our earlier studies would
> have led us to expect ... The most likely explanation for this stylistic shift is that we have here
> the woodenly imitative work of some supplementary editor ...

---

[14] The same cannot be said of his point about the עם־הארץ. It does not follow that because two kings who were elevated by this group receive favourable judgements (Jehoash, 2 Kgs 11:18-19; 12:3; and Josiah, 2 Kgs 21:24; 22:2), the negative judgement on Jehoahaz implies that a different author wrote his formulae. This is to assume a link between means of accession and judgement which cannot be demonstrated.

The problem, however, with this argument, which Nelson himself sees (p. 33), is that rigidification of formulae is to be found elsewhere in Kings:

> While these verdict formulae for Israel's kings are highly varied at first, near the end of Israel's history, they rigidify into a more static pattern (2 Kgs 13:10; 14:24; 15:8,18,24,28).

The last four of the formulae mentioned here are reproduced below so that they may be compared with the four above:

2 Kgs 15:9   ויעש הרע בעיני יהוה כאשר עשו אבתיו לא סר מחטאות ירבעם בן־נבט אשר החטיא את־ישראל

2 Kgs 15:18   ויעש הרע בעיני יהוה לא סר מעל חטאות ירבעם בן־נבט אשר־החטיא את־ישראל כל־ימיו

2 Kgs 15:24   ויעש הרע בעיני יהוה לא סר מחטאות ירבעם בן־נבט אשר החטיא את־ישראל

2 Kgs 15:28   ויעש הרע בעיני יהוה לא סר מן־חטאות ירבעם בן־נבט אשר החטיא את־ישראל

The point of interest here is how Nelson differentiates these two series, having accepted that both show evidence of rigidification when compared to earlier formulae of their type. Essentially he does this partly by denying that the northern series is in fact as rigid as the southern one after all; and partly by explaining the rigidity of the northern series on different grounds to that of the southern. Thus even the more rigid formulae for the northern kings are "... nowhere nearly as frozen as the last four for Judah", while "... the minor differences that do occur in these last four were actually forced upon the exilic editor ..." (p. 38). In the case of the northern formulae, "... hammering repetition expresses the stubbornness of the disobedience ..." (p. 33), but in the case of the southern formulae, repetition is just wooden imitation, and evidence of the hand of a second editor (p. 38).

The extent to which Nelson's presupposition about the nature of Kings dictates his handling of the evidence is plain to see. Why is it that variations in the northern formulae are to be understood as due to the creativity of the author, while variations in the southern ones are to be understood as forced on him? On what grounds can the decision be made that repetition in the northern formulae is an authorial device, while the same in the southern formulae is the result of wooden imitation? In reality there are no good grounds for making such distinctions. Both series *could* have been written by the same author, and the explanations given for the northern formulae can equally apply to the southern. A comparison of the two series alone could not possibly yield the conclusion at which he arrives. Rather, it is only his presupposition that different authors are responsible which leads him to adopt different explanations for each. Since the present study does not assume the existence of a Josianic edition of Kings, however, Nelson's work on the judgement formulae cannot provide it with any foundation.

Weippert's analysis of the formulae also raises some interesting questions. In particular, her suggestion that some of the formulae are interested only in the centralization of Yahweh-worship, while others are more concerned with the worship of foreign gods, is a provocative one, and one which echoes the sentiments of some earlier scholars concerning the במה theme in Kings[15]. If such a difference in perspective does exist, it certainly requires explanation. Her own analysis of the formulae in general, however, is flawed in a way similar to that of Nelson. On the one hand, the separation of R^{III} from R^{II} is made entirely on the basis of the use of אבות in 2 Kgs 23:32, 37, the style of the redactors apart from this usage being acknowledged as very similar. In the case of the distinction between R^{I} and R^{II}, on the other hand, a presupposition appears to be at work which dictates her interpretation of the evidence, and without which her conclusions could not stand. The two main pillars of her position, given that, as Weippert admits and Cortese has convincingly argued, IN and IIN can scarcely be distinguished at all, are the presence of references to the במה in IS1 but not in IIS, and to David in IIS, but not in IS1. The evaluation of this part of Weippert's case requires the reproduction here of a selection of the formulae for the kings of Judah as described by her on pp. 304-305. All the references except 2 Kgs 16:2b-4 are given in full, 16:3b being omitted for reasons of space:

---

[15]   So, for example, Driver (*Introduction*, 199-200) and the other scholars whose views are discussed in 3.1 below.

Rehoboam   (1 Kgs 14:22): ויעש יהודה הרע בעיני יהוה ויקנאו אתו מכל אשר עשו אבתם בחטאתם אשר
חטאו

Abijam   (1 Kgs 15:3): וילך בכל־חטאות אביו אשר־עשה לפניו ולא־היה לבבו שלם עם־יהוה אלהיו כלבב
דוד אביו

Asa   (1 Kgs 15:11): ויעש אסא הישר בעיני יהוה כדוד אביו

Jehoshaphat (1 Kgs 22:43-44): וילך בכל־דרך אסא אביו לא־סר ממנו לעשות הישר בעיני יהוה אך הבמות
לא־סרו עוד העם מזבחים ומקטרים בבמות

Jehoram   (2 Kgs 8:18): וילך בדרך מלכי ישראל כאשר עשו בית אחאב כי בת־אחאב היתה־לו לאשה ויעש
הרע בעיני יהוה

Azariah   (2 Kgs 15:3-4): ויעש הישר בעיני יהוה ככל אשר־עשה אמציהו אביו רק הבמות לא־סרו עוד
העם מזבחים ומקטרים בבמות

Jotham   (2 Kgs 15:34-35a): ויעש הישר בעיני יהוה ככל אשר־עשה עזיהו אביו עשה רק הבמות לא סרו
עוד העם מזבחים ומקטרים בבמות

Ahaz   (2 Kgs 16:2b-4): ... ולא־עשה הישר בעיני יהוה אלהיו כדוד אביו וילך בדרך מלכי ישראל
ויזבח ויקטר בבמות ועל הגבעות ותחת כל־עץ רענן

Josiah   (2 Kgs 22:2): ויעש הישר בעיני יהוה וילך בכל־דרך דוד אביו ולא־סר ימין ושמאול

Weippert attributes the first three formulae, from Rehoboam to Asa, to IIS; the next five, from Jehoshaphat to Ahaz, to IS1; and the last (Josiah) to IIS again.

It should be noted first of all how selective Weippert is in her choice of the verses from each reign which are to be discussed. For some reigns she includes everything which is said about the cult, for others only certain statements. How little justification there is for this procedure can be seen if we note here 1 Kgs 15:14: והבמות לא־סרו רק לבב־אסא היה שלם עם־יהוה כל־ימיו. This verse is omitted completely from the tables of formulae provided by Weippert, and from the discussion in the main text of the article, although having clear affinities with both 1 Kgs 15:3 and 22:44. Such an omission must lead to a distortion of the evidence, and there are others like it.

Even on the evidence as presented in the article and contained above, however, it is, secondly, almost impossible to see how the analysis of the language and style of these verses could lead Weippert to her conclusion about the redactional blocks. The formulae for Azariah (2 Kgs 15:3-4) and Jotham (2 Kgs 15:34-35a) are certainly quite similar, and are similar also to two not quoted here, those for Jehoash (2 Kgs 12:3-4) and Amaziah (2 Kgs 14:3-4). The formulae for Jehoshaphat (1 Kgs 22:43-44), however, are really only similar to these in their second part. The structure of their first part is much more like the comment for Josiah (2 Kgs 22:2), which is assigned to R^{II}. The formulae for Ahaz, moreover, are quite dissimilar to 2 Kgs 15:3-4, 34-35a throughout. Yet all the formulae from Jehoshaphat to Ahaz are attributed to one redactor. If we now include 1 Kgs 15:14 in the discussion, we see immediately that the formulae for Asa are much closer to those for Azariah (2 Kgs 15:3-4) than are those for Ahaz, although attributed to a different redactor by Weippert. At the same time, they are quite dissimilar to those for Rehoboam, which are attributed to the same redactor.

On this last point, it must be said that Weippert is quite well aware of the problems which Asa and Ahaz cause for her hypothesis. It is the manner in which she deals with these problems, in fact, which gives greatest cause for concern. In the case of Ahaz, the complication is to be found in the reference to David, a feature supposedly of R^{II}, in 2 Kgs 16:2b. The first reference in her article to כדוד אביו in this verse is to be found on p. 314. Here it is stated that the phrase is to be denied to R^{I} on grounds which are to be discussed later. A footnote refers us to p. 331. On p. 331 we find a discussion of 2 Kgs 16:2b-4, which are said to contain elements of both R^{I} and R^{II}. The only mention of 16:2b, however, is the following:

> Den Eingriff des Redaktors II verrät auch die Bezugnahme auf David in Vers 2: כדוד ... לא אביו.

No reason is given for this assessment of the phrase in 16:2b, either on this page or anywhere else in the article. All that we have, then, is first of all a denial that the phrase is to be attributed to R^{I}, on grounds which are to be discussed later; and secondly, the attribution of the phrase to R^{II} on grounds which are unspecified. What we conspicuously lack are the grounds themselves.

A similar state of affairs exists with regard to the reference to the במה in 1 Kgs 15:14, which is only mentioned once, in a footnote on p. 318:

> Eventuell ist bei der Kommentierung Asas in 1 Kön 15,11 eine ursprüngliche Beurteilung nach dem Schema IS1 verdrängt. Vers 14 mit והבמה לא סרו wäre in diesem Fall als Bestandteil des Schemas IS1 zu beurteilen. Derartige Überlegungen kommen aber über einen geringen Wahrscheinlichkeitsgrad nicht hinaus.

Here again, assertion stands in place of argument, and no grounds are given for the decision taken about the significance of the linguistic and stylistic data. What is it that makes it so improbable that R^I is present in 1 Kgs 15:14? It is not the language or the style of the verse. This is similar to others attributed to R^I, as Weippert herself accepts. What we see in her treatment of both 1 Kgs 15:14 and 2 Kgs 16:2b, in fact, is that a presupposition that her overall case is correct actually dictates the position to be adopted on these verses. Since the overall case is based entirely on the language and style of the formulae in the first place, however, such an approach is circular. The fact is that it seems impossible to separate the David and במה elements of the judgement formulae as Weippert attempts to do, attributing each element to different authors. The במה theme noted by her, as Barrick has shown, reaches back at least as far as Asa's reign, and extends at least as far as Hezekiah's reign. The use of David as a comparative figure, while it does not occur for most of the intervening kings, is found at both ends of this block (1 Kgs 15:11; 2 Kgs 16:2; 18:3). There is absolutely no indication that this element was introduced secondarily to a text containing the במה element, nor that the במה element was introduced secondarily to a text containing the David element[16]. The most natural conclusion to be drawn from this is that the block of formulae from Asa to Hezekiah is from one author. Campbell is therefore surely correct to ignore Weippert's distinction between IS and IIS in his own study, and to regard all the formulae as basically from one hand, though attracting some additions at a later stage in their redaction. Given the similar weaknesses in Weippert's case for a distinction between IN and IIN; the fact that the validity of her comments on the differing ideologies of the formulae depends for the most part on the acceptance of the linguistic and stylistic distinctions; and the general implausibility of the idea that an edition of Kings could ever have begun with Jehoshaphat[17], it must be said that her case is not convincing.

Campbell's explanation of the variations within the judgement formulae has the merit of removing some of the difficulties associated with Weippert's thesis. His inclusion in pattern B of IS and some of IIS is welcome, while the existence of a "Prophetic Record" such as he describes would help to explain why the earliest formulae in both his hypothesis and Weippert's should commence in the middle of the books of Kings rather than at their beginning. Nevertheless, Campbell's case depends to a large extent on a distinction within the northern formulae (patterns A and C) which is virtually identical to that between IN and IIN in Weippert's thesis. Study of his A and C does not encourage one to dissent from Cortese's assessment that these formulae are best understood as the work of one author. Of

---

[16] McKenzie (*Use*, 104) regards the במה statements as secondary on the highly dubious ground that Chronicles frequently lacks parallel statements. For a critique of the McKenzie's whole approach to Chronicles, see the review by H. G. M. Williamson in *VT* 37 (1987) 107-114.

[17] J. van Seters ("Histories and Historians of the Ancient Near East: The Israelites", *Or* N.S. 50 (1981) 137-185) rightly describes this notion (p. 169, n. 103) as "most curious", particularly since repeated reference back to Jeroboam and his sin is made in the material attributed to the first redactor.

the four principal component elements listed by him for A, all but one are shared by C in significant frequency, while even the fourth ("he did not depart from") is found once in B and once in C. On five other occasions, C has the idiom "he walked in the way of", and on one occasion "he walked in the sins of". There is certainly stylistic variation here, but it is within C as well as between A and C, and whether it is sufficient to separate A and C in terms of authorship is questionable. Nor is the fact that C uses two phrases not found in A sufficient of itself to lead to such a conclusion. What Campbell fails to demonstrate is that the slight variations in language and style which exist are related to differences in ideology such as would imply different authorship. Such minor variations by themselves, when so much of the rest of the material shares common language and style, can easily be understood in terms of a single author, as Nelson and Cortese have argued. There seems little reason on the basis of Campbell's analysis, then, to view the northern formulae as from more than one hand, nor, since his argument here depends upon the distinction between A and C, to abandon the almost universal view that all the judgement formulae are Dtr compositions rather than insertions from a source.

With regard to pattern B, it is interesting to note that Campbell is yet one more scholar who sees the account of Hezekiah's reign as a significant climax within the books of Kings. The case for distinguishing B as a separate document, however, is not at all strong. B's view of the kings of Israel is only inconsistent with that of A if it is insisted that the author of B made a very sharp distinction between Jeroboam's sin and Baal-worship, an assertion for which there is little evidence; while the lack of any mention of the northern במות can be understood as resulting from the differing interests of a single author in relation to the cults of north and south. Here again, there is no convincing evidence in favour of ascribing the patterns to different authors. It is much more likely that A, B and C were part of one document from the beginning, than that B was independent, but influenced by A and closely related to C, as Campbell would have it. There seems little reason, then, to dispute that the bulk of the judgement formulae from Rehoboam to Hezekiah are from one Dtr hand, as the overwhelming majority of scholars have believed.

In view of the detailed critique of Weippert's work given above, little needs to be said about Lemaire's article, which essentially offers a rather minor modification of her position. It is true that his analysis, like Campbell's, explains why Weippert's R^{II} begins in the middle of the books of Kings. The fine distinctions which he draws between the formulae within this group, however - and it is clear that he cannot even demonstrate that all the formulae within his two sub-groups share the same features - cannot provide a sure basis for the conclusions at which he arrives, particularly when Weippert's separation of R^I and R^{II} from which he begins is so open to question. The existence of an edition of Kings dating from around 850 B.C. must therefore be regarded as unproven, although Lemaire's general thesis as to the context in which historiographical work of the kind found in Kings was carried out deserves serious consideration.

In summary, then, it must be said that recent discussion of the judgement formulae in Kings has produced no hypothesis which is completely convincing. It has, however, identified several curious features within this material, suggesting that further study of the structure of Kings which is centred here might yet provide us with reliable evidence as to the way in which the books were composed. It is to such further study that chaps. 3 and 4 are devoted. Both chapters begin from the generally accepted premise that the judgement formulae are an intrinsic part of the Dtr Kings[18]. Chap. 3 re-examines the במה theme of the books, relating the various occurrences of במה/במות within the formulae to those elsewhere in Kings, and attempting to build up a coherent picture of the במה throughout the books. Chap. 4 re-examines the David theme, relating the comparative use of David in the formulae to similar occurrences elsewhere, and discussing the closely associated use of David as a promissory figure, which has always been important in redactional studies of Kings. Examination of these two themes will suggest that variations within the judgement formulae do imply that more than one Dtr author is at work, and that those scholars are correct who have argued that the first Dtr edition of Kings was pre-exilic and ended with an account of Hezekiah's reign. Chap. 5 will provide further evidence from the regnal formulae that this is the case, but will argue that this edition of Kings was nevertheless produced, as most scholars who support the hypothesis of a pre-exilic edition have thought, in Josiah's reign. The chapter will also suggest that there is little evidence that it was revised before the exile. Chap. 6 will then briefly address the wider question raised by chap. 1, namely the question of the nature and extent of the first edition of the DH. We begin, then, with a detailed study of the במה theme in the books of Kings.

---

[18] Peckham (*History*) is almost unique, in that he omits the judgement formulae from his first Dtr Kings (see the figures towards the end of the book). As he himself comes close to admitting, however (p. 79 n. 31), his first edition can scarcely be described as Dtr at all.

3. THE במות THEME IN THE BOOKS OF KINGS

3.1 Introduction

The במות referred to in the books of Kings have attracted scholarly interest from two points of view. On the one hand, there has been much discussion of them in the context of the wider debate about the type of structure or place which a במה was historically. This debate is of great interest in itself, but is of little relevance in the context of the present study[1]. On the other hand, there has been some interest in the theological significance attached to the במות, and the precise attitude expressed towards them by the author(s). A review of the commentaries on Kings and of the standard introductions to the OT reveals an interesting diversity of opinion here. All are agreed that the Dtr material on the במות in Kings rejects them as illegitimate. There is no such consensus, however, when it comes to explaining why the author(s) adopted this attitude. A wide divergence of opinion exists as to whether it was because the Temple was regarded as the only legitimate place of worship; because the במות were syncretistic; because they were devoted to the worship of other gods; or for a combination of these reasons. Nor is there agreement as to whether all cults outside Jerusalem are equally forcefully rejected, or whether a distinction is made between northern and southern במות. Thus Montgomery[2], for example, regards the במות as "heathenish shrines" throughout Kings, whether in Judah or Israel, while Gray and Robinson[3] find the practice of fertility rites to be a characteristic of their cult, again in both Israel and Judah. Oesterley and Robinson, Eissfeldt and Fohrer[4] likewise find no distinction between Dtr's treatment of במות in the different kingdoms, and Fichtner[5] thinks that Dtr saw all sacrifice at them as an "*ein Greuel*". Jones[6] also finds the criterion of evaluation to be the same for both kingdoms.

---

[1] For a comprehensive discussion of the issues here, and a bibliography, see P. H. Vaughan, *The Meaning of 'Bāmâ' in the Old Testament: A Study of Etymological, Textual and Archaeological Evidence* (SOTSMS 3; London, 1974); and, more recently, J. T. Whitney, "'Bamoth' in the Old Testament", *TynBul* 30 (1979) 125-147; W. B. Barrick, "What Do We Really Know about 'High Places'?", *SEÅ* 45 (1980) 50-57; and M. D. Fowler, "The Israelite *Bāmâ*: A Question of Interpretation", *ZAW* 94 (1982) 203-213.

[2] J. A. Montgomery and H. S. Gehman, *A Critical and Exegetical Commentary on the Books of Kings* (ICC; Edinburgh, 1951) 103, 268, 468.

[3] Gray, 120, 317; J. Robinson, *The First Book of Kings* (CNEB; London, 1972) 49, 156.

[4] Oesterley and Robinson, *Introduction*, 104-105; Eissfeldt, *Einleitung*, 320; Fohrer, *Einleitung*, 250.

[5] J. Fichtner, *Das erste Buch von den Königen* (BAT 12/1; Stuttgart, 1964) 69-70.

[6] Jones, 29.

Driver[7], on the other hand, explicitly draws a distinction between the worship on the במות described in the case of the six Judaean kings from Asa to Jotham, which is regarded by the author as the worship of Yahweh, and "practices actually heathen", like those which were part of the northern cult. The former is viewed only with disapproval by Dtr, whereas the latter are condemned without qualification. Similarly, Burney[8] finds the disapproval of the במות in the case of the same kings to be principally directed at their location in the provinces rather than in Jerusalem. He contrasts this disapproval, on the one hand, with the condemnation of Rehoboam's worship, which may have been mixed with definite idolatry, and, on the other, with the wholesale reprobation of the calf-worship of Israel. The same distinction between concern for centralized worship and condemnation of idolatry is also found in Bentzen and Hobbs[9]. Benzinger and Pfeiffer[10] take the argument a stage further, maintaining that this difference in perspective is evidence of different Dtr redactions. Benzinger finds in 1 Kgs 3:2-3 a first redactor who viewed Solomon's sacrifice as acceptable because it took place before the building of the Temple, and a second who found it offensive and sought to excuse him from blame. This is related to a more general distinction in Kings between a first redaction which regards the sin of Israel as consisting in the worship at the במות, and a second which regards it as consisting in the worship of Canaanite gods (2 Kgs 17:7-23). For the second redactor, במה worship was associated with the worship of these gods, and was thus offensive even in the case of Solomon. The same general picture is painted by Pfeiffer, who finds the first edition of Kings to be mainly concerned with the worship of Yahweh at the במה instead of at Jerusalem, and only occasionally with the adoption of heathen gods and practices, as in the time of Manasseh. A second edition shares the concern of later Dtr authors at work in Judges, who were preoccupied with the worship of the deities of Canaan instead of Yahweh alone[11].

It is clear even from this selective and brief survey of scholarly opinion that in spite of general agreement that the במות stand at the centre of Dtr concern in Kings, there has been a variety of opinion about the Dtr attitude to them, to the extent that differing perspectives, in some passages at least, have been explained in terms of different Dtr authors. It is somewhat surprising, then, that in the recent debate about the redactional development of Kings, although there has been some discussion of the במה in terms of linguistic patterns, and although Weippert has hinted at a theological difference between redactional layers in terms of במה, no thoroughgoing attempt has been made to address the theological issue. The

---

[7]   Driver, *Introduction*, 199-200.

[8]   C. F. Burney, *Notes on the Hebrew Text of the Books of Kings* (Oxford, 1903) 27-28.

[9]   A. Bentzen, *Introduction to the Old Testament*, 2: *The Books of the Old Testament* (Copenhagen, 1948) 97; Hobbs, 151, 178-179, 193, 232, 251.

[10]   I. Benzinger *Die Bücher der Könige* (KHC 9; Freiburg, 1899) xiii-xv, 14-15; R. H. Pfeiffer, *Introduction to the Old Testament* (revd. ed.; New York, 1948) 377-381.

[11]   Jepsen (*Quellen*, 81) makes the same distinction between his priestly and prophetic editors.

present chapter will attempt a more detailed analysis of the במה theme in Kings, beginning with the block of formulae in the centre of the books (1 Kings 22-2 Kings 15), where the case for common authorship is virtually undisputed, and where the recurrence of a particular kind of statement about the במה makes it legitimate to speak of a "במה theme". Examination of this section of the books will provide us with the foundation for further study.

3.2 The במות in 1 Kings 22-2 Kings 15

במות/במה occurs in Kings in the following places:

	במה	הבמה	במות	הבמות	והבמות	בבמה	במחיו
1 Kgs 3:2	-	-	-	-	-	1	-
1 Kgs 3:3	-	-	-	-	-	1	-
1 Kgs 3:4	-	1	-	-	-	-	-
1 Kgs 11:7	1	-	-	-	-	-	-
1 Kgs 12:31	-	-	1	-	-	-	-
1 Kgs 12:32	-	-	-	1	-	-	-
1 Kgs 13:2	-	-	-	1	-	-	-
1 Kgs 13:32	-	-	-	1	-	-	-
1 Kgs 13:33	-	-	2	-	-	-	-
1 Kgs 14:23	-	-	1	-	-	-	-
1 Kgs 15:14	-	-	-	-	1	-	-
1 Kgs 22:44	-	-	-	1	-	1	-
2 Kgs 12:4	-	-	-	1	-	1	-
2 Kgs 14:4	-	-	-	1	-	1	-
2 Kgs 15:4	-	-	-	1	-	1	-
2 Kgs 15:35	-	-	-	1	-	1	-
2 Kgs 16:4	-	-	-	-	-	1	-
2 Kgs 17:9	-	-	1	-	-	-	-
2 Kgs 17:11	-	-	1	-	-	-	-
2 Kgs 17:29	-	-	-	1	-	-	-
2 Kgs 17:32	-	-	1	1	-	-	-
2 Kgs 18:4	-	-	-	1	-	-	-
2 Kgs 18:22	-	-	-	-	-	-	1
2 Kgs 21:3	-	-	-	1	-	-	-
2 Kgs 23:5	-	-	-	-	-	1	-
2 Kgs 23:8	-	-	1	1	-	-	-
2 Kgs 23:9	-	-	-	1	-	-	-
2 Kgs 23:13	-	-	-	1	-	-	-

2 Kgs 23:15	-	3	-	-	-	-	-
2 Kgs 23:19	-	-	-	1	-	-	-
2 Kgs 23:20	-	-	-	1	-	-	-

Our attention is immediately drawn by such a chart to the group of occurrences in the centre, noted by Weippert, where the same pattern is followed in each verse:

1 Kgs 22:44   אך הבמות לא־סרו עוד העם מזבחים ומקטרים בבמות

2 Kgs 12:4   רק הבמות לא־סרו עוד העם מזבחים ומקטרים בבמות

2 Kgs 14:4   רק הבמות לא־סרו עוד העם מזבחים ומקטרים בבמות

2 Kgs 15:4   רק הבמות לא־סרו עוד העם מזבחים ומקטרים בבמות

2 Kgs 15:35a   רק הבמות לא סרו עוד העם מזבחים ומקטרים בבמות

Each verse is identical in structure and virtually so in language (only the אך of 1 Kgs 22:44 deviating from the pattern)[12], and each acts as a restrictive clause to the basic judgement of the preceding verse, that the king "did what was right" (עשה הישר). Closely associated with these verses by their use of סור with the negative, which provides the backbone of the structure of this entire section of Kings, are the evaluations of the northern kings from Ahaziah to Pekah (1 Kgs 22:53 to 2 Kgs 15:28). Of none of these kings is the phrase עשה הישר used[13], all but Jehu and Shallum being explicitly described as "doing what was evil" (עשה הרע: 1 Kgs 22:53-54; 2 Kgs 3:2-3; 13:2-6, 11; 14:24; 15:9, 18, 24, 28)[14]. The negative

---

[12] Barrick ("Removal", 258) sees in the use of אך and רק, along with ו in 1 Kgs 15:14, evidence of a progression of thought, and cites Deut 28:29, 33 and 1 Kgs 11:12-13 as parallels. It is difficult, however, to see any real progression in the first example, and the difference in usage in the second may simply be dictated by stylistic considerations, the author avoiding a double use of רק. אך and רק seem merely to be synonyms in this context. For a general discussion of רק, see B. Jongeling, "La particule רק", *OTS* 18 (1973) 97-107.

[13] It does, of course, appear in 2 Kgs 10:30 in relation to Jehu. However, the judgement formulae for Jehu, as the repetition in vv 29 and 31 indicates, seem to have been secondarily expanded. Since 10:29a, like all the other northern formulae in this section, uses the full name ירבעם בן־נבט, and since there is no other reference in these to תורה as the standard of behaviour (10:31), it is more than probable that those scholars are correct who regard vv 30-31 as the addition (so Dietrich, *Prophetie*, 34; Jepsen, *Quellen*, appendices; Weippert, "Beurteilungen", 317; and Gray, 562). Such an understanding of the verses is supported by the fact that the fulfilment-notice (2 Kgs 15:12) which relates to v 30 lies outside the framework around which the first edition of Kings is constructed.

[14] Shallum, inexplicably, has no judgement formulae at all, and so does not enter into the discussion. The omission of the phrase from the formulae for Jehu (2 Kgs 10:29a) must be explained in terms of stylistic variation by the author, since the intention of the verse is clearly not to to differentiate Jehu from the remainder of the northern kings in this section. The verse implies that the author regarded him as just as guilty as, for example, Joram (2 Kgs 3:2-3), for whom עשה הרע does appear. Neither king departed from Jeroboam's sin, and both are therefore indicted, in spite of the fact that both took action against Baal-worship.

evaluation is then expanded by the claim that the king participated in Jeroboam's sin(s), which in every case except that of Ahaziah is expressed by לא סר, "he did not depart (from it/them)", and sometimes also by another phrase[15]. In the case of Ahaziah, the reference to participation in Jeroboam's sin is followed by the claim that he also worshipped Baal (1 Kgs 22:54). It may be that it was the desire of the author to focus attention on this which led to the omission of a further reference here, utilizing לא סר, to Jeroboam's sin. Whatever is the case, and given that there are slight variations in the formulae for the Israelite kings, the two basic patterns of this section of the books may be described as follows:

Southern: X did what was right in Yahweh's sight, with the exception that the במות were not removed (לא סרו).

Northern: Y did what was evil in Yahweh's sight, by failing to turn aside from Jeroboam's sin(s) (לא סר).

The judgement formulae for two Judaean kings do not follow the southern pattern. Both Jehoram (2 Kgs 8:18) and Ahaziah (2 Kgs 8:27) are said to have done evil. The negative evaluation is expanded in their case by "he walked in the way of the kings of Israel as the house of Ahab had done" (8:18), and "he walked in the way of the house of Ahab" (8:27). The specific reference to the house of Ahab in both cases suggests that the sin in question is Baal-worship, rather than the imitation of Jeroboam's sin, although no clear distinction seems to exist between these two types of sin in 2 Kgs 8:18, nor is any difference in classification between these kings and the Israelite kings apparent. Their behaviour is רע just the same. No reference to במות exists in the formulae for Jehoram and Ahaziah, emphasizing that the במות statements function as qualifications of the basic judgement ישר, and have nothing to do with the judgement רע.

The judgement formulae for the kings between 1 Kings 22 and 2 Kings 15 taken together, therefore, seem to imply that their author did not consider the toleration of the במות sufficient reason to condemn a king, whereas he did consider participation in Jeroboam's sin(s), and/or Baal-worship, sufficient reason for so doing. There are two possible explanations for this difference in evaluation. Either the author did not think of worship at the במות and walking in Jeroboam's sin(s)/worshipping Baal as equally reprehensible in Yahweh's sight; or he did not hold the Judaean kings who tolerated the במות to be as responsible for what took place there as he did the condemned kings for the sins associated with them. That is to say, the author must have perceived a difference either in the nature of the offences described, or in the degree of responsibility for them on the part of the kings.

---

[15]   So Ahaziah "walked in the way of ... Jeroboam" (הלך בדרך, 1 Kgs 22:53); Joram "clung to the sins of Jeroboam" (דבק בחטאות, 2 Kgs 3:3); and Jehoahaz "followed the sins of Jeroboam" (הלך אחר חטאת, 2 Kgs 13:2).

The latter might be suggested by his use, in the case of the kings pronounced ישר, of במות with לא סרו, followed by a reference to the people. Weippert[16] has argued that this is a device which leaves the question of the implied agent of סור open, moving the blame away from the king and on to the people. The argument is unconvincing, however. The statement about the במות appears, after all, in an assessment of the king, which itself implies that the king is responsible for their existence, and could have removed them had he so wished. Such action is indeed taken by both Hezekiah and Josiah, at least one of whom must be seen as the king towards whom the statements about the במות earlier in the books point. It is, furthermore, a mistake to assume that the use of לא סרו leaves the question of the agent "open" in any sense. A similar use of סור may be found in Isa 6:7; 10:27 and 14:25, where no such intention is evident, the context clearly designating Yahweh as the agent. In the same way, there is no question in Kings as to who the agent is. Finally, there is no other evidence that the author of the judgement formulae makes any distinction between kings and their subjects in terms of their responsibility for sin. In the case of Jeroboam, indeed, the king is thought to be completely responsible for the behaviour of his people, as the frequent reference to the "the sin(s) of Jeroboam son of Nebat *which he caused Israel to sin*" demonstrates. This statement refers back to the account of Jeroboam's religious reforms in 1 Kgs 12:25 ff., a passage which in some form must be regarded as deriving from the same author as the section of Kings under discussion here[17]. In this passage we find a similar juxtaposition of the actions of the king and the actions of the people, with no causal link explicitly made between them. That our author nevertheless held Jeroboam responsible for the sins of the people is quite clear from his use of the formula just mentioned. If the lack of an explicit causal link between king and people in 1 Kings 12 cannot therefore be interpreted as absolving the king from responsibility, but the evidence is that the author of the formulae saw the behaviour of king and people as closely connected, there is little justification for arguing that the same author intended something different in the case of the righteous Judaean kings. It is far more likely that the choice of לא סרו has been made on purely stylistic grounds, so as to neatly parallel the accounts of north and south (לא סרה/לא סר).

We must therefore consider the alternative, that the author perceived some difference in nature between worship at the במות and participation in Jeroboam's sin or worship of Baal which led him to assess differently the kings connected with each. The most obvious grounds for a distinction of this kind have already been described by some of the scholars mentioned in the introduction to the chapter. They argued that the five kings of Judah under discussion were regarded by the author as faithful Yahwists, whose only fault was that they sanctioned

---

16   Weippert, "Beurteilungen", 310-311. Similarly also Noth, 337; and Gray, 349. Weippert, however, sees all the material attributed to the first redactor as refraining from blaming the individual kings, and allows no contrast between north and south.

17   This point seems to have been overlooked both by Weippert and by those who follow her in limiting the original Kings to a central section of the present books alone.

such Yahweh-worship at the provincial sanctuaries. For this reason, these kings were distinguished from other northern and southern monarchs, who were regarded as having sanctioned idolatry. Such an explanation of this section of Kings makes very good sense. It is indeed almost inconceivable that the author could have regarded the five kings as ישר in any sense had he also believed that they tolerated the worship of other gods in their kingdom. It is significant in this context that it is precisely the two Judaean kings in this section who are associated with the house of Ahab, and thus with idolatry, who are described as "doing what was evil" (2 Kgs 8:18, 27), and concerning whom there is no reference to the במה. That the sin of Jeroboam is likewise regarded as idolatry, and not just as uncentralized worship of Yahweh, is suggested in the judgement formulae themselves by the easy way in which the author places side by side references to walking in Jeroboam's sin and references to Baal-worship. Thus Ahaziah (1 Kgs 22:53) "walked in the way of his father and in the way of his mother (cf. 1 Kgs 16:31-32) and in the way of Jeroboam". Joram's assessment (2 Kgs 3:2-3) is not affected by his removal of the pillar of Baal, because he "clung" (דבק) to Jeroboam's sin, the verb being one frequently used in Deuteronomy of the relationship between deity and people[18]. What is implied in the formulae is clearly spelled out in 1 Kgs 12:28-30, where Jeroboam's fundamental sin and its consequences are described[19]. Jeroboam constructs two "gods"[20], which the people worship, thereby falling into sin. A link with the worship of Baal here is of course indicated by the fact that the symbol chosen by Jeroboam to represent his "gods" is the bull[21]. There is thus ample evidence that the condemnation of Jeroboam's sin in

---

[18]   So Deut 4:4; 10:20; 11:22; 13:5; 30:20, all in relation to Yahweh. Further, Josh 22:5; 23:8 and 2 Kgs 18:6, also in relation to Yahweh. The choice of the verb in Joram's case is, within the context, hardly accidental, and must be taken as a reference to the relationship which he had with gods other than Yahweh (cf. 1 Kgs 11:2, where דבק also occurs in relation to other gods).

[19]   A discussion of 12:31-13:34 follows below. The fundamental sin, however, which lies behind the others described - the creation of new sanctuaries, new priests, and a new festival - is clearly the construction of the calves.

[20]   It may well be the case, as most at present accept, that the calves were not understood as gods by "the Jeroboam of history" (although E. Danielus, "The Sins of Jeroboam Ben-Nabat", *JQR* 58 (1967-1968) 95-114, 204-223, thinks that they were). They have been variously explained as pedestals connected with the place of God's presence (so H. T. Obbink, "Jahwebilder", *ZAW* 47 (1929) 264-274); as the heads of standards carried in processions (so O. Eissfeldt, "Lade und Stierbild", *ZAW* 58 (1940-1941) 190-215; J. Debus, *Die Sünde Jerobeams: Studien zur Darstellung Jerobeams und der Geschichte des Nordreichs in der deuteronomistischen Geschichtsschreibung* (FRLANT 93; Göttingen, 1967) 39); and as escorts of the deity used in cultic ritual (so M. Weippert, "Gott und Stier: Bemerkungen zu einer Terrakotte aus *jáfa*", *ZDPV* 77 (1961) 93-117). It may also be the case, as some have argued (for example, E. Nielsen, *Shechem: A Traditio-Historical Investigation* (Copenhagen, 1959), 195-197), that historically no calf was erected at Dan (although this seems unlikely, as B. Halpern, "Levitic Participation in the Reform Cult of Jeroboam I", *JBL* 95 (1976) 31-42, has pointed out (p. 32), in view of passages like Amos 8:14). What seems certain from the juxtaposition of אלהיך, עגלי זהב and the plural verb העלוך in 12:28, however, is that the author of this verse *thought of*, or at least intended to portray the calves as gods, whatever was actually the case (so H. Donner, "Hier sind deine Götter, Israel", in H. Gese, and H. P. Rüger (eds.), *Wort und Geschichte: Festschrift für Karl Elliger zum 70. Geburtstag* (AOAT 18; Neukirchen-Vluyn, 1973) 45-50; H. Motzki, "Ein Beitrag zum Problem des Stierkultes in der Religionsgeschichte Israels", *VT* 25 (1975) 470-485, on pp. 472-477; J. Hahn, *Das "Goldene Kalb": Die Jahwe-Verehrung bei Stierbildern in der Geschichte Israels* (EHS 23/154; Frankfurt-am-Main, 1981) 309-311).

[21]   The bull functioned as a symbol for fertility deities among the Canaanites, and Baal is often represented as a bull copulating with the goddess Anat, who is portrayed as a young heifer (as, for example, at Ras Shamra, cf. *CTA* 10, col. 2:13-29; col. 3:2-11, 20-38: see A. S. Kapelrud, *The Violent Goddess: Anat in the Ras Shamra Texts* (Oslo, 1969) 92-98 for translation and discussion).

the judgement formulae of 1 Kings 22-2 Kings 15 is upon the grounds that he committed idolatry and led Israel to do the same, his sin being closely associated in the author's mind with the worship of Baal. The basic רע/ישר distinction of these formulae, therefore, seems best understood as a distinction between kings who committed idolatry and kings who did not.

We must conclude, then, that the difference in treatment of the kings in the judgement formulae from 1 Kings 22 to 2 Kings 15 is due to the fact that the author understands worship at the במח and Jeroboam's worship/the worship of Baal as fundamentally different. The latter are regarded as idolatry, while the former is, as some scholars have argued, correct in its content but illegitimate in terms of where it is practised. The kings who are true Yahwists are commended, with the qualification that they failed to centralize Yahweh worship: the kings who are not true Yahwists, but are guilty of idolatry, are condemned. No reference to the failure to centralize Yahweh worship occurs in the case of Judaean kings who are condemned, for the obvious reason that such criticism of a non-Yahwist would be meaningless. The extent to which the remainder of Kings shares the ideology described here will be the subject of the remainder of this chapter.

3.3 Asa and the במוה (1 Kings 15:11-15)

Asa has traditionally been seen as a member of the group of Judaean kings which has just been discussed[22], and Barrick has recently reasserted his membership on linguistic grounds over against Weippert[23]. Examination of 2 Kgs 15:11-15 reveals that its perspective is consistent with that of the formulae in 1 Kings 22-2 Kings 15, and indeed that the passage explicitly confirms that the understanding of the במוה accepted there is correct. Asa, too, "did what was right", with the exception that "the במוה were not removed" (1 Kgs 15:11, 15). In his case, however, additional notes make it especially clear what the author means by these two statements. That the first refers to true Yahwism, uncorrupted by idolatry, is demonstrated by 15:12-13, where we are informed that the cult-prostitutes were removed, as well as all the idols, and a cult-object[24] made for Asherah. For the author, "doing what was right in Yahweh's sight" thus refers to the worship of Yahweh in a cult which is free of all cult-objects related to other gods, the king being clearly responsible for ensuring that such worship takes place throughout the land (15:12a). The statement about the במוה is followed by two notices (15:14b-15). First of all, it is reaffirmed that Asa's heart was wholly true (שלם) to Yahweh, the existence of the במוה notwithstanding. The phrase היה לבב שלם עם יהוה occurs in the DH only in 1 Kgs 8:61; 11:4; 15:3 and 15:14. In 1 Kgs 8:61, Solomon urges the people to make sure that their hearts are "wholly true to Yahweh", meaning that they should "walk in his statutes and keep his commandments" (ללכת בחקיו ולשמר מצותיו). Solomon and Abijam are subsequently described as not being wholly true to Yahweh. In Solomon's case, this is specifically related to the worship of other gods (11:4), ולא־היה לבבו שלם עם־יהוה being a parallel statement to נשיו הטו את־לבבו אחרי אלהים אחרים (11:4), and ויעש שלמה הרע בעיני יהוה (11:6)[25]. We may infer that the author intended by his use of the phrase in 15:3 to accuse Abijam of the same fault, since 15:12 includes him among the worshippers of idols. As the negative form of the phrase refers to idolatry, so its positive form here in 15:14 implies freedom from the same. 15:14 thus places worship at the במוה firmly within the camp of true Yahweh-worship, and over against the worship of other gods, and the author, in adding 15:14b to 15:14a, seems to be at pains to ensure that the reader understands that this

---

[22] Thus Driver, *Introduction*, 199, and Burney, 27.

[23] Barrick, "Removal", 257-258.

[24] מפלצת occurs only here and in the parallel 2 Chr 15:16, and its precise nature is unclear. It is connected to the verb פלץ, "to shudder" (Job 9:6). A neutral translation "cult-object" seems best under the circumstances.

[25] 1 Kgs 11:6, however, as is discussed below, may well be a secondary addition.

is so[26]. 15:15 reinforces further the king's piety, by telling us that he himself worshipped in the Temple[27], and that he brought into the Temple the קדשי אביו, which were probably offerings made by his father at other shrines[28].

The perspective of 1 Kgs 15:11-15 is thus exactly the same as that of the judgement formulae already discussed. עשה הישר refers to what the author understands as pure Yahwism, which involves the removal of any idolatry present, while the במות are provincial, but Yahwistic sanctuaries. There is no good reason to doubt, then, that these verses derive from the same author as the later formulae. This being the case, there is a presumption in favour of the view that the formulae for the Israelite kings in 1 Kings 15-16 also derive from this author. The attempts by Weippert and Campbell to dispute this widely accepted position on the basis of linguistic variations have been criticized in chap. 2. Here it may simply be pointed out that the ideology behind the northern formulae in 1 Kings 15-16 is perfectly consistent with that behind the same formulae in 1 Kings 22-2 Kings 15. All the kings receive negative assessments for participating in Jeroboam's sin (1 Kgs 15:26, 34; 16:18-19, 25, 30-31)[29], which is specifically referred to in 16:26 as idolatry, and none are criticized in terms of their failure to remove any במות. Common authorship is therefore most likely. A similar case may be made for the judgement formulae for Abijam (1 Kgs 15:3-5). It may be inferred that here, too, the absence of a positive assessment, which is paralleled by the absence of any reference to במות, is connected with the king's participation in idolatry (ולא־היה לבבו שלם עם־יהוה, 15:3, cf. 15:12). Although there are slight linguistic variations among them, then, the central ideas of the whole section 1 Kings 15-2 Kings 15 remain consistent throughout, to the extent that all the judgement formulae here may confidently be ascribed to a single author.

---

[26] Jones (284) misses the point when he says that the insertion of 15:14a is badly placed, because it breaks the sequence in a judgement otherwise favourable to Asa. It is precisely *because* of the position of 15:14a that the question of the author's view of the במות is posed with such force in these verses.

[27] I follow K, with 2 Chr 15:18 and the Versions, against Q in the interpretation of this verse.

[28] So R. Kittel, *Die Bücher der Könige* (HKAT 1/5; Göttingen, 1900) 125; Montgomery, 275. Jones (284) thinks that this suggestion is "without foundation". קדשים is frequently used in the OT of things consecrated at sacred places, however (BDB, 872), and the mere fact that Asa brought the קדשים of his father into the Temple implies that they had originally been consecrated somewhere else. The author probably has in mind offerings made to Yahweh rather than those made to the גללים of 15:12.

[29] Elah (1 Kgs 16:8-14) has no judgement formulae of his own. The way in which he is condemned along with Baasha (16:13), however, makes clear that the author regarded him as conforming to the same pattern.

3.4 Solomon and the במה (1 Kings 3:2-15, 11:1-8).

Solomon is unique among the kings described in the books of Kings in having two sets of judgement formulae. The first is found near the beginning of the books, in 1 Kgs 3:3[30], and relates to the early part of his life, when he is regarded by the author as having been righteous; while the second appears near the end, in 1 Kgs 11:4-5, 7a, 8[31], and is related to a period of apostasy. Both contain references to במה (3:3, 4; 11:7a, and 11:8 by implication). The references in 11:7a, 8 have little in common with those which have been discussed hitherto. They share none of their linguistic or structural features, and tell us nothing about their author's view of במה in general. They concern only the particular במה built by Solomon for Chemosh and the במה built for his foreign wives, which were clearly idolatrous. 1 Kgs 11:1-8 therefore fits into the pattern described in 3.2 and 3.3 above in its negative aspect, the king being condemned for idolatry, and no general reference to במה being made in that context. 1 Kgs 3:3-15 fits into this same pattern in its positive aspect. The judgement formulae here (3:3) have several points of contact with the formulae for the later, righteous Judaean kings, although the complete pattern of these formulae is not adopted. As in the later examples, the רק clause qualifies the commendation of the king which precedes it, here expressed as ויאהב שלמה את־יהוה ללכת בחקת דוד אביו rather than the more stereotyped עשה הישר, with a general notice that worship at the high places was common. In this instance, however,

---

[30] In spite of its linguistic connection with the later judgement formulae, 1 Kgs 3:2 is unlikely to have formed part of the original edition (contra H. A. Kenik, *Design for Kingship: The Deuteronomistic Narrative Technique in 1 Kings 3:4-15* (SBLDS 69; Chico, California, 1983) 186-187). The רק of 3:2 has no real antecedent, and has rightly been taken by most commentators (Benzinger, 14-15; Kittel, 23-24; Burney, 28; J. Skinner, *Kings* (CenB; Edinburgh, n.d.) 84; B. Stade and F. Schwally, *The Book of Kings* (SBOT 9; Leipzig, 1904) 4; Montgomery, 103; Noth, 45-46; Gray, 120; Würthwein, 28-29; M. Rehm, *Das erste Buch der Könige* (Eichstätt, 1979) 42; Jones, 122; S. J. DeVries, *1 Kings* (WBC 12; Waco, Texas, 1985) 48) as evidence that the verse is a later gloss.

[31] It has long been recognized that 1 Kgs 11:1-8 do not read at all well. The preference here has been for a rearrangement of the material after the pattern of the LXX, which seems to reflect a different verse order (vv 1a, 3a, 1b, 2, 4aα, 4b, 3b, 4aβ, 7, 5a, 8, 6), rather than for a redactional solution. This certainly removes the obvious disorder and duplication of the MT. It is, however, difficult to understand how the MT came to be in such a disordered state if the LXX represents something close to the original Hebrew. On the other hand, it is quite conceivable that the LXX would rearrange the MT precisely because the MT was in such a state, and give it a more logical order (for similar reordering of the MT by the LXX in Solomon's reign, see D. W. Gooding, "Pedantic Timetabling in 3rd Book of Reigns", *VT* 15 (1965) 153-166; idem, "The Septuagint's Version of Solomon's Misconduct", *VT* 15 (1965) 325-335; idem, "Temple Specifications: A Dispute in Logical Arrangement between the MT and the LXX", *VT* 17 (1967) 143-172). It seems better, therefore, to retain the order of the MT, and to understand its present form as the result of redactional activity. 11:6, which breaks into the description of the gods worshipped by Solomon and virtually repeats the general statement of 11:4, is probably best omitted. It may be noted that the phrase לא מלא אחרי יהוה appears nowhere else in the judgement formulae of Kings, and indeed is restricted in the whole of the OT to the Caleb narratives (Num 32:11; and in its positive form, 14:24; 32:12; Deut 1:36; Josh 14:8, 9, 14). 11:7b, which refers to the god of the Ammonites under a different name to that in v 5, and is in a very awkward position syntactically, is probably also an addition (so Benzinger, 78; Stade and Schwally, 14; Noth, 249).

it is the king himself who is described as worshipping at the במה, rather than the people, and there is no occurrence of הבמה לא סרו. Weippert[32] argues that the reference to the king, as well as the fact that the Hiphil of קטר is used, instead of the Piel of the later formulae, is sufficient reason to ascribe 1 Kgs 3:3 to a different author. The case is not compelling, however. The difference in the form of קטר, which reflects no difference in meaning, is quite insignificant in view of the general similarity between this verse and the later formulae; while the focussing of attention on the king can be explained as the result of the fact that the formulae for Solomon introduce a story in which a particular instance of במה worship involving the king alone is described[33]. As with the additional material on Asa and the cult in 1 Kgs 15:11-15, indeed, this story is of great importance to the case being made in the present chapter, since it settles beyond doubt the question of how the author of these במה statements regarded the במה to which he refers. Whereas the formulae in 1 Kgs 3:3 alone, like all the other general references to the במה in connection with righteous Judaean kings, creates only a strong presumption that Yahwistic shrines are in view, on account of the unlikelihood of a verse like 3:3a (... ויאהב שלמה את־יהוה) being followed by a statement suggesting that Solomon worshipped at idolatrous shrines, the story which follows makes the matter quite clear. It is Yahweh who is worshipped at the במה in Gibeon, and Yahweh who appears to Solomon there, promising the righteous king wisdom, riches, honour and a long life. The criticism of 3:3 therefore cannot have had anything to do with the critique of idolatry, but must have been penned with only the idea of the centralization of Yahweh-worship in mind. The understanding adopted above of the general במה references of this type is therefore confirmed as correct.

---

[32]   Weippert, "Beurteilungen", 314-315.

[33]   The absence of הבמה לא סרו may likewise be explained in terms of the particular position of the judgement formulae for Solomon. While it is clear that the author of this verse regarded במה worship at any time as less than ideal, it is also clear that to criticize Solomon for failing to remove them would have made little sense before the construction of the Temple. The author of the gloss in 3:2, then, has correctly interpreted the thought which lies behind 3:3.

3.5 The במה in 2 Kings 17:7-23

Examination of the judgement formulae for Solomon and for the kings of Israel and Judah in 1 Kings 15-2 Kings 15 has revealed that they represent a consistent ideology. A clear distinction is made between Yahwistic and idolatrous worship, with references to worship at the במה in general occurring only within the context of the former. Another view of the במה is also to be found in Kings, however, and requires our attention at this point. It is clearly expressed in 2 Kgs 17:9-11, a passage which Benzinger[34], it will be recalled, assigned to a redactor later than the one responsible for the judgement formulae discussed above. 2 Kgs 17:7-23 have, of course, been much discussed, especially in relation to redactional theories about Kings. Some preliminary discussion is therefore required here, before we can move on to examine the במה references in 17:9-11 in particular.

The fundamental disagreement among scholars with regard to 2 Kgs 17:7-23 is to be found in the question of whether the passage is basically pre-exilic or exilic. As it stands, it is clearly exilic. 17:20 refers to the exile of "all the seed of Israel", implying all twelve tribes[35], and vv 7-19 prepare the ground for this by cataloguing the sins of both Israel and Judah (v 13, 18-19), and comparing these to the sins of the nations whom Yahweh had already driven out of the land (vv 8, 11, 15). This much is agreed by all. The majority of scholars, however, have also found pre-exilic elements in the passage. It has frequently been noted that nothing about vv 21-23 taken alone demands an exilic date; and, further, that vv 19-20 seem to break the connection between v 18 and vv 21-23, implying that they have been inserted secondarily[36]. Moving on from this, some have argued[37] that the original text of 17:7-17 must have concerned only the northern kingdom, ביהודה in 17:13 being a later gloss. There is by no means a consensus on this last point, however, since other scholars have noted that the cataloguing of sins in the manner of vv 7-17 is not characteristic of the author of the framework of Kings, whose constant point of reference so far as Israel is concerned is "the sin of Jeroboam", and that some of the sins in particular (cf. vv 16b, 17a) are

---

[34] Benzinger, xiii-xv

[35] Cf. Gen 46:6, 7; 48:4, and, for exactly the same phrase as in 2 Kgs 17:20, Isa 45:25; Jer 31:37; Ps 22:24, where Judah is always at least included within the scope of the "seed" (contra Montgomery, 470).

[36] Kittel (274-275), Burney (330-331), N. H. Snaith ("The First and Second Books of Kings: Introduction and Exegesis", IB 3:3-338, on pp. 281-282), Gray (649-650) and J. Robinson (The Second Book of Kings (CNEB; Cambridge, 1976) 157) all regard vv 18, 21-23 as pre-exilic. Benzinger (174), Skinner (375-378) and A. Šanda (Die Bücher der Könige (EHAT 9; 2 vols.; Münster, 1911-1912), 2:235) regard only vv 21-23 as pre-exilic. Jepsen (Quellen, appendices) accepts only vv 21, 23b as such. Those who follow Noth, of course, including those of the Göttingen school, find no pre-exilic Dtr composition at all.

[37] Burney, 331; Montgomery, 469.

characteristic of Judah under Manasseh, rather than Israel under her kings (2 Kgs 21:3, 6)[38].
Nelson[39] has argued more generally that the linguistic affinities of 2 Kgs 17:7-17 are not with
the "historian" of the books of Kings, but rather with other passages which have usually been
accepted as from a second hand. He denies that v 18 is necessarily pre-exilic, and considers
that it could just as easily have come from the hand of a later author, referring back to the
situation as it was after 722 B.C. He thus sees all of 17:7-20 as from an exilic author, and
explains the connection between v 18 and vv 21-23 by positing another editor, who attached
vv 21-23 at a later date.

To begin with that which appears most certain about the passage, it seems indisputable
that 17:18 belongs with 17:7aα, as the apodosis of the sentence which begins in that verse[40].
It also seems fairly certain that vv 21-23 were originally connected to v 18 and not to vv 19-
20. The text as it stands makes little sense of the כי of 17:21, which can hardly refer back to
17:20. It fits far more happily with 17:18a, the four verses together giving a theological
explanation of the fall of the northern kingdom:

> Yahweh was very angry with Israel and removed them from his sight. For when he tore
> Israel from the house of David, they made Jeroboam son of Nebat king. Jeroboam drove Israel
> from following Yahweh ...

It is most probably the case, then, that 17:18b-20 are a secondary insertion, and that the
original passage concerned, as one might expect after 17:1-6, only the downfall of Israel. If
so, it also seems likely that 17:7aβ-17 are to be understood as from a later hand. That most
of this material could not have derived from the author of 17:7aα, 18a, 21-23 is suggested in
any case by the great distance which it places between the protasis of the sentence in 17:7aα
and its apodosis in 17:18a[41]. It is also suggested by the relative positions of 17:7aβ-17 and
17:21-23. A single author would hardly have omitted all reference to Jeroboam in the main
part of the passage, where he would fit in most naturally as the one who occasioned the

---

[38] B. Stade, "Miscellen: Anmerkungen zu 2 Kö. 15-21", *ZAW* 6 (1886) 156-189, on pp. 163-167; Benzinger,
174; Gray, 648.

[39] Nelson, *Redaction*, 55-63.

[40] So Skinner, 376; Šanda, 2:220; Montgomery, 468, 478; Snaith, 280; Nelson, *Redaction*, 55. No justification
exists from the syntax for taking ... כי ויהי with the RSV as a retrospective causal clause. The
protasis/apodosis pattern is followed in every other occurrence of this form (Gen 26:8; 27:1; 43:21; 44:24;
Exod 1:21; 13:15; Josh 17:13; Judg 1:28; 6:7-8; 16:16, 25; 2 Sam 6:13; 7:1-2; 19:26; Job 1:5).

[41] The difficulty of 2 Kgs 17:7-18 in this respect has often been felt by scholars. Skinner (376) describes the
long protasis with apodosis as "un-Hebraic", and Snaith (280) as "a very unlikely Hebrew construction".
Both propose an emendation to 17:7 in accordance with LXX[L], which suggests a Hebrew text as follows:
ויהי אף יהוה בישראל כי חטאו. Burney (331) thinks that LXX[L] is "superior", and Gray (645) also emends in line
with it. LXX[L] is virtually unsupported, however, and Montgomery (478) is more likely to be correct when
he maintains that its text is an attempt to smooth out the difficulty, and is not representative of the original
Hebrew. We may in turn object to Montgomery's claim (*op. cit.*, 468) that "... the long period belongs to
the Deuteronomistic rhetoric". The example he quotes is only four verses long, and is hardly comparable to
what we have here. It is much more likely that the form of 2 Kgs 17:7-18 is the result of insertion into an
already existing sentence, than that an author would have composed it from the start in this way.

building of במה in the north (vv 9 ff., cf. 1 Kgs 12:31-32; 13:2, 32-33) and the worship of
idols (vv 12, 16), and have introduced him only at the end, where such a reference provides
a very tame climax to the catalogue of sins listed beforehand. That the passage as a whole
must be an insertion is confirmed, however, if we note that the object of attack throughout
vv 7aβ-17 is "all Israel" rather than just the northern kingdom. This is clear from v 13,
where no textual evidence exists to support the removal of ביהודה as a gloss, and from vv
7aβ-8, which introduce Israel as the people of exodus and conquest, thus implying that the
passage is going to treat all twelve tribes together. The observation made by others that some
of the sins mentioned in vv 7aβ-17 are described elsewhere in Kings only in relation to
Judah is also of relevance here. Thus worship of the צבא השמים (17:16) is ascribed to
Manasseh, and to the priests installed by the kings of Judah generally (2 Kgs 21:3, 5; 23:4-
5); Molech-worship (17:17) to Ahaz, Manasseh and the people of Judah generally (2 Kgs
16:3; 21:6; 23:10); and practising sorcery (נחש : 17:17) to Manasseh alone (2 Kgs 21:6).
None of these sins are mentioned in Kings in relation to the Israelite kings or people. What
we have in 2 Kgs 17:7aβ-17, then, is a catalogue of sins which relate in part to both
kingdoms, as v 13 states. These verses therefore provide the grounds upon which both Israel
and Judah, rather than Israel alone, are condemned, and as such were most probably
introduced by the author of 17:18b-20.

The passage which originally followed 2 Kgs 17:1-6, then, comprised only 17:7aα, 18a
and 21-23:

> Because Israel sinned against Yahweh their god, Yahweh was very angry with Israel, and
> removed them from his sight. For when he tore Israel from the house of David, they made
> Jeroboam son of Nebat king. Jeroboam drove Israel from following Yahweh, and made them
> commit great sin. And the people of Israel walked in all the sins which Jeroboam did. They did
> not depart from them, until Yahweh removed Israel from his sight, as he had spoken by his
> servants the prophets ...

The points of contact between this passage and the judgement formulae discussed above are
clear. Jeroboam's sin is the focus of concern, here as there, and as it is said there of the
kings of Israel from Joram to Pekah that they "did not depart from it" (לא סר), so here the
same is claimed of the people of Israel in general (17:22). It may be assumed, then, that we
have in this passage the conclusion of the northern pattern, the author cleverly bringing his
history of Israel to a close with a play on words in vv 22-23 (הסיר/לא סרו). Equally clear is
the great difference in perspective with regard to the במה between these same judgement
formulae and the later 2 Kgs 17:9-11. Whereas in the formulae the במה were explicitly
disassociated from idolatry, here they are explicitly associated with it. Thus, where the

formulae use ישר of the kings of Judah who tolerated them, 17:9-11 pronounces the verdict רע upon their cult (17:11). Where the idolatrous גללים and מפלצת לאשרה are clearly distinguished from the cult at the במה (1 Kgs 15:12-14) by the author of the formulae, this passage describes במה in conjunction with מצבות and אשרים (17:9-10), and in close association with גללים (17:12). The worship at the במה is characterized as that which the nations did whom Yahweh carried away before Israel (17:11), and described as "provoking Yahweh to anger" (להכעיס את־יהוה). This latter phrase occurs in the formulae, of course, only in relation to the idolatrous northern worship, and never of the cult in Judah[42]. Yet that the Judaean במה are at least included in the condemnation of 17:9-11 is clear not only from the general nature of the passage as an attack against both Judah and Israel, but also and specifically from the use of קטר (17:11). This verb is characteristic of the *Judaean* formulae in 1 Kings 15-2 Kings 15, where it is used of the worship of the people at the במה.[43] No reader could fail to grasp the allusion here, where the people are condemned for exactly the same activity. The use of קטר and כעס together in this way is consistent with the intention of the whole passage, which is to present the history of both kingdoms as equally sinful and without merit. It is hardly consistent, however, with the usage of the author of the formulae, who keeps the verbs quite separate, and maintains a distinction between the righteous Judaean kings and the rest.

A quite different view of במה, then, from that to be found in the Judaean judgement formulae is apparent in 2 Kgs 17:9-11. A later editor, reviewing the history of Israel and Judah from an exilic perspective, understood the two kingdoms to be equally guilty of idolatry, and saw the worship at the במה in Judah as indicative of Judah's participation in this.

---

[42] 1 Kgs 15:30; 16:2, 7, 13, 26, 33; 22:54.
[43] 1 Kgs 22:44; 2 Kgs 12:4; 14:4; 15:4, 35.

3.6 Rehoboam and the במות (1 Kings 14:22-24)

Examination of 2 Kgs 17:7-23 has led to the conclusion that a different editor is
responsible for 17:9-11 than is responsible for the judgement formulae in 1 Kings 15-2 Kings
15. This conclusion is certainly not original, for it has been the common view among
students of Kings. Nevertheless, our digression from the discussion of the formulae has been
essential, since it has shown that in at least one case, a difference in perspective where the
במות are concerned is almost certainly due to a difference in authorship. It is important to
stress this point precisely because its implications have never been consistently carried
through in scholars' thinking about the במות in general. While a distinction in Kings between
an emphasis on centralization and an emphasis on idolatry has often been made in studies of
Kings where dual or multiple authorship is accepted, discussion of this in terms of the
redactional development of the books has been confined to passages like 2 Kgs 17:7-23,
where there is already a wide consensus that there is primary and secondary material. Since,
with the exception of those for the last four kings of Judah, the judgement formulae have
usually been assumed to be from one hand, they have never been thoroughly analysed from
this point of view, even though similar differences in emphasis have been noted within them.
If it is now no longer acceptable simply to assume that one author is responsible for most of
the formulae, then the question arises as to whether variations within these with regard to the
view taken of the במות are also best understood as the result of redactional activity.

Nowhere is this question more in need of an answer than in 1 Kgs 14:22-24. This passage
is designed by its author as a programmatic statement about the cult in Judah, describing the
genesis of what we read about as we progress through the books. Scholars have therefore
very often formed their impression of the במות in the remainder of Kings from the way in
which they are portrayed here. We may note the following as one early example:

> The deuteronomic author and the subsequent editor of Kings apply the name to the
> sanctuaries of Judah outside of Jerusalem, which they unhistorically represent, not as holy places
> older than the temple of Solomon, but as originating in the apostasy of Rehoboam's time (I K.
> 14:22-24 II K. 23:5, cp 8f.) ...[44]

---

[44] T. K. Cheyne, and J. Sutherland Black (eds.), *Encyclopaedia Biblica: A Critical Dictionary of the Literary,
Political and Religious History, the Archaeology, Geography and Natural History of the Bible* (4 vols.;
London, 1899-1903) 2066.

That the במות in 14:22-24 are indeed regarded as idolatrous places of worship is clear from
the judgement רע in 14:22, and from the context in which they are described in 14:23-24.
They are closely associated with Asherim and cult-prostitutes, and the whole cult of which
they form a part is characterized as the תועבת הגוים.[45] We have seen, however, that such an
understanding of במה is suggested neither by the judgement formulae for Solomon, nor by
those for the Judaean kings from Asa to Jotham. 14:22-24 and 15:11-15 may indeed be
usefully contrasted at this point. In the latter, worship at the במות (15:14) is explicitly
dissociated from the Asherah cult and male cult-prostitutes (15:12-13), the author stressing,
in spite of his retention of the במות, Asa's purity of heart. Far from setting the scene for later
discussion of the Judaean במה, then, 14:22-24 actually appear to introduce a note of
disharmony into what is otherwise a perfectly consistent picture of them in 1 Kings 3-2
Kings 15. It is always possible, of course, that the same author has used the general term
במה in two entirely different ways, referring to idolatrous shrines in 14:23 and to Yahwistic
shrines in 15:14. This does not seem very likely, however. The reader's natural assumption,
particularly since the verses are in such close proximity, is, as the history of scholarship itself
illustrates, that the במות referred to in 15:14 are the same shrines as those referred to in
14:23. It seems much more likely, purely on the ground of narrative coherence, that the
difference in perspective between the verses, and between 14:23 and the rest of the
judgement formulae already discussed, is to be explained, as it was in 2 Kgs 17:7aβ-17, in
terms of an addition by a later editor.

The secondary nature of 1 Kgs 14:23, and indeed of most of the material which
immediately surrounds it, is confirmed by closer study of the whole unit 1 Kgs 14:22-24. In
the first place, it may be noted that the judgement formulae of 14:22-24 are unique within
Kings in having anything other than the king as the subject of discussion. In every other
case, as one would expect, an assessment of the king himself, rather than an assessment of
the nation, follows his introductory formulae. What is even more interesting is that both 1
Kgs 15:3 ("he walked in all the sins which his *father* did before him") and 1 Kgs 15:12 ("he
removed all the idols which his *fathers* had made") imply that there was originally such an
evaluation of Rehoboam himself where 1 Kgs 14:22-24 now stand. Furthermore, both 2 Chr
12:14 and the LXX seem to reflect a Hebrew text of Kings which contained רחבעם rather
than יהודה. All of this suggests at the very least, as others have noted[46], that the יהודה of 14:22
is not original to the passage. Either it has replaced an original רחבעם, which the LXX in this

---

[45] Here, as elsewhere in Kings, תועבה denotes Canaanite cultic practices (cf. P. Humbert, "Le substantif *to'ēbā*
et le verbe *t'b* dans l'Ancien Testament", *ZAW* 72 (1960) 217-237). Noth (324) regards its presence in this
verse as the result of a gloss, due to the impossibility of the definite article along with the construct state.
The more usual emendation, however, is simply to remove the article, on the assumption that it has been
added mechanically after כל, where it normally occurs (so GKC, §127g).

[46] Benzinger, 98; Stade and Schwally, 138; Šanda, 1:371; de Vaux, 91; Noth, 323-324; Gray, 341; Würthwein,
181; DeVries, 183.

case reflects[47]; or, as in 2 Chr 12:14, the רחבעם of 14:21 was originally the implied subject of the verb ויעש in 14:22, and both יהודה and Ροβοαμ have come into the text secondarily[48]. The question then arises as to how much, if any, of the remainder of the material in 14:22-24 also reflects an editorial hand. So far as 14:22 is concerned, the reading of some Greek texts has been appealed to as evidence that both the verb ויקנא and the suffix on אבתם were originally singular[49]. If this were so, then there would be no grammatical difficulty in taking all of 14:22b as part of an original statement about Rehoboam. The evidence in the case of the verb is certainly strong. Only LXX[A], the cursives g and u, and the Syro-hexaplar read the plural here, the majority of witnesses supporting the singular. The evidence for the singular suffix is slightly weaker, and here it must be noted that even if the original was אביו, the last part of the verse still could not have derived from the same author as the judgement formulae already discussed. In these, as chap. 4 will demonstrate, David appears as the ideal king (cf. 1 Kgs 15:11). A singular אבהיו in 14:22, however, would require the translation "he did what was evil ... more than his fathers (i.e. David and Solomon, cf. 1 Kgs 15:12) had done". It does not seem likely, then, that the comparison with his fathers was part of the earliest judgement formulae on Rehoboam. 14:23 certainly could not have been, given that the originality of the plural verb here is beyond doubt, and that the verse therefore could not have followed a v 22 with Rehoboam as its subject[50]. 14:24a is doubtless original, being the only element of 14:22-24 to be explicitly presupposed by later judgement formulae (cf. 15:12); while 14:24b, with its plural verb[51], belongs with 14:23. The evidence would appear to suggest, then, that a passage which originally concerned Rehoboam has been heavily overworked, with some original elements (a reference to Rehoboam's construction of idols (15:12), for example) perhaps being omitted, by an editor who introduced יהודה to 14:22a and added 14:22bβ-23, 24b.

The points of contact between 1 Kgs 14:22-24 and 2 Kgs 17:7aβ-17, secondly, also confirm the secondary nature of the former. Both passages, as we have seen, view the במה as idolatrous places of worship, and in both it is the people rather than the king who are under discussion. Both use the term אבות as a general term for the ancestors of the people,

---

[47]   So Gray, 341; DeVries, 183.

[48]   Thus Benzinger, 98; Stade and Schwally, 138; Šanda, 1:371; de Vaux, 91; Noth, 323-324; Würthwein, 181.

[49]   Thus Stade and Schwally, 138; de Vaux, 91; Gray, 341.

[50]   None of the attempts at explaining the plural of v 23 in the context of formulae for Rehoboam are convincing. It hardly seems likely, for example, that the author of the formulae would use a "plural of majesty" here and nowhere else. Nor is Würthwein's claim (182) that the plurals disguise a lack of concrete information about Rehoboam's reign convincing, since it is clear neither why the author should have been so bereft of information in only this case, nor why he would generalize about the king in the plural rather than the singular.

[51]   All Greek witnesses except LXX[L] and three other MSS reflect the plural here.

characterizing them as a group as evil-doers (14:22/17:14)[52]. Other linguistic contacts include the common occurrence of the phrase ויבנו להם במות (14:23/17:9); the mention of מצבות and אשרים in conjunction with במות (14:23/17:10); the location of the cult-places על כל־נבעה נבהה וחחת כל־עץ רענן(14:23/17:10); and the reference to the people behaving like הגוים אשר הוריש יהוה מפני בני ישראל (14:24/17:8). In addition, both passages equate the behaviour of Judah and Israel. The equation is expressed in 14:23 by the phrase גם־המה, which implies that the behaviour of Judah in constructing the במה and worshipping there was exactly the same kind of behaviour as that of Israel (1 Kgs 12:31). Furthermore, if 14:24b is understood as a retrospective reference from an exilic standpoint to the fate which will befall Judah, as in 2 Kgs 17:8, then we also have in each passage the advance intimation that Judah's fate will be the same as Israel's. In every way, then, 1 Kgs 14:22-24 functions as the overture for the reprise of 2 Kgs 17:7-17, and the finale contained in the last few chapters of the books, where the fall of Judah is recorded. Common authorship is thus strongly suggested.

The conclusion drawn on the basis of the view of במות reflected in 1 Kgs 14:23 is confirmed, then, by a closer analysis of 1 Kgs 14:22-24 as a whole. There is good evidence, first of all, that these verses have their present form as the result of secondary editing; and secondly, that the editor involved was the author of the exilic 2 Kgs 17:7aβ-17. The disharmony which 14:23 introduces to the picture of the Judaean במות in 1 Kings 3-2 Kings 15 is therefore best understood as the result of redactional activity in the text, and is not to be explained in terms of the work of a single author.

---

[52] Apart from 1 Kgs 14:22 and 2 Kgs 17:14, אבות occurs in the context of the fathers' sinfulness only in 2 Kgs 21:15 and 22:13. The first of these has been widely regarded as exilic and secondary to the main redaction of Kings (thus, for example, Benzinger, 188; Burney, 352-353; Šanda, 2:325), while the second is argued to be so in chap. 5 below. All regard the history of the people as one of unmitigated sinfulness, eliciting Yahweh's wrath, in sharp contrast to most of the material in Kings relating to David and Judah (cf. chap. 4 below).

3.7 Jeroboam and the במה (1 Kings 12:25-13:34)

Before the discussion of the במה in 1 Kings 3-2 Kings 15 may be drawn to a close, some attention must be given to the few references which appear in connection with Jeroboam. במה occurs six times in the material dealing with Jeroboam's idolatry: once in the expression בית במה (12:31); once in the expression בתי הבמות (13:32); and four times in the expression כהני (ה)במות (12:32; 13:2, 33 (twice)). There has been a wide divergence of opinion concerning the extent to which this material is to be understood as deriving from one hand. 13:2 and 13:32 have been distinguished by some, for example, on the ground that the former does not mention the provincial במה, while the latter does[53]. 12:32b has been regarded by others as a gloss from a hand later than 12:31[54]. Indeed, 12:31 has in general been distinguished from many or all of the remaining במה references in 1 Kings 12-13, both by those who have regarded chap. 13 as a secondary insertion into the Dtr books of Kings[55], and by some of those who have not[56]. Hölscher and Jepsen[57], however, reject this view. 12:30, they argue, is properly resumed in 13:34, while 12:31-13:33 display different interests to the material on either side of them. From 12:31 on, the creation of illegitimate priests and provincial במה appears as the major sin of Jeroboam, whereas the concern elsewhere is only with the construction of the calves. 12:31-13:33 (Hölscher) or 13:34 (Jepsen), therefore, represent an insertion into the original Dtr Kings. A recent article by Lemke[58] has sought to establish in more detail the correctness of the assertion that 12:31 marks the beginning of a redactional unit which extends to the end of 13. 13:33, Lemke argues, reflects the language and thought of 12:31. At the same time the phrase אחר הדבר הזה in particular presupposes knowledge of the prophetic material which precedes it. All of this implies that one editor was responsible for the composition of 12:31-33, 13:33, and for the insertion of the prophetic stories. The occurrence within 13:1-32 of the same Dtr phrases (כהני הבמות, 12:32, 13:2,

---

53 So Kittel, 113; Šanda, 1:357; Würthwein, 168.

54 So Burney, 177-179; Montgomery, 259; G. Vanoni, *Literarkritik und Grammatik: Untersuchung der Wiederholungen und Spannungen in 1 Kön 11-12* (ATSAT 21; St. Ottilien, 1984) 265.

55 For example, Wellhausen, *Composition*, 280; Eissfeldt, *Einleitung*, 326-327; Debus, *Sünde*, 35, n. 10; Dietrich, *Prophetie*, 114-120; F.-L. Hossfeld, and I. Meyer, *Prophet gegen Prophet: Eine Analyse der alttestamentlichen Texte zum Thema "wahre und falsche Propheten"* (BibB 9; Fribourg, 1973) 24-25.

56 Thus Noth (285-286), although he regards the insertion of chap. 13 as the work of Dtr, draws a sharp distinction between 12:31, which he thinks is from a source, and 13:33-34, which are from Dtr himself. For a similar analysis, see I. Plein, "Erwägungen zur Überlieferung von I Reg 11,26-14,20", ZAW 78 (1966) 8-24.

57 Hölscher, "Könige", 183; Jepsen, *Quellen*, 6.

58 W. E. Lemke, "The Way of Obedience: I Kings 13 and the Structure of the Deuteronomistic History", in F. M. Cross, W. E. Lemke and P. D. Miller, Jnr. (eds.), *Magnalia Dei: The Mighty Acts of God* (FS Wright; Garden City, 1976) 301-326.

13:33; בתי הבמוח, 12:31, 13:32[59]; לשוב ב/מן הדרך, (13:9, 10, 17, 26, 33)) as occur in 12:31-33 and 13:33 confirms that this is so, and shows that the Dtr editor not only inserted the stories, but also shaped their content. That the whole unified passage 12:31-13:33 is a secondary insertion into Kings is in turn demonstrated both by the example of *Wiederaufnahme*[60] to be found in 12:30/13:34[61], with their common phrase ויהי הדבר הזה לחמאת,[62] and by the linguistic links between 12:31-13:33 and other passages in Kings (2 Kings 17, 23) which have generally been accepted to have undergone secondary expansion. Lemke's view is therefore that 12:26-30; 13:34 is the work of the first Dtr redactor of Kings, while 12:31-13:33 is that of a second, who sought to illustrate and underscore the sin of Jeroboam by means of the insertion.

The general case argued by Hölscher, Jepsen and Lemke for taking 12:31 ff. as an insertion seems strong. Two further observations may now be made which may tell in its favour. In the first place, it may be noted that the form of 12:30 seems to demand some similar reference to the people in relation to Bethel in 12:31. The fact that such a reference does not appear in the present text may indicate that it has been displaced by 12:31 ff. It is, of course, possible that a reference to Bethel originally existed *before* that to Dan in 12:30, and that it has fallen out through homoioteleuton. If so, its absence in the present text will not carry this implication in terms of the redaction of the text. Secondly, however, it should be observed that 12:29 (and now perhaps the original form of 12:30) refers to both Bethel and Dan as the major sanctuaries of the cult, whereas Dan abruptly disappears after 12:30. A transition of some kind is, of course, essential as preparation for the stories of chap. 13, which relate only to Bethel. The abruptness of the change is, however, surprising. Leaving aside for the moment the ambiguous 12:31, the first intimation that we are now dealing with Bethel alone comes in 12:32a, with the statement that Jeroboam "went up to the altar". The altar at Bethel clearly must be meant, but has not been introduced beforehand. The statement therefore begs the question "which altar?". In the present form of the text, of course, it is explained by the following כן עשה בביחאל. This is syntactically awkward, however, and is

---

[59]   It is a fault in Lemke's case that he simply assumes with no discussion that ביח in 12:31 should be emended to בחי. This is certainly one of the options which scholars have chosen in dealing with 12:31, but it is by no means the only one. Nor is it particularly plausible, as will be argued below.

[60]   This literary-critical principle of resumption was first described in detail C. Kuhl, "Die 'Wiederaufnahme' - ein literarkritisches Prinzip?", *ZAW* 64 (1952) 1-11. The basic concept had, of course, been much used by scholars well before this time, as the comments of both Hölscher and Jepsen on 1 Kings 13 demonstrate. Of particular importance is the work of H. M. Wiener, *The Composition of Judges II 11 to I Kings II 46* (Leipzig, 1929). S. Talmon ("Polemics and Apology in Biblical Historiography - 2 Kings 17:24-41", in R. E. Friedman (ed.), *The Creation of Sacred Literature: Composition and Redaction of the Biblical Text* (UCNES 22; Berkeley, 1981) 57-68) also notes (pp. 58-59) rabbinic antecedents.

[61]   For a less convincing analysis of 12:25-13:34 which also employs this literary-critical principle, see Debus, *Sünde*, 35-47. R. L. Cohn ("Literary Technique in the Jeroboam Narrative", *ZAW* 97 (1985) 23-35), although he accepts (p. 31) that *Wiederaufnahme* is suggested here, rejects this explanation in favour of one in terms of "purposeful repetition" by a single author.

[62]   This point depends on the acceptance of the Qere (הדבר) in 13:34, which is usually thought to be correct.

best understood as a gloss from an editor[63] who himself felt the difficulty under discussion. The problem would be relieved so far as 12:32a is concerned if 12:31 were to be seen as a reference to a shrine at Bethel rather than as a reference to the provincial במה. Some preparation would then exist for the introduction of the altar. The majority of scholars, it is true, have not regarded 12:31 in this way, preferring to emend בית to בתי (the form in 13:32)[64], or to read בית as a collective plural (as it is in 2 Kgs 17:29, 32)[65], and to understand it as a reference to the construction of במה throughout the land. This interpretation of 12:31 has a difficulty attached to it, however, which seems to have gone unnoticed by scholars. It requires us to read 13:2 as a prophecy that the provincial priests, whom we must suppose to have been gathered at Bethel for Jeroboam's festival (12:32b)[66], will be sacrificed by Josiah on the altar at Bethel. It is extremely unlikely, however, given the well-known interest in Kings in prophecy and fulfilment, that this is what 13:2 means at all, since the fulfilment in 2 Kgs 23:19-20 notes only that the provincial priests were sacrificed on their *own* altars, and yet consciously uses the language of 13:2 to record the event. It is far more likely that 13:2 means to say that the *Bethel* priests will be sacrificed at Bethel, and that 2 Kgs 23:15-20 means to include Bethel in its description of what happened at all the במה of Israel. If this is accepted, it follows that it is much better to retain the MT of 12:31, reading בית, and to understand it as a singular[67]. 12:31 then refers to Jeroboam's construction of the Bethel sanctuary, and the institution of its priesthood, and the replication of the cult elsewhere in Israel is not introduced until 13:33-34. Such an interpretation of 12:31, however, only moves the general problem under discussion here back from 12:32 to 12:31. We have still shifted suddenly into a narrative about Bethel, where before we had a narrative about Bethel and Dan. If for 12:32a the question which the text begged was "which altar?", the question in the case of 12:31 is clearly "where did he build the shrine?". The impression is thus created that different authors are at work in 12:26-30 and 12:31 ff., the latter being so preoccupied with the Bethel material which he is introducing to the narrative that he fails properly to integrate it.

---

[63] So Burney, 178-179; Montgomery, 259; Vanoni, *Literarkritik*, 265.

[64] Stade and Schwally, 131; Gray, 313; Lemke, "Way", 308; DeVries, 161.

[65] Kittel, 111; Burney, 178; Šanda, 1:344; Montgomery, 259; Noth, 268.

[66] Too much weight cannot be placed on 12:32b, however, since it seems highly likely that it is part of a gloss, as some scholars have suggested. 12:32-33 are heavily overloaded, with Jeroboam described as going up to the altar three times, and reference being made to the month and to the creation of the festival on two occasions. The best solution would seem to be to accept the first reference with עלה as original, and regard the other two as an attempt at *Wiederaufnahme* by the editor(s) who introduced the notes in 12:32b, 33a, bα. The original text would then run: "Jeroboam appointed a festival on the eighth month like the festival which took place in Judah, and went up to the altar to burn incense" (so Montgomery, 259).

[67] So de Vaux, 84; Talmon, "Polemics", 62-63. Noth (268) admits the possibility that a singular is intended here, but affirms that it is more probable that the plural is meant, without giving any reasons. He allows (285) for the possibility that 12:31 refers to the particular במה at Bethel and Dan rather than במה in general, and that the latter understanding of the text is a later development.

The evidence therefore suggests that 12:31-13:34[68] represent an insertion into the original Dtr text of Kings[69]. Lemke is underplaying the significance of the addition, however, when he describes it simply as "illustrating and underscoring" Jeroboam's sin. The emphasis of 13:33-34, as scholars other than Hölscher and Jepsen have noted, is quite different to that of 12:28-30[70]. These verses represent an attempt to direct the attention of the reader away from the issue of the calves and on to the issue of the במות, making the latter the more important of the two. Indeed, there is no trace of the במות theme of which they are the culmination in the Dtr material before 12:31, and no hint of it in that which follows 13:34. Although 14:7-10 and 13:33-34 give explanations for exactly the same event (the fall of Jeroboam's house), the former show no awareness of precisely that sin, the patronage of the provincial cult, which 13:33-34 blame for this, taking their cue instead from 12:26-30 (cf. 14:9, "other gods"). Nor do any of the northern judgement formulae presuppose the material in 12:31-13:34. Rather than this passage merely illustrating and underscoring Jeroboam's sin, then, it seems to be the case that a second Dtr wished to focus attention on an aspect of Jeroboam's idolatry which was not even referred to in the original account. The במות *are* referred to in relation to the northern kingdom, of course, in 2 Kgs 17:7aβ-17[71], and knowledge of 12:31-13:34 is implied by 1 Kgs 14:23 (נמ־זמה). It may therefore be suggested that this whole section has been introduced by an editor later than the original Dtr author of Kings, who at the very least shared the perspective of the editor of 1 Kgs 14:22-24 and 2 Kgs 17:7aβ-17, and who may be identical with him.

---

[68] Jepsen (*Quellen*, 6) is doubtless correct to take the addition as including 13:34. It is difficult to see how Lemke's attribution of both 12:30 and 13:34 to one hand, with no material intervening between them, could possibly be correct. Hölscher also thought that 13:34 belonged to the first redactor, but assigned 12:30a to the second. Kuhl's analysis of *Wiederaufnahme*, however, now makes it unnecessary to remove 12:30a from the original at all, since both references can be accounted for.

[69] The affirmation that 12:31-13:34 as a whole is an insertion does not necessarily entail that every part of the passage must be seen as from the same editorial hand. As noted above, it seems highly likely that 12:32-33 has undergone subsequent glossing and expansion, and therefore that the במות reference in 12:32b is not from the same author as the remainder. The suggestion which has sometimes been made by scholars, on the other hand, that 13:2 and 13:32b should be distinguished, does not seem to stand up under close examination. It is certainly true that 13:2 does not mention the במות in the cities of Samaria, but concerns only Bethel. However, it must be remembered that the editor already had a narrative before him which contained a prophecy against Bethel. The difference is explicable if we assume that the author decided to retain the structure of the story at 13:2 (similarly S. J. DeVries, *Prophet against Prophet: The Role of the Micaiah Narrative (I Kings 22) in the Development of Early Prophetic Tradition* (Grand Rapids, 1978) 110, n. 19, who argues that the form of the narrative placed certain constraints on the Dtr editor), and then to extend the scope of the prophecy in 13:32, just before describing the proliferation of the cult in general (13:33-34).

[70] Montgomery (262), Noth (285-286) and Jones (268-269) all detect a difference in emphasis. DeVries (169) goes further, regarding 13:33-34 as "... directly conflicting with 12:30 ...". He therefore posits two Dtr redactors.

[71] 2 Kgs 17:29-34a may also be noted. Here the deportees from outside Israel are said to have put their gods בבית הבמה and to have appointed כחני הבמות who sacrificed for them there. This material clearly depends on 1 Kgs 12:31-13:34, and neither it, nor the interpretative passage which follows it (17:34b-40), can therefore have been present in the original Dtr Kings.

3.8 The במות Theme in the Closing Chapters of Kings

Examination of the במות material in Kings thus far has revealed that the במות in 1 Kings 15-2 Kings 15 are in all probability regarded by the author of the judgement formulae as places of true Yahweh-worship (3.2-3.3). This author's criticism of them derives from concern for centralization of Yahweh-worship, rather than from concern about idolatry. Such an interpretation of the central section of Kings is supported by the Solomonic במות material (3.4), which is to be regarded as from the same author. A different understanding of the במות may be found in 2 Kgs 17:7aβ-17. The author of this passage regards all the במות of north and south as idolatrous shrines (3.5). The judgement formulae in 1 Kgs 14:22-24 are closely related to 2 Kgs 17:7aβ-17 in language and ideology, and seem to have been reworked by the same editor (3.6). Furthermore, there are good grounds for taking 1 Kgs 12:31-13:34, which is the only passage apart from 2 Kgs 17:7aβ-17 to mention the במות in relation to the northern kingdom (3.7), as a secondary addition to the Dtr Kings. A primary במות theme can thus be differentiated on a redactional level from additional במות material in 1 Kings 3-2 Kings 15.

The question now arises as to where this במות theme comes to a conclusion. Given that it obviously looks forward to and presupposes a king who takes action against the provincial Judaean במות, the activities of only two kings, Hezekiah and Josiah, could have provided it with a focal point and climax. It is traditionally the latter, of course, who has been seen as the "hero" of the books of Kings, and whose reform has been regarded as the crucial event towards which their judgement formulae point. Careful examination of the במות notices for each king, however, indicates that it is the former who was originally the central figure of the narrative, and whose reign was seen as the zenith of Judaean history.

במות are mentioned in relation to Josiah's reform on 10 occasions (2 Kgs 23:5a, 8a, 8b, 9, 13, 15(thrice), 19, 20). Of these, only 23:8a, 9 could plausibly be argued to represent the

---

[72]   The במות of 23:5a are clearly viewed by the author of this verse as idolatrous. We may note the use of the noun כמרים, and the immediate context in 23:5b. The במת השעירים (following, with the majority of scholars, the emendation of G. Hoffman, "Kleinigkeiten", *ZAW* 2 (1882) 175) of 23:8b are equally clearly not Yahwistic shrines. Nor are the במות of 23:13. The references in 23:15, 19, 20 do not come into consideration here, both because they concern the northern במות, and because they presuppose the presence in Kings of the secondary 1 Kgs 12:31-13:34.

climax of the במה theme described in 3.2-3.4 above[72]. Examination of 2 Kgs 23:8a[73], however, reveals that this reference is extremely ill suited to be the climax of the במה theme found in the formulae. The earlier material is reproduced here for the purpose of comparison:

1 Kgs 3:3	רק בבמות הוא מזבח ומקטיר
1 Kgs 15:14	והבמות לא־סרו
1 Kgs 22:44	אך הבמות לא־סרו עוד העם מזבחים ומקטרים בבמות
2 Kgs 12:4	רק הבמות לא־סרו עוד העם מזבחים ומקטרים בבמות
2 Kgs 14:4	רק הבמות לא־סרו עוד העם מזבחים ומקטרים בבמות
2 Kgs 15:4	רק הבמות לא־סרו עוד העם מזבחים ומקטרים בבמות
2 Kgs 15:35a	רק הבמות לא סרו עוד העם מזבחים ומקטרים בבמות
2 Kgs 23:8a	ויבא את־כל־הכהנים מערי יהודה ויטמא את־הבמות אשר קטרו־שמה הכהנים מגבע עד־באר שבע

Several differences between the earlier במה statements and 23:8a are immediately apparent. We may first of all note the dual reference to כהנים in 23:8a. The term does not appear in the earlier material, where the emphasis is usually on the people, nor is there any hint of any priestly intermediary there. In itself, of course, this is not necessarily very significant, since it may be argued that in the earlier references a priesthood is implicitly present. When it is realized, however, that apart from 2 Kgs 23:8a and 23:9 כהנים are only mentioned in relation to the במה in 1 Kgs 12:31-13:34 and 2 Kgs 17:29-33, which were introduced secondarily to the first Dtr Kings (3.7), and in 2 Kgs 23:19-20, which presuppose the presence of 1 Kgs 12:31-13:34, then the difference between 23:8a and the earlier material becomes more important. We may note, moreover, the structure of the sentence. In the verses already assigned to the first editor, the structure of the sentence always draws attention to the non-removal of the במה by placing במה at the beginning. In 23:8a, however, mention of the במה is delayed, with the emphasis falling on the priesthood rather than on the shrines themselves. It will be recalled that the primary concern of the editor of 1 Kgs 12:31-13:34 was also the priesthood rather than the במה themselves (1 Kgs 13:33). The dual occurrence

---

[73] 2 Kgs 23:9 is of little help in assessing the likelihood that 23:8a, 9 were part of the original Kings, since it is ambiguous. It has been common to assume that it reflects an awareness on the part of the author that the instructions of Deut 18:6-8 have not been carried out. In this case, it might well imply that 23:8a concerns the centralization of true Yahweh-worship rather than the eradication of idolatry, since the author would then be seen to have no qualms about provincial priests serving in the Temple. Several scholars, however, (for example, G. von Rad, *Das fünfte Buch Mose: Deuteronomium* (ATD 8; Göttingen, 1964) 87-88; A. H. J. Gunneweg, *Leviten und Priester: Hauptlinien der Traditionsbildung und Geschichte des israelitisch-jüdischen Kultpersonals* (FRLANT 89; Göttingen, 1965) 118-126; J. Lindblom, *Erwägungen zur Herkunft der josianischen Tempelurkunde* (Lund, 1971) 22-33; E. Würthwein, "Die josianische Reform und das Deuteronomium", *ZTK* 73 (1976) 395-423, on p. 417; Mayes, *Deuteronomy*, 278-279) have questioned this linking of 23:8-9 and Deut 18:6-8; and it may be observed that a notice that Josiah failed in even one aspect of his reform would be out of place in a narrative which otherwise exalts this king, claiming that he did "according to all the law of Moses" (23:25). The verse can, in fact, be read in quite a different way. It can be taken as reflecting no expectation that the priests *should* have come up to the Temple, but merely emphasizing that they *did* not. The concern of its author would then have been to stress that the Temple cult and the במה cult had nothing to do with each other. 2 Kgs 23:9 can thus be interpreted in two entirely different ways, depending upon one's view of the nature of reform in 23:8a.

of כהנים in 2 Kgs 23:8a thus presents a problem in two respects for those who would wish to assign the verses to the primary editor of Kings. Its very appearance in the verse is unexpected in view of the earlier references; and the stress of the verse on the כהנים, rather than on the במה, is also unexpected. Both of these things are explicable, however, if the verse derives from a later editor.

A second difference between 2 Kgs 23:8a and the earlier verses is to be found in the term which is used for Josiah's action against the במה. Where an explicit statement about inaction in this respect is made in the earlier material, the verb used is always סור. The very consistency with which it recurs would lead us to expect that the account concerning the king who at last acted against them would also use סור. This is not the case with 23:8a, which utilizes a verb (טמא) unique in Kings to this chapter (23:8, 10, 13, 16)[74]. This again suggests that we are dealing here with a different author. Confirmatory evidence is provided by the other verses in 2 Kings 23 where טמא occurs. In all three cases it is used of action against idolatry. Given that 23:8a itself follows an account of action against idolatry (23:4, 6-7), it therefore seems most natural to understand the במה here as idolatrous places of worship. This corresponds to the view of the Judaean במה found in 2 Kgs 14:22-24, of course[75], but not to that found in the other Judaean judgement formulae. The occurrence of טמא in 2 Kgs 23:8a, then, like the occurrence of כהנים, makes it unlikely that 23:8a is to be seen as the climax of the במות theme.

The third difference which may be detected between 23:8a and the earlier במות references is in the expression used for the worship at these shrines. In all the earlier references where worship at the במה is mentioned, we find that זבח and קטר are used together. In 2 Kgs 23:8a, however, קטר is used alone, something which is paralleled only in 23:5 and in passages already distinguished as secondary additions to Kings[76]. We may thus again say that the language of the verse corresponds more closely to that of later passages than to that of the first edition.

2 Kgs 23:8a is therefore well-suited neither linguistically, nor structurally nor ideologically to be the climax of the במות theme. The notice concerning Hezekiah's action against the במה (2 Kgs 18:4a) on the other hand, fits, at least in part (18:4aα), extremely well into the pattern

---

[74] It is also unattested anywhere else in the Dtr/Dtn literature. It is widely used in P and in Ezekiel, however. occurring, for example, 82 times in Leviticus (in the Piel, as in Kings, 17 times), and 29 times in Ezekiel (Piel, 14 times).

[75] It also corresponds to the view in 2 Kgs 21:3a, the verse which prepares for the defilement of the במה in 23:8a. Manasseh's rebuilding of the במה here comprises part of his doing what was evil in the sight of Yahweh כתועבת הגוים אשר הוריש מפני בני ישראל (21:2, cf. 1 Kgs 14:24; 2 Kgs 17:8), and is described in the same breath as his building of altars for Baal, his construction of an Asherah, and his worship of the host of heaven.

[76] So 2 Kgs 17:11 (Piel, as here); and 1 Kgs 12:33; 13:1-2 (Hiphil), of the Bethel במה.

of the preceding material, as Barrick[77] has noted. A similar table to that provided for 23:8a should make this clear:

1 Kgs 3:3	רק בבמות הוא מזבח ומקטיר
1 Kgs 15:14	והבמות לא־סרו
1 Kgs 22:44	אך הבמות לא־סרו עוד העם מזבחים ומקטרים בבמות
2 Kgs 12:4	רק הבמות לא־סרו עוד העם מזבחים ומקטרים בבמות
2 Kgs 14:4	רק הבמות לא־סרו עוד העם מזבחים ומקטרים בבמות
2 Kgs 15:4	רק הבמות לא־סרו עוד העם מזבחים ומקטרים בבמות
2 Kgs 15:35a	רק הבמות לא סרו עוד העם מזבחים ומקטרים בבמות
2 Kgs 18:4aα	הוא הסיר את־הבמות

The persistent theme of this material (הבמות לא סרו) is now provided with the perfect conclusion: הוא הסיר את־הבמות, "*he* it was who removed the במה". Such a reference is exactly what the reader has been led to expect, both in terms of its structure and in terms of its language. The closely related reference in 2 Kgs 18:22[78], furthermore, stresses the climactic nature, so far as the author was concerned, of Hezekiah's action. This verse binds the story of the siege and deliverance of Jerusalem to that of the reform[79], emphasizing the risk (in terms of possible divine disapproval) which the king took in removing (הסיר) the במה, and inviting the reader to see the events which followed as a vindication of his (and the people's) trust[80]. It thus strongly implies that the במה referred to in 18:4aα are truly Yahwistic shrines, as one would expect in view of the linguistic relationship of this verse to the earlier במה statements. There can be little doubt, then, that 2 Kgs 18:4aα provides a much more appropriate ending for the במה theme than does 2 Kgs 23:8a.

A problem is immediately apparent, however. Whereas 18:4aα taken alone fits the pattern of the previous במה statements perfectly, the same cannot be said of 18:4 taken as a whole. The addition of 18:4aβ, b to 18:4aα has the effect of associating the במה mentioned here very clearly with idolatry - with מצבה, an אשרה and the worship of the serpent Nehushtan. The במה reference for Ahaz (2 Kgs 16:4), moreover, is also out of step with the pattern. With the exception of 1 Kgs 14:22-24, במה are only referred to in the earlier material, it will be recalled, in relation to kings who "did what was right". Ahaz, however, "did not do what was right" (2 Kgs 16:2), but walked בדרך מלכי ישראל (16:3, cf. 2 Kgs 8:18), and did כתעבות הגוים (16:3). It is in this context that his worship at the במה is referred to, not as a

---

[77] Barrick, "Removal".

[78] It is assumed here that the story of Jerusalem's deliverance was in some form already part of the first edition of the books of Kings. For a defence of this view, see 4.4.3 below.

[79] This is so even if 18:22 is an insertion (so, for example, Benzinger, 180; Stade and Schwally, 50; Würthwein, 421). The link between the reform and the deliverance of Jerusalem is consciously made.

[80] We may note here the recurrent use of בטח in 2 Kgs 18:5, 19-22, 24, 30.

qualification of his righteousness, therefore, but as evidence of his apostasy. If, then, the במות theme described in 3.2-3.4 runs as far as Hezekiah, as 18:4aα, 22 suggest, it must be assumed that the judgement formulae for both Ahaz and Hezekiah have been reworked by a later editor, and their original orientation obscured. That this is indeed what has happened is confirmed both by the linguistic affinities of 16:3b-4 and 18:4aβ, b with 1 Kgs 14:22-24 and 2 Kgs 17:7aβ-17, and by literary-critical evidence in 16:3b and 18:4aβ.

The evidence in the case of Ahaz may be briefly stated. Most of the phraseology of 16:3b-4 is paralleled in the secondary passages mentioned[81]. Thus the comparison of the behaviour of Judah with the התעבות הגוים אשר הוריש יהוה מפני בני ישראל in 16:3b is almost exactly paralleled in 1 Kgs 14:24b; while the phrase וחחת כל־עץ רענן (16:4b) is found elsewhere in Kings only in 1 Kgs 14:23 and 2 Kgs 17:10, where it is also associated with במות and נבעות.[82] In addition, 2 Kgs 17:17 includes a reference to the "passing of sons and daughters through fire" (cf. 16:3b). There is good reason on linguistic grounds, then, to suppose that 16:3b-4 are from the hand of a later editor; and the presence of וגם in 16:3b is further evidence of a break in the text at this point. The removal of this material leaves judgement formulae for Ahaz which are perfectly consistent with the earlier pattern.

2 Kgs 18:4aβ, b are also closely related to 2 Kgs 14:22-24 and 2 Kgs 17:7aβ-17, both by their association of במות with מצבת and אשרה/ים (1 Kgs 14:23, 2 Kgs 17:9-10), and by the occurrence of קטר alone in the Piel (2 Kgs 17:11). They are, furthermore, related to these passages by their view of the history of Judah as one of continuous idolatry, here signified by the devotion of the people to Nehushtan. The beginning of the expansion is marked in this instance by the waw-copulative (ושבר) of 18:4aβ. While this tense-form appears nowhere in the judgement formulae before this point, it does occur both in 2 Kgs 21:1-9 (21:4, 6) and in the account of Josiah's reform in 2 Kgs 23:4-20 (23:4bβ-5, 8b, 10, 12bβ, 14aα, 15bβ). In both passages, a strong case can be made in favour of taking the material which it introduces as secondary to a surrounding context in which waw-consecutive uniformly appears[83].

---

[81] The exception is 16:4aα, ויזבח ויקטר בבמות. This phrase is similar to the earlier במות references, in that זבח and קטר appear together of worship at the במות. It differs from most, of course, in having the king rather than the people as the subject of the verbs, and from all in its structure. In addition, it is not accompanied by any statement concerning the failure to remove these shrines.

[82] For a full discussion of this phrase, see W. L. Holladay, "On Every High Hill and under Every Green Tree", *VT* 11 (1961) 170-176.

[83] Hoffman (*Reform*, 215-217) rather misses the point when he argues that the work of R. Meyer ("Auffallender Erzählungsstil in einem angeblichen Auszug aus der 'Chronik der Könige von Juda'", in L. Rost (ed.), *Festschrift: Friedrich Baumgärtel zum 70. Geburtstag, 14. Januar 1958* (ErF A/10; Erlangen, 1959) 114-123) shows that the division of the text on the basis of the appearance of the waw-copulative is illegitimate in principle. Meyer argued that the waw-copulative had been used in classical Hebrew as far back as the pre-Israelite period. Even if he is correct in this claim (and it is by no means clear that his "early OT examples" are anything more than isolated emendations by copyists, cf. A. Rubinstein, "The Anomalous Perfect with *Waw*-Conjunctive in Biblical Hebrew", *Bib* 44 (1963) 62-69), it does not necessarily follow, as Spieckermann (*Juda*, 120-130) has pointed out, that waw-copulatives are never best understood as marking insertions into the text by a later hand. Meyer's work requires only that we do not automatically assume that this is the case without confirmatory evidence. The matter must be settled, then, on the basis of what is most likely in any given text.

So far as 2 Kings 21 is concerned, it has frequently been noted that v 4 reads rather strangely in view of vv 5 and 7, which it seems to duplicate. Indeed, it interrupts the specific connection between vv 3 and 5: "he worshipped all the host of heaven and served them ... he built altars for all the host of heaven". 21:6 likewise breaks a connection between vv 3, 5 and v 7: "he made an Asherah, as Ahab king of Israel had done, and worshipped all the host of heaven and served them ... he built altars for all the host of heaven ... and put the graven image of Asherah which he had made in the Temple ...". Furthermore, while the sins referred to in 21:3, 5, 7 are all picked up in 2 Kings 23 (vv 4, 6, 12), there is no reference there to those mentioned in 21:4, 6. Both verses, therefore, are best understood as additions to the Dtr account of Manasseh's reign[84].

Moving on to 2 Kings 23, 23:4bβ-5 interrupt the account of the removal of alien cult objects from within the Temple, and have generally been regarded as an insertion[85]; and 23:8b likewise breaks the connection between 23:8a and 23:9, and is best understood as such[86]. 23:10, which begins with a waw-copulative and names the Ammonite god as מלך, and 23:13, which begins with waw-consecutive, and calls him מלכם, are clearly in some tension,

---

[84] So Benzinger, 188; Stade and Schwally, 53; Šanda, 2:324-325; Gray, 705-706; Würthwein, 439-440. Jepsen (*Quellen*, appendices) sees the verses as Dtr additions to his priestly text. Montgomery (519), Dietrich (*Prophetie*, 31-34), Veijola (*Verheissung*, 157), Spieckermann (*Juda*, 162-164, 421) and Jones (596-597) regard only v 4 as an addition. It is unlikely, however, that two examples of a relatively rare tense-form in such close proximity to one another derive from different hands. Burney (353) thinks that the form of both of the verses is due to the style of the sources employed. This does not seem very likely in the case of 21:6, which is thoroughly Dtr (cf. Deut 18:9-14, 2 Kgs 17:17), and is therefore not likely in 21:4 either.

[85] Benzinger, 189; Kittel, 300; Stade and Schwally, 55; Šanda, 2:362-363; Montgomery, 529; de Vaux, 228; Gray, 732; Würthwein, "Reform", 413-415; H. Hollenstein, "Literarkritische Erwägungen zum Bericht über die Reformmassnahmen Josias 2 Kön. xxiii 4ff.", *VT* 27 (1977) 321-336, on pp. 330-331; Würthwein, 453, 456; M. Rehm, *Das zweite Buch der Könige* (Eichstätt, 1982) 216, 221-222; Nelson, *Redaction*, 80-81; C. Levin, "Joschija im deuteronomistischen Geschichtswerk", *ZAW* 96 (1984) 351-371, on p. 361, n. 42; Jones, 617. A. Jepsen ("Die Reform des Josia", in L. Rost (ed.), *Festschrift: Friedrich Baumgärtel zum 70. Geburtstag, 14. Januar 1958* (ErF A/10; Erlangen, 1959) 97-108), who resolves the disorder of the text by rearranging the verses into an "original" order, finds insertion into a pre-existing text neither here nor generally in the passage. It is difficult to find any justification for such rearrangement, however, which seems mainly to proceed from the assumption that a more logical order must *ipso facto* be the original order. Furthermore, it is extremely difficult to understand how the rearranged text could have subsequently become so disorganized.

[86] So Benzinger, 189, 193 (tentatively); Stade and Schwally, 55; Šanda, 2:362-363; Würthwein, "Reform", 415; Hollenstein, "Reformmassnahmen", 333-334; Würthwein, 453, 458-459; Rehm, 2:216, 223; Spieckermann, *Juda*, 99-101, 426; Jones, 617, 621. Not a few scholars have argued that 23:8b is an annalistic notice (thus, for example, the influential article by J. A. Montgomery, "Archival Data in the Book of Kings", *JBL* 53 (1934) 46-52), and therefore that 23:8, 9 as a unit comes from one editor. Nelson (*Redaction*, 81), however, who himself supports this position, admits that the combining of the material in this way represents "... rather odd editorial procedure ...". In addition, it must again be asked whether it is very likely that material containing a tense-form which has appeared only sporadically throughout the books should, in a passage where there are no less than seven occurrences in twelve verses, be understood as deriving from different authors (so Rehm, 2:216). It is much more likely that 23:8b is an addition from the same hand as 23:4bβ-5.

and are unlikely to have derived from the same author[87]. 23:15bβ is also best explained as a redactional addition to 23:15[88]. Its intention seems to be, like that of the other additions to the verse[89], to associate the reform at Bethel with that at Jerusalem, in this case by introducing the burning of an Asherah there. Indeed, the same intention is also implicit in the insertion of 23:4bβ, and may perhaps lie behind that of 23:5, which can be taken to mean that the idolatrous priests of Judah, like their counterparts in Israel (23:20), were executed[90]. There is good reason in all these cases, then, to suppose that a redactor is at work, and this being the case, it seems more than probable that the remaining two occurrences (23:12bβ, 14aα) are also to be explained in the same way[91]. It may be noted that none of the material introduced by waw-copulative in the chapter is reflected by Chr, which may imply that it was not present in his Vorlage[92].

If there is compelling evidence, then, that a redactor whose distinguishing feature is his use of the waw-copulative has worked over other material on the cult in the closing chapters of Kings, it seems likely in principle that the occurrences of the form in 18:4aβ, b are also due to his editorial work. A specific connection between his additions in these other passages and 18:4aβ, indeed, is to be found in the phrase ושבר את־המצבות, which occurs in Kings only in 18:4aβ and 23:14aα. Together with the linguistic data already discussed, then, the form of the verbs in 18:4aβ, b provides weighty evidence that 18:4aα has been expanded secondarily.

In summary, it may be said that while the description of Josiah's action against the provincial Judaean במה (2 Kgs 23:8a, 9) has no points of contact with the במה references found in the judgement formulae for most of the kings of Judah, part of the notice concerning Hezekiah's action against the same (2 Kgs 18:4) does fit their pattern extremely

---

[87]   A similar situation is found in 1 Kgs 11:7, which is the only other verse in Kings to mention מלך (cf. 3.4 above). Here 11:7b (מלך) duplicates 11:5b (מלכם), and clearly seems to be an addition to 11:7a. 11:5, 7a are then picked up in 11:33 (which has the same trio of names as 2 Kgs 23:13), while 11:7b is unreflected. This fact, and the fact that 23:10 is so closely related to Deut 18:9-14, 2 Kgs 17:17, makes it unlikely, quite apart from the general consideration mentioned in the previous note, that the conflict is to be explained in terms of the editing of a source (23:10) by a Dtr author (23:13). It is much more likely that 23:10 is an addition to a text which already contained 23:13 (so Stade and Schwally, 55-56; Würthwein, "Reform", 415-416; Hollenstein, "Reformmassnahmen", 334; Würthwein, 453, 459; Rehm, 2:216, 224; Jones, 617, 622. Benzinger, 193, argues somewhat implausibly that it is only the waw-copulative which is secondary, the result of careless editing).

[88]   So Stade and Schwally, 56; Šanda, 2:362-363; Montgomery, 534; Dietrich, *Prophetie*, 119; Würthwein, 453, 460; Rehm, 2:216; Jones, 624.

[89]   A coherent text may be obtained in 23:15 if we remove the references to במה in the verse (so Benzinger, 194; Ogden, "Reforms", 34, n. 12; and Würthwein, 453) and view these as later glosses designed to emphasize the relationship between the destruction of Bethel and the activities of Josiah just mentioned. Bethel, it is emphasized, was one of the במה destroyed by this king. There is no need to excise all of 23:15aβ (with Stade and Schwally, 56, and others).

[90]   So BDB, 992, cf. שבט (Hiphil) in Hos 1:4; Amos 8:4; Ps 8:3; 119:119.

[91]   23:12bβ is accepted as an addition by Benzinger (193), Stade and Schwally (55), Hollenstein ("Reformmassnahmen", 335), Rehm (2:216, 225), and Spieckermann (*Juda*, 111, 427). The tendency among scholars has been to take all of v 14, which is introduced by ושבר, as the addition, rather than simply 23:14aα. There is nothing to compel such a conclusion, however, and it seems better simply to regard the first part of the verse as the gloss.

[92]   So Würthwein, "Reform", 415; Hollenstein, "Reformmassnahmen".

well. The extent to which this latter verse, and the preceding judgement formulae for Ahaz, reflect an ideology alien to the earlier references may be explained in terms of the reworking of the text by later editors. The במה theme identified in 3.2-3.4 above, then, finds its most appropriate climax in the account of Hezekiah's reign in 2 Kings 18-20, rather than in the account of Josiah's reign in 2 Kings 22-23.

3.9 Conclusion

Analysis of the במה material of the books of Kings has suggested that it is best understood as having derived in the main from two different hands. A primary theme may be found in 1 Kings 3-2 Kings 18. The במה are viewed as Yahwistic shrines, and Hezekiah as the good king who removed them, centralizing Yahweh-worship in Jerusalem. That this was Yahweh's will is confirmed for the author by the events recorded in 2 Kings 18-19, in which it is demonstrated that he is still with his people. A different and later view of the במה is detectable elsewhere in Kings, both in redactional additions within 1 Kings 3-2 Kings 18, and in material towards the end of the books. Here they are viewed as idolatrous places of worship. There is some evidence to suggest that not all of this material is from one hand, although for the most part there seems little reason to see more than one, exilic editor at work. The question of the redactional development of the secondary sections will be taken up again in chap. 5. For the moment, it is sufficient to note that the fact that the primary במה theme comes to a conclusion in 2 Kings 18, and that after this point the perspective of Kings with regard to these shrines completely changes, is evidence both that there was a pre-exilic edition of the books, and that it ended with Hezekiah rather than Josiah or some later king. Analysis of the other major theme of the judgement formulae, the David theme, will further support this thesis.

4. THE DAVID THEME IN THE BOOKS OF KINGS

4.1 Introduction

References to David appear on 96 occasions in the books of Kings, although by no means all these are of relevance to this study. Of particular importance here are those which appear in conjunction with the evaluation of each king, and others associated with these by language or interests. This chapter will consequently centre its attention on two uses of David in Kings, which may be described as "comparative" and "promissory". The comparative is, of course, that which Weippert has concentrated upon in her own redactional study of the books, and it may be illustrated in its positive form by 1 Kgs 15:11,

> Asa did what was right in Yahweh's sight as David his father had done

and in its negative form by 1 Kgs 15:3:

> He walked in all the sins which his father did before him, and his heart was not wholly true
> to Yahweh his God, as was the heart of David his father.

The promissory may be illustrated by 1 Kgs 15:4-5:

> Nevertheless, for David's sake Yahweh his God gave him dominion[1] in Jerusalem, setting up
> his son after him and establishing Jerusalem; because David did what was right in Yahweh's
> sight ...

In the following analysis the pattern adopted will be that of chap. 3. Different blocks of

---

[1] The possibility that ניר has a similar meaning to the Akkadian *nīru(m)* was first mooted by J. W. Wevers, "Exegetical Principles Underlying the Septuagint Text of 1 Kings ii 12-xxi 43", *OTS* 8 (1950) 300-322, on p. 316, n. 13. P. Hanson ("The Song of Heshbon and David's *Nîr*", *HTR* 61 (1968) 297-320) has now elaborated the case for this suggestion in more detail. In view of the fact that the roots ניר and נור were always carefully distinguished in those languages which preserved them both, and that the translation "dominion" makes better sense than the more common "lamp", which assumes that ניר is equivalent to נר, it seems best to adopt this view. For a brief but detailed survey of scholarly opinion on ניר, see Vanoni, *Literarkritik*, 179-180, n. 620, who also follows Hanson. M. Görg ("Ein 'Machtzeichen' Davids 1 Könige xi 36", *VT* 35 (1985) 363-368) accepts Hanson's basic case, and suggests in addition that the Egyptian *nir~w* has influenced Dtr usage. He understands Dtr as interpreting "yoke of dominion" as "symbol of power", Judah being the "sceptre of David".

material will be studied in turn, beginning with the central section of the books (1 Kings 15-
2 Kings 15).

4.2 The David Theme in 1 Kings 15-2 Kings 15

4.2.1 David as a Comparative Figure

David appears as a comparative figure in these chapters in 1 Kgs 15:3, 11 and 2 Kgs 14:3. רק לא כדוד אביו in 2 Kgs 14:3, however, seems almost certainly to be a secondary addition to the verse[2], and therefore does not enter into a discussion of their original shape. Of the two references which remain, one (15:3) is negative and the other (15:11) positive: Abijam is said to have been unlike David, and Asa like him. The behaviour of David may thus be seen to be the paradigm which has influenced the author's assessment of both kings. The question which immediately arises, in view of the fact that there exist no similar comparative statements for the later kings of this section of the books, each (with the exception of Jehoash, 2 Kgs 12:3) being compared to his immediate predecessor rather than to David, is how these references are related to the basic רע/ישר pattern discussed in 3.2-3.3 above. Does the author[3] intend an evaluative distinction between Abijam and the other bad kings, and between Asa and the other good kings, by his use of David; or does this same paradigm lie behind the evaluations of all the kings in 1 Kings 15-2 Kings 15, even though explicit mention of David is not made? The first alternative does not seem very likely. It has already been argued in 3.3 that Abijam, although he did not worship Baal, was regarded by the author in the same way (i.e. as an idolater) as Jehoram and Ahaziah; and the presence of ניר references (see 4.2.2 below) for both Abijam and Jehoram (1 Kgs 15:4, 2 Kgs 8:19) demonstrates that a similar explanation for Yahweh's forbearance was felt necessary in each case. The lack of a reference to David in 2 Kgs 8:19 does not therefore seem to signify any distinction between Jehoram and Abijam. Similarly, it is difficult to find any theological

---

[2] The presence of two excepting statements in vv 3-4, both beginning with רק, makes the passage syntactically awkward, and disrupts the pattern of the positive judgement formulae for the whole section, in which uniformly only one such statement, relating to the non-removal of the במה, exists (1 Kgs 15:14, with ו; 22:44 with אך; and 2 Kgs 12:4; 15:4, 35 with רק). The removal of the first (with Šanda, 2:161, 174; Montgomery, 439; Gray (1st ed.), 547; Weippert, "Beurteilungen", 314; Würthwein, 371; Jones, 507) leaves the form of the verse identical to that of 2 Kgs 15:34, ויעש הישר בעיני יהוה ככל אשר־עשה עזיהו אביו עשה, or, if the final עשה is to be regarded as secondary (Stade and Schwally, 246; and Šanda, 2:161-162, 174) to that of 2 Kgs 15:3.

[3] Weippert, of course, has taken the difference between 1 Kings 15 and 1 Kings 22-2 Kings 15 in this regard as evidence that different authors are at work. She sees in the use of David a lack of interest in history on the part of the author of the former, since he is interested in the "ideal king" rather than the historical predecessor of the monarch under consideration. Her case is generally implausible, however, given the unlikelihood that any edition of Kings ever began with Jehoshaphat, and the evidence adduced in chap. 3 that 1 Kings 15-2 Kings 15 comprise a unit. In addition, examination of 1 Kgs 15:3 rather calls her assertion about the significance of David in 1 Kings 15 into question, since both the immediate predecessor and the ideal king are referred to in this verse. The variation must rather be accounted for in terms of a single author, as the overwhelming majority of scholars accept.

reason why Asa should be compared positively to David and his successors not. It is true, as Cortese[4] notes, that Asa carried through a reformation, while none of the other good kings in 1 Kings 15-2 Kings 15 did so. Since the author portrays the cult in Judah as free from idolatry upon the accession of each of these kings[5], however, and thus would not have thought of any of them as having the opportunity for such reform, 1 Kgs 15:11 can hardly be intended to praise Asa more highly than them for this reason; and otherwise the pattern of his assessment is exactly the same as the pattern of theirs. Furthermore, it must be noted that the positive comparison of Jehoshaphat to Asa in 1 Kgs 22:43 stands as evidence against any proposal that the David reference in 1 Kgs 15:11 is designed to elevate Asa above his immediate successors. Jehoshaphat, it is claimed here, "walked in *all* [my emphasis] the way of Asa his father". It seems more likely, then, that although David is not mentioned as a comparative figure after 1 Kings 15, the author of 1 Kings 15-2 Kings 15 is still operating with him as the ideal figure who sets the standard for all the succeeding kings. Having stated that Abijam did not meet this standard, and that Asa did, he has contented himself with describing succeeding kings who have done הישר in relation to their immediate predecessor rather than to David. David, who himself did הישר (1 Kgs 15:11) in following Yahweh, is thus to be seen as the model of the faithful Yahwist which lies behind the assessment of the various Judaean kings in this section as having done good or evil.

4.2.2 David as a Promissory Figure

David appears as a promissory figure in this section of Kings in 1 Kgs 15:4-5 and 2 Kgs 8:19. On the latter occasion it is stated, on the former implied, that Yahweh took no action in response to the sin of the king because he had promised ניר, dominion, to David. Together with a third ניר passage in 1 Kgs 11:36, these references to the Davidic promise have played an important part in the debate about the date and nature of the books of Kings and of the DH as a whole, since they provide strong evidence for a pre-exilic edition of those books. Noth and those who follow his view of the DH as an exilic work have found it difficult to deal with this evidence convincingly. Noth himself had two different attempts at explaining the ניר references within the context of his overall thesis, first of all in *Studien*, and then later in his commentary on Kings.

In *Studien*, he argued that only 2 Kgs 8:19 actually came from the hand of Dtr, 1 Kgs 11:36b being part of the pre-exilic Ahijah story, and 1 Kgs 15:4 a post-Dtr addition[6]. He

---

[4]   Cortese, "Schema", 44.

[5]   This is so even in the case of Jehoash (2 Kgs 12:1-4), whose reign is properly introduced after the account of the priest Jehoiada's reformation in 2 Kings 11.

[6]   Noth, *Studien*, 72, n. 5; 82, n. 1; 84, n. 1.

explained 2 Kgs 8:19 as follows:

> Die Reflexion von Dtr in V. 19 geht von der geschichtlichen Tatsache des Weiterbestehens
> des Staates Juda aus und nimmt auf einen Satz aus der Ahiageschichte (I. Kön. 11,36b) Bezug.

It is not clear, however, that this "explanation" actually explains anything. The distinction which Noth appears to be trying to draw between 1 Kgs 11:36b and 2 Kgs 8:19 is that between a statement which regards the Davidic dynasty as eternal, and which in his view therefore must be pre-exilic and pre-Dtr; and a statement which is concerned with the survival of the state rather than the dynasty, and which may therefore be exilic and Dtr. Such a distinction cannot be maintained, however, since both verses clearly regard the Davidic dynasty in the same way, as surviving כל־הימים. If 1 Kgs 11:36 must be regarded as pre-exilic because of this, then so must 2 Kgs 8:19. By the same token, there can be little doubt that if 2 Kgs 8:19 is Dtr, then 1 Kgs 11:36b must be Dtr also.

Noth himself must have realized the weakness of his position on this point, since in the commentary he abandons the attempt to distinguish between the two verses, and accepts 1 Kgs 11:36b as Dtr[7]. His method of dealing with the verse is now to argue that since כל־הימים can mean "a very long time" as well as "forever", its occurrence here, and presumably also in 2 Kgs 8:19, is not certain proof that the sentence about the Davidic dynasty was formulated before the disappearance of the last Davidic king from Jerusalem. Rather, it could equally well have been used by an exilic author. Since the complexity of the structure of 1 Kgs 15:3-5 demonstrates that 15:4-5 are post-Dtr additions[8], all of the ניר references may thus be accommodated within the framework of Noth's theory of an exilic DH with isolated additions.

Even in this revised form, Noth's treatment of the ניר material in Kings is not very convincing. First of all, it is highly unlikely that 1 Kgs 15:4 is to be regarded as from a different author to the other two references, when in content and intention it is so similar to them. Nor is there any good reason to accept Noth's contention that the verse is secondary. The structure of 15:3-5 is only complex if we insist, with Noth, that the כי of v 4 *must* be taken as causal. A more obvious alternative, however, is that the כי is adversative, and thus to be translated "nevertheless, however"[9]. The literary-critical ground for the distinction between 1 Kgs 15:4, on the one hand, and 1 Kgs 11:36 and 2 Kgs 8:19 on the other thus disappears. Secondly, and more importantly, Noth's explanation of the meaning of כל־הימים in

---

[7]   Noth, 261-262.

[8]   Ibid., 334. In *Studien*, Noth had argued that only 15:4 was a secondary addition, and this because it interrupted the connection between 15:3 and 15:5.

[9]   This usage is well-known (cf. GKC, §163a), and Noth's insistence that כי can only be causal is therefore quite remarkable.

1 Kgs 11:36 seems very weak. On no other occasion in the OT is the translation "a very
long time" the most obvious for this phrase. In the vast majority of cases, the translation
demanded is "forever"[10]; and in the remainder, where the immediate context makes this
translation inappropriate, the best alternative appears to be "continually"[11]. Since nothing in
the immediate context of 1 Kgs 11:36 requires us to adopt the latter, less common usage, and
since we know that the Davidic promise was widely regarded in Judah, both before and after
the events of 587 B.C., as of eternal validity[12], there seems little reason to doubt that כל־הימים
here means "forever", as Noth originally accepted in *Studien*.

Noth's attempt to explain the ניר references within the context of his theory of a
pessimistic, exilic Dtr must therefore be seen as a failure, and it is significant that his
position on this point has been abandoned by many of those who have followed him in
accepting a basically exilic Kings. Many scholars would accept that the "eternal" aspect of
the ניר material must somehow be accommodated within the exilic theory of the books if it is
to have any credibility. Thus it is that the attempt has been made to explain these verses in
terms of a Dtr "future hope" in the restoration of the Davidic dynasty, either on the part of
the Dtr author of Kings himself[13], or on the part of the later Dtr redactor, DtrN[14]. On this
view, the ניר material was not written by an author who knew nothing of the events of 587
B.C., but by an author who still held on to the Davidic promise even after those events. The
stronger form of this argument, since there is no convincing literary-critical evidence that 1
Kgs 11:36; 15:4 and 2 Kgs 8:19 are secondary additions to the books of Kings, is that which
attributes the ניר references to Dtr himself, rather than to a later redactor. Even in this
stronger form, however, there are problems with it. It is difficult to understand why an exilic
author who was composing a work from the start, even if a future hope was in his mind,
would have used the ניר material in the way in which we find it used in Kings. It should be
noted that what we have in these verses is not just a vague hope which is unconnected to the
story of the monarchy as it unfolds. What we have is rather a means of historical
explanation, which is an intrinsic part of the structure of the books. The ניר material is used
to explain why it was that there remained a continuous succession of Davidic kings in Judah
in spite of the fact that a few sinned. The plain implication of the way in which it is thus
used is that no matter what a future king does, the promise will stay in force, for it is a

---

[10]   So, for example, Deut 6:24; 11:1; 14:23; 18:5; 19:9; Jer 31:36; 32:39; 33:18; 35:19.

[11]   So, for example, Judg 16:16; 1 Sam 23:14; 2 Sam 13:37; 1 Kgs 14:30.

[12]   The most pertinent example so far as the exilic material is concerned is Jer 33:14-26, which actually
       utilizes the phrase כל־הימים (v 18) in its discussion of the eternal nature of the covenants with David and the
       Levites.

[13]   This modification of Noth may be found as early as von Rad, *Studien*, 52-64, and has been taken up by
       many scholars, including E. Janssen (*Juda in der Exilszeit: Ein Beitrag zur Frage der Entstehung des
       Judentums* (FRLANT 69; Göttingen, 1956) 75), Amsler (*David*, 61-64), Fichtner (187-188) and Zenger
       ("Rehabilitierung", 29).

[14]   So Dietrich, *Prophetie*, 142-143; Veijola, *Dynastie*, 141-142; Würthwein, 500-501.

promise "forever". That is, there will always be a Davidic king on the throne, and Judah will never be destroyed (השחית, 2 Kgs 8:19). Given this, it must be asked whether it is really plausible to suggest that the ניר references are from the hand of an exilic editor who would have known that Judah had been destroyed (cf. האביד, 2 Kgs 24:2), and that no Davidic king ruled in Jerusalem any longer. Why would he have referred to the Davidic promise in such an historical context, when his aim was to look to the future, and when he could easily have found some other means of explaining the delay of Yahweh's judgement on Judah which did not involve recourse to an everlasting promise? The theory that in the exilic period the ניר references were reinterpreted so as to refer to a future hope is perhaps plausible. To argue that this is what they referred to originally is, in the light of their context in Kings, unconvincing. It is more likely that the obvious conclusion to be drawn from the ניר material is the correct one, namely that it derives from a pre-exilic author[15] who knew nothing of the fall of Jerusalem and the deportation of the king.

The existence of a pre-exilic edition of Kings has already been suggested by analysis of the במות theme in chap. 3, and it may be pointed out that the fact that two of the verses identified there as pre-exilic (1 Kgs 15:3, 2 Kgs 8:18) are closely associated with two of the ניר references (1 Kgs 15:4, 2 Kgs 8:19), and that no literary-critical evidence exists to suggest that this association is secondary, is confirmatory evidence that these references are from a pre-exilic author. Conversely, the presence of the ניר references in the evaluations for Abijam and Jehoram (1 Kgs 15:3-5, 2 Kgs 8:18-19), and their absence in the evaluations for all the kings described as having "done what was right", is confirmatory evidence that the analysis of the structure of this section of Kings offered in 3.2-3.3 above is correct. It was argued there that the basic distinction רע/ישר in 1 Kings 15-2 Kings 15 is a distinction between Yahwism and idolatry, and that the במות were regarded by the author as Yahwistic places of worship. What is significant about the ניר references is that the author clearly felt a need to explain why judgement did not fall in the case of the first two Judaean kings whom he judges negatively, whereas he felt no such need in the case of any of the kings said to have "done what was right", in spite of the fact that they all tolerated the במות. The difference between במות worship and the activities of the kings who are not said to have "done right" is thus once more emphasized. The former may be a fault, but it is not so serious a fault as to elicit Yahweh's wrath. The kings who failed to take action against the במות were still within the Yahwistic camp, "like David" (15:11, 14). The latter, however, is serious enough to lead to an expectation of judgement, and an explanation is therefore required as to why the kings concerned, who were not like David (15:3), escaped. The ניר references supply this: they escaped because of the promise to David, which was itself grounded in the fact that he *did*

---

[15]   So Benzinger, xiii; Kittel, vi-viii, 123; Burney, xv-xvii, 170, 195, 294; Skinner, 18-23, 183, 207, 317; Šanda, 1:xxxvi-xlii, 323, 2:88 (but with 1 Kgs 15:4 as exilic, 1:395); de Vaux, 15-17, 93; Cross, *Myth*, 281-285; Gray, 288, 296-297, 349, 535; Nelson, *Redaction*, 108-118.

do what was right (15:5)[16]. The lack of righteousness, or David-likeness, on the part of these kings is thus compensated for by the merit of David himself.

In summary, then, it may be said that the appearance of David as a promissory figure in 1 Kings 15-2 Kings 15 is best understood within the context of a pre-exilic edition of the books of Kings, and that the way in which the Davidic material is used in the section provides support for the interpretation presented in chap. 3 of its structure and its theological perspective.

---

[16] The fact that we only have נֵיר statements in the case of the first two evil kings of Judah, and not in the case of Ahaziah (2 Kgs 8:27) and Ahaz (2 Kgs 16:2-4), is of no great importance, since the author has made his philosophy of history clear by this point.

4.3 The David Theme in 1 Kings 1-14

4.3.1 David as a Comparative Figure

David appears as a comparative figure in this section in 1 Kgs 3:3, 14; 8:25; 9:4; 11:4, 6, 33, 38; 14:8. Of the positive and negative references, as opposed to the neutral statements which will be discussed shortly, it has sometimes been argued that 11:33b is a secondary addition to the Dtr passage, on the ground that it shares the concerns of other secondary material in the passage which seeks to account for the continuation of the Davidic rule over Judah[17]. This view is unconvincing, however. The mere contrasting of David with Solomon does not of itself connect v 33b to verses like 11:32, 36, and there is no literary-critical evidence for a break between 11:33a and 11:33b. The only secondary working apparent in the verse is in the pluralization of the verbs[18], which may be understood as an attempt to associate the whole of Israel with Solomon's sin and its consequences, or perhaps even to blame the northern tribes for the schism[19].

The positive and negative comparative references in the Solomonic material (1 Kgs 3:3; 11:4, 6, 33; 14:8) confirm the impression gained by study of 1 Kings 15-2 Kings 15. Here, as there, a positive comparison of the king to David (3:3) is thought consistent with the charge that the king tolerated, and worshipped at, the במה. The negative contrast with David is reserved for the accusation against Jeroboam in 14:8, where the worship of other gods is the issue, and for the account of Solomon's apostasy at the end of his reign (1 Kgs 11:4, 6, 33), when he too turned and worshipped other gods. At this point, "his heart was not wholly true to Yahweh his God, as was the heart of David his father" (11:4, cf. 15:3)

---

[17] Dietrich (*Prophetie*, 15-20, 28-29) and Würthwein (139-140, 144, 500) take the whole of v 33b as an insertion from DtrN. Weippert ("Ätiologie", 373-374) and DeVries (149) see all of v 33 as secondary. It makes little sense, however, to suggest that one author would have inserted a verse with plural verbs and a singular כדוד אביו, when he could easily have compared the people to their "fathers" as is done elsewhere (cf. 1 Kgs 14:22). Furthermore, it is inadmissible simply to change *one* of the verbs to the singular, and leave the other two in the plural, as DeVries does.

[18] The plural verbs are out of step with the כדוד אביו at the end of the verse; with the whole context of the passage, which concerns Solomon rather than the people; and with the broader context in 1 Kgs 11:1-8, where it is also Solomon alone who is accused (11:5, 7a). The majority of scholars (Kittel, 100; Burney, 171; Stade and Schwally, 126; Šanda, 1:319; Noth, *Studien*, 72, n. 8; Montgomery, 247; de Vaux, 79; Fichtner, 184; Plein, "Erwägungen", 18; Gray, 291; Robinson, 1:143; Würthwein, 139) therefore accept that the verbs were originally singular, and were subsequently emended.

[19] It seems best to take 1 Kgs 11:32 as an insertion which breaks the connection between 11:31 and 11:33 (Stade and Schwally, 126; Šanda, 1:319, 323-324; Dietrich, *Prophetie*, 16-17; H. Seebass, "Zur Teilung der Herrschaft Salomos nach I Reg 11,29-39", ZAW 88 (1976) 363-376, on p. 364; Würthwein, 139, 144; Vanoni, *Literarkritik*, 72). This being the case, the subject of the plural verbs in the secondary overworking may have been understood as עשרה השבטים in 11:31, and the changes to 11:33 could then be taken as a later tendentious attempt to move the blame for the schism on to the northerners.

In addition to these references, there are in 1 Kings 1-14 four occasions when, because the passage concerns a promise of Yahweh for the future, rather than the assessment of the king in retrospect, David is used as a model without any evaluation being made (1 Kgs 3:14; 8:25; 9:4; 11:38). Such a usage has no parallel in the central section of Kings. On one occasion (11:38), however, where the promise is directed to Jeroboam, the founder of a dynasty, it seems to be quite compatible with the positive and negative usage there, since the king is being promised that he will have a house like David's if he behaves like David. It is also possible to interpret 1 Kgs 3:14 in a sense consistent with this material, since it deals only with the circumstances of the individual king ("I will lengthen your days"), and not necessarily with the dynasty[20]. It is not so clear, however, that the comparative statements in 1 Kgs 8:25 and 9:4 are compatible with those in 1 Kings 15-2 Kings 15, since in the latter chapters, as we have seen, the message is that the Davidic dynasty survives *in spite of* the fact that some kings are unlike David, because those kings are David's successors. In 1 Kgs 8:25 and 9:4, on the other hand, it seems to be the case that even though the king is David's successor, he *must* behave like David if the dynasty is to survive. Discussion of this inconsistency is best postponed, however, until the discussion of David as a promissory figure in the Solomonic material, when the whole issue of the Davidic promise with regard to Solomon will be examined in detail.

4.3.2 David as a Promissory Figure

David appears as a promissory figure in this section in 2:4; 2:24; 3:6, 7; 6:12; 8:15-18, 20, 24-26; 9:5; 11:12-13, 32, 34, 36, 38, 39. We must also consider here the comparative statements mentioned above, in 8:25 and 9:4. Perhaps the best place to begin the examination of this aspect of the David theme in the Solomonic material is with 1 Kgs 11:29-39, since certain verses from this passage have already been discussed above.

4.3.2.1 The Davidic Promise in 1 Kings 11:29-39

It is generally agreed among scholars that 1 Kgs 11:29-39 do not derive from a single author or editor. As Mayes says:

---

[20]   It seems clear that 1 Kgs 3:14 (cf. אֶת־יָמֶיךָ וְהַאֲרַכְתִּי, 3:14b) reflects the law of the king in Deut 17:14-20 (cf. לְמַעַן יַאֲרִיךְ יָמִים עַל־מַמְלַכְתּוֹ הוּא וּבָנָיו בְּקֶרֶב יִשְׂרָאֵל, Deut 17:20b). The question of whether 1 Kgs 3:14 implies more than just that Solomon will live a long life must therefore be settled with regard to the phrase הוּא וּבָנָיו in Deut 17:20. Assuming that the phrase is original (a proposition denied by K. Galling, "Das Königsgesetz im Deuteronomium", *TLZ* 76 (1951) 133-138; and von Rad, *Deuteronomium*, 85-86), does this verse mean that if one king obeys, his dynasty will continue for a long time (so Weinfeld, *Deuteronomy*, 4-5); or that if each successive king obeys, each will have a long reign? Examination of the other occurrences in Deuteronomy in which a promise of long life is made (הַאֲרִיךְ with יָמִים: 4:26, 40; 5:16, 33; 6:2; 11:9; 22:7; 25:15; 30:18; 32:47) seems to indicate that the latter is the correct way in which to take 17:20, and thus that the promise of 1 Kgs 3:14 concerns only Solomon's fate, and has no dynastic implications.

There is no doubt that vv. 29-39 are overfull, repetitious and characterized by changes of emphasis which are occasionally illogical ...[21]

There is little consensus, however, when it comes to the detailed literary criticism of the passage. The analysis which is presented here proceeds in the first instance from decisions already taken above about certain of its verses. It was accepted there that 11:32 is a secondary insertion which breaks into the original Dtr passage represented by 11:31 and 11:33; that 11:33 originally concerned Solomon rather than the people; and that 11:36, with its unconditional promise of ניר to David, is to be understood as from the same primary Dtr author as 1 Kgs 15:4-5 and 2 Kgs 8:19. Such an analysis suggests, of course, that 11:32 and 11:36 are to be understood as deriving from different Dtr authors. This has not been the general opinion among scholars, who have pointed to similarities between them - the concentration on the one tribe which is to be left to the Davidic dynasty and the common phrase העיר אשר בחרתי - which suggest common authorship[22]. While it cannot be denied that a general similarity exists, it must also be pointed out that the differences between the verses are significant. 11:32 contains no reference to David's ניר, and nothing which is equivalent to the כל-הימים of 11:36 - nothing, in fact, which would necessitate a pre-exilic date. An exilic author could well have explained a *temporary* retention of Judah by the Davidic dynasty as due to Yahweh's regard for David's virtue. In addition, the originality of the final phrase of 11:36, which includes the phrase העיר אשר בחרתי, has been questioned by some scholars[23]; and if it is secondary, then the dissimilarity between the two verses is even more striking. Even as they stand, indeed, the use of "Jerusalem" seems to be quite different in each. In 11:36, the stress of the verse is on the ניר promised to David, and Jerusalem is merely the place where this ניר is centred. This priority is reflected even more clearly in 15:4, where Jerusalem is established because of David, and in 2 Kgs 8:19, where Jerusalem is not even mentioned, but Judah is saved from destruction because of David. In 11:32, however, no such priority exists. Rather, the *choice* of Jerusalem is stressed equally with David's role in the retention of Judah by the dynasty. Not only is the idea of the everlasting continuity of the dynasty lacking in 11:32, then, but a cultic explanation of Judah's survival is present which is not present in the ניר material. Taking all this evidence together with the fact that 11:32 seems

---

21 Mayes, *Story*, 117.

22 Burney, 170-171; Skinner, 180-183; Montgomery, 243-247; Gray, 288; Noth, 259-262; Dietrich, *Prophetie*, 15-20; Würthwein, 139-142, 144; Rehm, 1:122-123, 126-127; Mayes, *Story*, 118; Jones, 241, 244-246; DeVries, 149.

23 So Šanda, 1:320; Noth, *Studien*, 72; Plein, "Erwägungen", 20.

clearly to disrupt the Dtr context 11:31, 33, the attribution of the verse to a later hand than is responsible for 11:36 seems justified[24].

Turning now to the remainder of 11:29-39, we discover two uses of the Davidic promise which are distinct from its use in 11:36. The first of these is to be found in 11:34-35, where David is referred to in the context of the delay of Yahweh's judgement until the reign of Rehoboam. Yahweh takes no action against Solomon because of David. Such a use of David is not, of course, logically incompatible with that of 11:36, and it is entirely possible that a single author could have been responsible for both. Indeed, some commentators[25] seem to have had little difficulty in taking all of 11:34-36, with two minor exceptions[26], as from the same hand. Other scholars have noted, however, that the way in which the two themes of delay and limitation of punishment are combined in 11:34-36 is somewhat strange. 11:34a clearly leads us to expect a following, antithetical statement about limitation, whereas what we actually have is a statement about delay (vv 34b-35), which seems to separate v 34a from its natural conclusion in v 36: "I will not take the whole kingdom from his hand (v 34a) ... but to his son I will give one tribe (v 36) ...". Kittel puts the problem well when he says:

> Das ganze Reich 34a entspricht natürlich nicht der Lebenszeit Salomos 34b und der Nennung seines Sohnes 35, sondern erst dem einen Stamm in 36. Entweder also müssen 34b-35 Zusatz sein oder ist כל zu streichen[27].

Kittel prefers the latter solution, because it is simpler, and in this preference he has been followed by most scholars[28]. This is surprising, since, according to Noth

> Die Streichung von כל־, die aus sachliche Gründen notwendig ist ... hat keine Grundlage in der Textüberlieferung, sondern ist reine Konjektur[29].

This is a slight overstatement, in fact, since one LXX manuscript (a_2) does support the omission. Nevertheless, it cannot be denied that this is far from solid evidence. Lacking as it

---

[24] The view that 11:32 is later than 11:36 is shared by Noth (*Studien*, 72) and Plein ("Erwägungen", 20), both of whom regard 11:36a, bα as part of a pre-Dtr account, and 11:32, 36bβ as Dtr; by Vanoni (*Literarkritik*, 261-262); and by Stade and Schwally (15), Šanda (1:320) and Jepsen (*Quellen*, appendices), who see the first author as a Dtr author. Benzinger (83-84) and Nelson (*Redaction*, 114) see v 32 as prior to v 36, a position which is implausible in view of the comments on 11:33 above.

[25] Thus, for example, Burney, 170-172; Skinner, 180-183.

[26] It is almost universally agreed that את עמרת השבטים (v 35) is a late gloss (for example, Montgomery, 247), and generally accepted that the second of the two אשר clauses of v 34b, אשר שמר מצותי חקתי, may also be secondary (for example, Burney, 171). I would agree that it is likely that one of the אשר clauses is secondary, but think it better to omit the first. The idea of the choice of David is otherwise lacking in the passage, and may have come into it under the influence of נשיא, which is discussed below.

[27] Kittel, 100.

[28] So, for example, Šanda, 1:319; Noth, 261; Gray, 291; Dietrich, *Prophetie*, 21; Würthwein, 140; Weippert, "Ätiologie", 359, n. 29.

[29] Noth, 243.

does any real textual basis, the decision to excise כל must therefore rest upon the conviction that the evidence suggests the originality of the connection between v 34a and vv 34b-35. In fact, however, as Noth himself sees[30], the evidence in at least the case of v 35 suggests the opposite. Instead of the ממלכה of vv 31, 34a, we find in v 35 that what is to be taken away from Solomon is the מלוכה. Even with the removal of כל from v 34a, then, v 35 still does not function well as the antithesis of that half verse[31]. Further evidence that vv 34b-35 are most probably from a different hand to v 34a may be seen in the presence of נשיא in v 34b. This term is used in an Israelite context elsewhere in the DH only to refer to the tribal heads of Israel, and never to the king in general or to David in particular[32]. It has therefore often been assumed in translations, and sometimes explicitly stated in comments on 11:34[33], that in this context it must signify Solomon's demotion from king to a more subordinate role. It is not clear, however, what could have been in the author's mind if this were his intention. The whole story, and indeed v 35 itself, makes quite clear that Solomon remained ruler of all Israel until his death, and that no loss of power or position occurred with regard to the kingship until the reign of Rehoboam. נשיא in 11:34b, then, is better understood simply as a synonym for מלך. This being the case, it seems probable that Noth[34] is correct in his suggestion that its use here is influenced by Ezekiel's concept of the future Davidic ruler[35]; and thus that v 34b must be exilic rather than pre-exilic. It could not therefore have belonged to the original Dtr passage which contained v 36. It seems best, then, to retain the כל of v 34a, and to adopt the alternative explanation offered by Kittel for the tensions inherent in 1 Kgs 11:34-36, namely, that vv 34b-35 are a later insertion into the passage[36].

The third occurrence of the Davidic promise theme in 1 Kgs 11:29-39 is to be found in 11:38, a verse which is usually assigned to the same Dtr layer as 11:36. The thinking behind it is indeed consistent with that of the author of the ניר material. Jeroboam is promised that if he is faithful to Yahweh as David was, Yahweh will treat him in the same way. He will build him a "sure house" (בית־נאמן). The allusion is clearly to the promise of Yahweh to David in 2 Sam 7:16: "your house and your kingdom shall be made sure forever ..." (ונאמן

---

[30] Ibid., 261.

[31] For a detailed discussion of the distinction between ממלכה and מלוכה as evidence for a redactional break between vv 34a and 35a, see Vanoni, *Literarkritik*, 155-168.

[32] Josh 9:15, 18, 19, 21; 17:4; 22:14, 30, 32; 1 Kgs 8:1.

[33] So Montgomery, 243-244; Nelson, *Redaction*, 112. Plein ("Erwägungen", 18) agrees that נשיא has a lower status than מלך, but sees these verses as applying to the kings of Judah rather than to Solomon himself. This can hardly be correct, however, when it is clearly Solomon himself who is under discussion.

[34] Noth (261), followed by Würthwein (140, n. 4) and Jones (245).

[35] It should be noted here that in Ezekiel 37 נשיא and מלך are used interchangeably for "ruler" (37:24-25). These verses are something of a stumbling-block to attempts (such as that of E. A. Speiser, "Background and Function of the Biblical Nāśî'", *CBQ* 25 (1963) 111-117) to distinguish sharply between the use of מלך and the use of נשיא in Ezekiel. Whatever their original connotations, the words seem to function as synonyms here, both describing the ruler of all Israel.

[36] Similarly Vanoni (*Literarkritik*, 261-262), who views 11:34a, bα, 36a, bα, as earlier than both 11:34bβ and 11:35a, bα.

ביתך וממלכתך עד־עולם). It therefore seems likely that the author intends us to understand here that Jeroboam is being promised an eternal dynasty in the northern kingdom to match that of David in the southern. If this is so, however, then v 39 as it stands can hardly be from the same hand. This verse implies that the schism is not a permanent one, but will last for a limited period only (אך לא כל־הימים), at the end of which David's descendants will once more possess Israel. It may be suggested, then, that at least this final phrase must be a later addition; and it is perhaps better, with the majority of scholars[37], to regard the whole verse as such, taking ואענה את־זרע as itself implying a chastisement of limited duration along the lines of 2 Sam 7:14-15 (cf. זרע in 7:12), rather than an irrevocable judgement. The Dtr 1 Kgs 8:35-36, where affliction leads to repentance and forgiveness, may be cited in support of this understanding of the verb here, while the fact that the only other occurrence of ענה את־זרע in the DH is to be found in the exilic (cf. 3.5 above) 2 Kgs 17:20 is further evidence that the verse is a later addition. 11:38 thus represents the viewpoint of the primary Dtr author of Kings, while 11:39 reflects the hopes of a later editor. Both authors seem to be dependent on the Davidic promise material in 2 Sam 7:1-17, although they interpret it differently[38]. The author of 11:38 has evidently interpreted the promise of dynasty as applying to Judah alone, rather than, as 2 Sam 7:16 seems to intend it, to all Israel. He is thus able to claim that the Davidides will never lose Judah (1 Kgs 11:36; 15:4-5; 2 Kgs 8:19), while at the same time allowing that the possibility existed that Jeroboam's dynasty would possess Israel. The author of 11:39, on the other hand, has taken the promise as applying to all Israel, and explains the loss of the northern kingdom as chastisement which will one day come to an end. In thus accounting for the loss of the ten tribes, however, he too has departed from the apparent intention of the Samuel passage, which seems clearly to be concerned with *continuity* of government over all Israel after David's time, and to envisage no interruption of this. 11:38 and 11:39 thus represent attempts from different perspectives to bring the original promise into harmony with the historical reality of the schism.

---

[37] Benzinger, 84; Kittel, 101; Burney, 171; Skinner, 183; Stade and Schwally, 126; Šanda, 1:320; Noth, *Studien*, 72, n. 9; Jepsen, *Quellen*, appendices; Fichtner, 188; Plein, "Erwägungen", 20; Noth, 262; Dietrich, *Prophetie*, 19; Würthwein, 140; Rehm, 1:128; Weippert, "Ätiologie", 374; DeVries, 149; Vanoni, *Literarkritik*, 102, 262. Many of these scholars would also take v 38bβ, ובנתי לך אך־ישראל, as part of the insertion, on the ground that it repeats what is said in v 37. This seems unnecessary, however, since v 37 can be understood as referring to Jeroboam himself, and v 38bβ as referring to his dynastic possession of Israel in perpetuity. Cross (*Myth*, 279) differs from the majority in regarding v 39 as original, and Nelson (*Redaction*, 115-116) has sought in detail to justify this position.

[38] I assume here, with the majority of scholars, that the present form of the Nathan Oracle of 2 Sam 7:1-17 is at least substantially that which was known to the first Dtr author of Kings, and that vv 12-16 were certainly present (so Rost, *Thronnachfolge*, 47-74; M. Noth, "David und Israel in II Samuel, 7", in *Mélanges bibliques rédigés en l'honneur de André Robert* (TICP 4; Paris, n.d.) 122-130; E. Kutsch, "Die Dynastie von Gottes Gnaden: Probleme der Nathanweissagung in 2. Sam 7.", *ZTK* 58 (1961) 137-153; A. Weiser, "Die Tempelbaukrise unter David", *ZAW* 77 (1965) 153-168; D. J. McCarthy, "II Samuel 7 and the Structure of the Deuteronomic History", *JBL* 84 (1965) 131-138; Cross, *Myth*, 241-260; Veijola, *Dynastie*, 68-79; M. Görg, *Gott-König-Reden in Israel und Ägypten* (BWANT 105; Stuttgart, 1975) 188-233; T. N. D. Mettinger *King and Messiah: The Civil and Sacral Legitimation of the Israelite Kings* (ConBOT 8; Lund, 1976) 48-63; McCarter, *2 Samuel*, 210-231; H. Kruse, "David's Covenant", *VT* 35 (1985) 139-164, to name but a few).

If this analysis of 1 Kgs 11:29-39 is correct, the original Dtr narrative therefore consisted of vv 29-31, 33 (in the singular), 34a and 36-38. It proclaims a twofold message - that the Davidic dynasty is to have Judah "forever" because of David (11:36), and that Jeroboam's dynasty will similarly possess Israel if Jeroboam behaves like David (11:38) - and functions as the necessary background for the reader's understanding of the central section of Kings which has been examined above. Together with 1 Kgs 12:25-30 and 14:1-13, it explains why Yahweh's treatment of the kings of Israel is fundamentally and justly different from his treatment of the kings of Judah. Because the conditions attached to the dynastic promise to the first non-Davidic king were not fulfilled, there is nothing in the case of the northern kings to prevent Yahweh's wrath against sin. In the south, however, the Davidic promise always averts such wrath against sin. The additions to the passage, excluding here the glosses in 11:34bβ, 35bβ, seem to form a consistent pattern, and may be regarded as deriving from a single editor. If they did, then the most obvious candidate is the exilic editor identified in chap. 3. A specific connection between this author and these additions has already been noted in the use of עבה אחזרע in 11:39, implying that we are dealing in this verse with a "Messianic" understanding of the Davidic promise rather than one grounded in the pre-exilic history of Judah, while the probable influence of the exilic Ezekiel 37 on 11:34b-35 has also been mentioned. The thrust of the editorial work is not difficult to grasp. As well as providing some explanation for the delay in the judgement on Solomon, which he may well have felt necessary in view of the emphasis in 1 Kgs 3:14 that a long reign is dependent upon obedience, the editor also wished to provide an interpretation of its limitation which did not imply, as the original passage did, that the Davidic dynasty would continue regardless of the behaviour of its kings. By inserting before 11:36 an explanatory statement which is similar to it, and yet which uses language which does not imply the everlasting continuity of the Davidic dynasty, it may be suggested that he hoped to rob this verse of its force. Yahweh's regard for David had certainly been a factor, in his view, which influenced the divine attitude in the case of Solomon, but there is no hint, as there is in 11:36, that a promise is in force which will always avert his wrath from Judaean kings in the future. Such a qualification of the ניר material is, of course, quite understandable in the contribution of an author writing during the exile. The Davidic promise, insofar as it is regarded as unconditional, is thus transformed from a means of historical explanation into the ground of a future hope (11:39). The present form of 1 Kgs 11:29-39, then, is best understood, as the books of Kings as a whole were seen to be in chap. 3, as the result of the editing of a primary pre-exilic text by an exilic editor.

4.3.2.2 The Davidic Promise in 1 Kings 2:4; 8:25; 9:4-5

The נִיר material discussed in 4.2.2 and 4.3.2.1 above is not the only material in Kings in which reference to a promise to David is made. We also find such a promise referred to in 1 Kgs 2:4; 8:25 and 9:4-5. 1 Kgs 2:4aβ, b may be cited as an example of its form:

> If your sons take heed to their way, to walk before me in faithfulness with all their heart and
> with all their soul, there shall not fail you a man on the throne of Israel.

It is immediately apparent that if these verses refer back to 2 Sam 7:1-17, as most have believed, then they represent an interpretation of the passage which is very different from that found in the נִיר material. In 1 Kgs 11:36; 15:4-5 and 2 Kgs 8:19, it will be recalled, the Davidic dynasty is viewed as surviving in Judah, because of Yahweh's promise to David (2 Kgs 8:19), in spite of the sins of some of its kings. The promise of everlasting kingship is thus understood as being conditional, not upon the obedience of the individual Judaean kings, but upon that of David himself (1 Kgs 15:4-5). In 1 Kgs 2:4; 8:25 and 9:4-5, however, the promise of continuing kingship is conditional upon the obedience of Solomon and successive kings rather than that of David, who plays no crucial role. It is very difficult to believe that both types of material derive from one hand, even though many scholars[39], including those who have explained thematic tensions elsewhere in Kings in terms of the redactional development of the books[40], have found little difficulty with this idea. On this view, a single author must have wished to tell his readers that Yahweh's promise to David contained two elements which were contradictory. The dynasty would continue "forever, in spite of disobedience on the part of the kings"; and it would continue "forever, only if the kings obey". Since it does not seem very likely that the original author of Kings would deliberately have undercut the message communicated in the first element by introducing the second, two alternative explanations of the text must considered.

The first of these is to be found in the work of Nelson[41]. Nelson resolves the tension in the text, while retaining the idea that a single author is responsible for both נִיר and conditional material, by positing a second Davidic promise which is unrelated to the promise of 2 Samuel 7, and the giving of which is unrecorded in the DH. None of the words of 2 Sam 7:13b-16 are quoted, he notes, nor any of the circumstances in which the Nathan Oracle

---

[39]   So, for example, Wolff, "Kerygma"; Janssen, *Juda*, 13-14; Amsler, *David*, 61-64; Nicholson, *Deuteronomy*, 109-112; Weinfeld, *Deuteronomy*, 4-5, 23-24.

[40]   Thus the two types of material have been assigned to one Dtr hand both by many of those who adhere to a pre-exilic/exilic distinction within Kings (for example, Šanda, 1:244, 271, 323; 2:72; and Gray, 213-214, 288, 349), and by those who subscribe to a history/prophecy/law distinction (Dietrich, *Prophetie*, 72-73, n. 35; Veijola, *Dynastie*, 141-142; Würthwein, 498-501; and Jones, 200-201, 209, who find both types in DtrN).

[41]   Nelson, *Redaction*, 99-105.

was given recalled, in the first of the three references (2:4) which allude to a conditional promise. Precisely because the promise of kingship given in this verse is clearly conditional, indeed, it is difficult to believe that it is this oracle which was in the author's mind. Further evidence that the references do not represent an interpretation of 2 Samuel 7 is to be found in their location only in the Solomonic material, and in the application of the promise to Solomon alone in 1 Kgs 9:4-5. In these verses,

> ... the obedience required in a general way of David's "sons" in 1 Kings 2:4 and 8:25 is specifically required of Solomon, and of Solomon only, for the eternal security of the "royal throne over Israel"[42].

It is Solomon, then, who is in the author's mind, rather than the descendants of David in general, and it is in Solomon's reign that the outworking of the threat implicit in the promise must have taken place. Since the phrase "throne of Israel" can refer to the throne of the northern kingdom, and never refers to the throne of Judah, the promise is clearly meant to apply only to Davidic kingship over the north, which is lost because of Solomon's disobedience[43]. Davidic kingship over Judah, however, continues, since it is governed by a different promise, which is unconditional in nature (2 Samuel 7).

Nelson's appreciation of the need to give full weight to both types of promise in Kings, and his refusal to merge one into the other, as has so often been done in the past, is welcome. His solution to the problem, however, is far from satisfactory. In the first place, his interpretation of the phrase כסא ישראל must be questioned. Apart from the verses under discussion, this phrase appears elsewhere in Kings, as Nelson correctly notes, only in 1 Kgs 8:20 and 10:9, where it refers undoubtedly to the throne of the united kingdom, and in 2 Kgs 10:30 and 15:12, where it refers to dominion over the north. The weakness of taking the phrase in 1 Kgs 2:4; 8:25 and 9:4-5 in the latter sense is immediately apparent. Not only is it the case that in the other two references in the Solomonic material it refers to the throne of all Israel; it is also the case that one of these references is a mere five verses distant from 1 Kgs 8:25. Any reading of the context of 8:25 (1 Kgs 8:14-26) will immediately make clear how unlikely it is that כסא ישראל in 8:25 could mean "throne of the northern kingdom". The sequence of the passage is plain: Yahweh made a promise to David (v 15) which has now been fulfilled (קם, v 20), in that Solomon sits on the כסא ישראל and has built the Temple. Solomon now prays that Yahweh will keep (שמר) what he promised David, that he would always have a successor on the כסא ישראל, if his successors obeyed the law (v 25). Even if 8:25 is an insertion into the passage, as will be argued below, it is inconceivable that any

---

42   Ibid., 102.

43   Friedman ("Egypt", 175-176) makes the same distinction between kingship over the north and kingship over the south.

author who wished to say something about the northern throne alone would have inserted the verse at this point without some clarificatory statement that he did not mean the same throne as in v 20. It is much more likely that the phrase is to be taken uniformly throughout the Solomonic material as referring to the throne of the united kingdom, the throne of David, which is indeed the only throne of which 1 Kings 1-11 as a whole seems to know[44].

A second objection to Nelson's solution is that it requires us to believe that the verses under consideration refer to a Davidic promise which is not recorded anywhere else in the DH. It is unlikely, however, that an author who intended these verses to be understood in this way would not have made it much clearer that this is what he meant, either by being more definite about the circumstances in which the supposed promise was made, or by introducing another speech of Yahweh to David, like that in 2 Samuel 7, which contained the promise. As the text stands, the most natural reference point for 1 Kgs 2:4, 8:25 and 9:4-5 is 2 Sam 7:1-17. Indeed, while Nelson's specific contention that none of the words of 2 Sam 7:13b-16 are quoted in 1 Kgs 2:4 is correct, it must not be overlooked that 1 Kgs 9:4-5 contain the unusual phrase כסא הממלכה (הקמתי את־כסא ממלכתך על־ישראל לעלם, 9:5a), which occurs in the OT only here and in Deut 17:18; 2 Sam 7:13 and 2 Chr 23:20. In view of the rarity of the phrase, it is difficult to avoid the conclusion that the promise to Solomon recorded in 9:4-5 is quite deliberately intended to be a reinterpretation of the promise about the "seed of David" in 2 Sam 7:12-13: וכננתי את־כסא ממלכתו עד־עולם (7:13b). 2 Sam 7:13 promises, without any conditions being attached, that this "seed" will be established on the throne of his kingdom forever, while 1 Kgs 9:4-5 promises that this will happen only if he obeys Yahweh's "statutes and ordinances" (9:4). 1 Kgs 2:3 defines the standard of obedience more closely as that which is written בתורת משה. The occurrence of כסא הממלכה in Deut 17:18, then, is surely no coincidence, for Deut 17:18-20 specifies that when the king "sits on the throne of his kingdom", he should write for himself a copy of "this law" (התורה הזאת), by which is best understood the whole Dtn code[45]. If he obeys this, then "his days will be lengthened in his kingdom". We thus have grounds for supposing that 1 Kgs 9:4-5 are an interpretation of 2 Sam 7:1-16 from the standpoint of the law of the king in Deut 17:14-20 and the Dtn code as a whole. That this kind of reinterpretation of the Davidic promise went on within Dtr circles is clearly demonstrated by Jer 33:14-26, where similar language to 1 Kgs 2:4; 8:25 and 9:4-5 is used in describing it (לא־יכרת לדוד איש ישב על־כסא בית־ישראל, 33:17) and the context, which refers to the covenant with the Levites (33:18, 21-22), makes it plain

---

[44] So 1 Kgs 1:13, 17, 20, 24, 27, 30, 35, 37, 46, 47, 48; 2:12, 24, 33, 45; 3:6; 5:19.

[45] So S. R. Driver, *A Critical and Exegetical Commentary on Deuteronomy*, (ICC; Edinburgh, 1902) 8-9, 212; Mayes, *Deuteronomy*, 116, 273. References to תורה in this absolute sense are almost entirely confined to the framework of the code (4:8, 44; 27:3, 8, 26; 28:58, 61; 29:20, 28; 30:10; 31:9, 11, 12; 32:46). It is therefore likely that Deut 17:18-19 are, as is commonly thought (so, for example, Weinfeld, *Deuteronomy*, 5, n. 1), an insertion from the Dtr editor of the framework. It is thus to the book of Deuteronomy as a whole that the conditional material in 1 Kgs 2:4; 8:25; 9:4-5 is related, rather than simply to the law of the king in isolation, a point whose significance will become clear below.

that the author is thinking of Deut 17:14-18:5. It is thus much better to regard 1 Kgs 2:4; 8:25 and 9:4-5 as representing a similar reinterpretation of the known promise to David recorded in 2 Sam 7:1-17, than to regard them, as Nelson does, as evidence of a different, purely hypothetical promise.

A objection must be raised, thirdly, with regard to Nelson's claim that 9:4-5 assert that it is only Solomon's obedience which is required if the dynasty is to be established forever. This is certainly a possible interpretation of 9:4-5, if they are taken alone. The plausibility of the explanation is somewhat reduced, however, when we consider 9:4-5 in the context both of the other two conditional references, and of the continuation of 9:4-5 in 9:6-9. The question which arises with regard to 2:4 and 8:25 is asked by Nelson himself:

> ... if it was the historian's point that it was specifically Solomon's obedience that was vital ...
> why is the misleading term "sons" used in 2:4 and 8:25[46]?

Why indeed?! Nelson's answer to the question is that the form of 2:4 and 8:25 were forced on Dtr, because it would have been ludicrous for a promise to David in the past to have anticipated Solomon's successful bid for the throne. It was therefore necessary for Dtr to expand the promise to include David's other natural sons. This is unconvincing, however, since the singular instead of the plural in these verses would have made perfect sense as referring to whichever son eventually succeeded to the throne. The best explanation of the plural "sons" in 2:4 and 8:25, as has long been recognized by scholars, is to take it as referring to descendants in general, as it does in 2 Kgs 8:19, where the Davidic promise is also referred to[47]. What 2:4 and 8:25 appear to be saying, then, is that the obedience of David's descendants in general is vital if the dynasty is to continue. If this is so, and if 9:4-5 are from the same author, then clearly 9:4-5 cannot mean that if Solomon obeys, then the future of the dynasty is secure *regardless* of the behaviour of his successors. 9:4-5 must be taken rather as meaning that if Solomon, as one of the kings to whom the promise is made, obeys Yahweh, then the promise of eternal kingship stands good. Taken in this sense, these verses could of course be applied to any of the kings who followed as well, since the obedience of every king is vital.

---

[46] Nelson, *Redaction*, 102.

[47] Here the MT reads לחת לו ניר לבניו, which is difficult. The witness of the LXX is mixed, LXX[B] omitting לבניו entirely, LXX[N] reading as the MT, and LXX[AL] apparently reading ולבניו. This last reading is also found in 2 Chr 21:7. It seems best to restore the ו before לבניו, and to explain both the loss of the entire word (LXX[B]) and the loss of the conjunction (MT, LXX[N]) as a haplography due to the similarity in the form of the ר and the ו in third-century orthography (so Hanson, "Song", 316).

That this is the sense in which 9:4-5 is to be taken is confirmed by 9:6-9, if we regard these verses, with the majority of scholars[48], but against Nelson, as the original continuation of vv 4-5. 9:6-9, containing as they do the reference to the descendants (ובניכם, 9:6) which is lacking in 9:4-5 but present in 2:4, 8:25, make clear that it is Solomon and all those who follow him who are in view, and not Solomon alone. It is certainly true, as Nelson notes, that the reference is in plural form (אם־שוב תשבון אתם ובניכם), whereas Solomon in 9:4-5 is addressed in the singular. If account is taken, however, of the relationship noted above between the conditional material and the law of the king in Deut 17:14-20, this is understandable. Concern for the obedience of the king in Deuteronomy is already closely linked, by the reference to תורה in its absolute sense in 17:18-19, to the more general concern for the obedience of the people as a whole which is found in the framework of the book. As the king is promised that obedience will result in his days being prolonged in Israel, so the people are similarly promised that obedience will mean long life in the land (4:40; 5:33; 6:2; 11:8-9; 30:15-20; 32:45-47). Since the two themes are linked in Deuteronomy, it is hardly surprising that they should also be linked in 1 Kgs 9:4-9, the אתם ובניכם referring both to the king and to the people, and reflecting both the appositional phrase in Deut 17:20 (הוא ובניו) and similar phrases in the framework (Deut 6:2 אתה ובנך ובן־בנך; 30:2 אתה ובניך). It is, indeed, the author's desire to introduce the people at this point which is the best explanation for the fact that 9:4-5 have a different form to 2:4 and 8:25. The delay of the reference to the descendants is necessary if the people are to be included within its scope.

Nelson's attempt, then, to hold the conditional and ניר material together by suggesting that they relate to entirely different promises must be judged unconvincing. At no point is his interpretation of the conditional material so compelling as to lead to the abandonment of the traditional critical view that it represents a reinterpretation of 2 Sam 7:1-17 and is concerned to introduce a conditional element to that promise. A better solution of the problem which is posed by the Davidic promise in Kings is that of Cross[49]: that the ניר material and the conditional material derive from different hands. Indeed, 1 Kgs 9:4-9 clearly imply that the latter is from the hand of an exilic editor, who knows of the fall of Jerusalem and the exile[50], and is thus driven by historical events to an interpretation of 2 Samuel 7 different to that

---

[48] Thus Wellhausen, *Composition*, 273; Kittel, 81-82; Stade and Schwally, 12; Šanda, 1:271; Jepsen, *Quellen*, 20; Montgomery, 203-204; Fichtner, 153-154; Noth, 195-196; Gray, 235-236; Dietrich, *Prophetie*, 72, n. 35; Rehm, 1:101; Jones, 209.

[49] Cross, *Myth*, 281-287.

[50] Thus all of the scholars mentioned in n. 48 above, except Šanda and Montgomery, who take the verses as from a pre-exilic author. Burney (129-130) also accepts that vv 6-9 do not necessarily imply an exilic standpoint, and notes that 9:3 implies a pre-exilic standpoint. I accept this latter claim, and it must also be admitted that the mere mention of exile does not necessarily entail an exilic date (cf. D. R. Hillers, *Treaty-Curses and the Old Testament Prophets* (BibOr 16; Rome, 1964)). It still seems preferable, however, particularly because of the points of contact between these verses and 2 Kings 21 (cf. 4.4 and chap. 5 below), to regard 9:4-9 as reflecting events which have already happened, and to explain v 3 (which conflicts with vv 7-9) as from a pre-exilic author, who also wrote vv 1-2. I thus agree with Cross (*Myth*, 287) that the break between pre-exilic and exilic authorship occurs at v 4.

found in the נִיר material. This editor believed that the continuation of the monarchy, the presence of Yahweh in the Temple, and the presence of the people in the land all depended upon obedience to the law (1 Kgs 9:4-9), and it is the fact that he worked over a pre-existing history of the monarchy in which this view did not appear which may be seen to have led to the tensions which we now find within the books. The נִיר material is now placed in a new context which makes it difficult to read it in the way in which the original author seems to have intended. It still functions to explain the delay of Yahweh's wrath on Judah, but can no longer be taken as implying that the everlasting continuity of the Davidic dynasty is not dependent upon the behaviour of its kings. If it is remembered that 11:32, 34b-5 also have such a qualifying effect on the particular נִיר reference in 11:36, and that this material, too, was assigned to an exilic hand, then it is possible to suggest that the same editor is at work in 1 Kgs 2:4, 8:25 and 9:4-5 as is at work in 1 Kings 11. The adjustments made to the latter passage are now clearly seen to be due to his underlying conviction that the Davidic promise contained an element of conditionality which better explained the history of Israel up until his day than the element of unconditionality which was central in the philosophy of his predecessor.

In conclusion, then, we may say that although many scholars have regarded 1 Kgs 2:4; 8:25 and 9:4-5 as from the same hand as the נִיר material, this position fails to explain adequately why the text is as it is at present. An adequate explanation is provided, however, if we consider that the author of the conditional material was editing a pre-existent text which already contained the נִיר material, and was therefore working under the constraints of that text. 1 Kgs 2:4; 8:25 and 9:4-5 may then be regarded as part of the attempt of a later editor to lead the reader to take the נִיר references in a more qualified way than they actually demand to be taken, in order to account for something which was beyond the experience of the original author: the fall of Jerusalem and the exile of Judah in 587 B.C.

4.3.2.3 Other References in 1 Kings 1-14

If the distinction between the pre-exilic and exilic Dtr view of the Davidic promise in 1 Kings 1-14 is accepted, then the way is clear to examine the remainder of the references to David as a promissory figure in this section of Kings. Perhaps the most important question which must be resolved here is the relationship between the references in 1 Kgs 8:15-18, 20, 24, 26, on the one hand, and the reference in 8:25 on the other. Most commentators[51] have assumed that the whole section 1 Kgs 8:14-26 is from one Dtr editor, although Benzinger[52] finds problems with the shift from the idea that Yahweh's promise to David has been

---

[51] Kittel, 70, 74-75; Burney, 112; Skinner, 144-146; Šanda, 1:221-226, 244; Montgomery, 193-194; Fichtner, 136-139; Noth, 182-184; Gray, 212-216; Rehm, 1:95-96; Würthwein, 95; Jones, 198; DeVries, 123.

[52] Benzinger, 60.

fulfilled (8:15, 20, 24) to the idea that it still has to be fulfilled (8:25-26), and consequently takes 8:25-26 as from a different hand to the one responsible for the rest of the material. There seems little justification for positing redaction for *this* reason, however, since it is clear that part of the promise has been fulfilled (Solomon sits on the throne, 2 Sam 7:12; and the Temple has been built, 7:13a), and part has yet to be fulfilled (that the dynasty should last forever, 7:13b-16). A problem with 1 Kgs 8:25-26 does exist, however, in that both verses appear to be a request for the same thing - that Yahweh would fulfil the rest of the promise - and both are introduced by ועתה, which marks the transition from the introduction (vv 22-24) to the petition (vv 25 and 26). Both seem to follow on most naturally, therefore, from 8:24, the sense of the passage being "you have done this ... now do this"; and the presence of both makes the passage read rather awkwardly[53]. Since it has already been argued on general grounds that the conditional material is secondary to Kings, and since nothing in the passage apart from 8:25 is inconsistent with the pre-exilic view of the promise to David, it seems best to interpret this inconcinnity in the text as the result of the insertion of 8:25 between the pre-exilic 8:24 and 8:26[54].

There remain to be discussed, then, 1 Kgs 2:24; 3:6-7; 6:12 and 11:12-13. As with 8:14-24, 26, there is nothing in either 2:24 or 3:6-7 to indicate that these are not pre-exilic. Indeed, the latter two verses belong to a passage (1 Kgs 3:3-14) which in the discussion of the במה theme in chap. 3 was attributed to the first editor. The situation is quite different with 6:12, however. Here the promise is clearly conditional, and the same link is made between king, people and land as occurs in 1 Kgs 9:4-9. The passage is most probably at least as late as the exilic editor, then, although its precise provenance is unclear[55]. Finally, 11:12-13 clearly assume the presence in 11:29-39 of the secondary 11:34b-35, which discuss the delay in Solomon's punishment (v 12), and they seem also to reflect the presence of

---

[53]   There is, indeed, no parallel to this double transitional ועתה in the DH as a whole. We do find more than one ועתה in other contexts where there is introduction and petition, but in all such cases the first ועתה marks the context in which the petition is made, and only the second the transition to the petition itself (so Josh 14:10, 12; 1 Sam 24:21-22, and most pertinently, 2 Sam 7:28-29, where the sense of the passage is exactly as in 1 Kgs 8:23-26).

[54]   Stade and Schwally (10-11) agree that 8:25 is an insertion, but do not think that the author of 8:14-24, 26 worked before the exile. How far the material which follows 8:26 may be attributed to the same author as this verse has been a matter of some debate among scholars. Given that 8:27 is certainly an insertion which breaks the connection between vv 26 and 28 (Benzinger, 60-61; Burney, 114, and most commentators); that this verse is closely associated with 8:30b and the rest of Solomon's prayer; and that 8:30b is attached awkwardly to 8:30a, Dietrich's division of the text at this point (*Prophetie*, 74, n. 39) seems best. The primary text (Dietrich's DtrN, my pre-exilic author) then consists of vv 28-30a, the expansion vv 27, 30b ff. Dietrich's attribution of 8:44-51 to a still later hand, however, does not seem so compelling; and his attribution of vv 53-61 to the same author as in vv 28-30a is most unlikely in view of the fact that Solomon is standing in v 22 and kneeling in v 53, and that v 59 refers back to the prayer. There seems little reason to doubt that 8:30b-61 derive from one hand. The pre-exilic text may then be seen as recommencing at 8:62.

[55]   It may well be from the hand of the exilic Dtr redactor. However, Burney (68-69) notes several instances in these verses of language which is reminiscent of P and the Holiness Code rather than of the Dtr redactors, and this perhaps signifies a later date. The absence of 6:11-13 from the LXX, however, cannot be taken as significant in this regard, given the tendency of the LXX towards logical ordering. 1 Kgs 6:11-13 is clearly intrusive at this point in the MT, and may well have been omitted for this reason.

11:32 rather than merely 11:36. We may note that as 11:32 lacks any reference to David's
ניר, and any indication that possession of Judah will continue "forever", so also does 11:13.
In addition, we find the same stress on the choice of Jerusalem as part of the reason for
Yahweh's action, while the structure of 11:13, although dissimilar to that of 11:36, is similar
to that of 11:32:

11:13b	למען דוד עבדי ולמען ירושלם אשר בחרתי
11:32b	למען עבדי דוד ולמען ירושלם העיר אשר בחרתי
11:36bα	למען היות־ניר לדויד־עבדי

It thus seems likely that 11:9-13 as a whole are from the hand of the exilic editor
identified above[56].

4.3.2.4 Conclusion

Examination of the use of David as a promissory figure in 1 Kings 1-14 has suggested
that the material in which he appears as such derives from two different authors. On the one
hand, the promise to David is cited as an unconditional promise which guarantees that the
Davidic dynasty will continue to rule in Judah. This perspective is exactly the same as is
found in 1 Kings 15-2 Kings 15, and is best seen as that of a pre-exilic author. On the other
hand, the promise is described as one which is conditional on the obedience of David's
successors, and which carries with it the threat of judgement and exile. This material, along
with other verses which are designed to place the ניר references in a new context, and to
make the unconditional element of the promise a matter of future hope rather than of present
experience, is best understood as the work of the exilic editor of Kings identified in chap. 3.
The David theme, then, like the במה theme, has arrived at its present form as the result of
redactional activity in the text.

---

[56]   Further evidence of the exilic date of 11:9-13 would, of course, be provided by v 10, which refers back to
the exilic 9:4-9, if this verse could be considered original. The presence of the waw-copulative ויצו,
however, may suggest a secondary insertion here (cf. 3.8 above).

4.4 The David Theme in the Closing Chapters of Kings

If the David theme in Kings has arrived at its present form through redactional activity, it follows that, as with the במה theme, the identification of the climax of its primary element should enable us to reach conclusions about the redactional development of the books as a whole. The present section will suggest that the climax of the primary David material is found in the account of Hezekiah's reign in 2 Kings 18-19.

4.4.1 David as a Comparative Figure

David appears as a comparative figure in the closing chapters of Kings in 2 Kgs 16:2; 18:3 and 22:2, verses which are similar in form to the comparative references of the earlier chapters. Ahaz did not behave like David, but committed idolatry like the kings of Israel (16:2), whereas Hezekiah and Josiah did behave like David in "doing what was right in Yahweh's sight" (18:3, 22:2). It is, of course, Josiah who has generally been regarded by scholars who support the idea of a pre-exilic version of Kings as the "second David" whose reign formed the high point of this edition:

> The historian ... has written a great sermon to rally Israel to the new possibility of salvation, through obedience to the ancient covenant of Yahweh, and hope in the new David, King Josiah[57].

There are, however, two problems associated with the attribution of 2 Kgs 22:2 to the pre-exilic author of Kings.

In the first place, the perspective of other comparative statements on either side of the verse (21:2; 23:32, 37) suggests that the whole section from Manasseh onwards derives from a later hand. The latter two verses both maintain that the king concerned "did what was evil in Yahweh's sight according to all that his fathers had done" (ויעש הרע בעיני יהוה ככל אשר־עשו אבתיו). These statements seem to accord ill with the earlier statements which compare a king favourably to David, or imply that he is the ideal figure behind the evaluation, since they express the view that the kings of Judah as a group were bad rather than good. Such a view

---

[57] Cross, *Myth*, 285.

of the history in general, of course, could well have accommodated the occasional exception of a king who "did what was right". It cannot therefore be assumed, purely on the ground that 23:32 follows immediately after a positive account of Josiah's reign, that a redactional break necessarily exists between Josiah and Jehoiakim[58]. It must be admitted, however, that it is extremely difficult to understand why an author who simply wished to characterize the Judaean kings *generally* as a bad lot would have written of more than half of them specifically that they "did what was right"[59]. This does indicate that a redactional break exists *somewhere* in the last few chapters of Kings, and that the section of which the judgement formulae for the last four kings of Judah form part does not derive from the pre-exilic Dtr. How extensive this section was is indicated by examination of 2 Kgs 21:2. This verse also stands out from the majority of the comparative statements, not so much because it necessarily has a different perspective from these so far as the previous kings are concerned, as because it is so different from them in its form. Whereas the other kings of Judah who are judged negatively are compared either with David (1 Kgs 15:3; 2 Kgs 16:2) or with the house of Ahab (2 Kgs 8:18, 27), the immediate focus of comparison in the case of Manasseh is with "the nations whom Yahweh drove out before the people of Israel" (הגוים אשר הוריש יהוה מפני בני ישראל). This phrase occurs elsewhere in Kings only in 1 Kgs 14:24; 2 Kgs 16:3 and 17:8, all of which were assigned in chap. 3 to the exilic editor of the books. Indeed, the phrase itself implies knowledge that Yahweh dealt with Judah in the same way that he dealt with הגוים, as is stated by 2 Kgs 21:10-15, which pick up the תועבת of 21:2 (cf. 21:10) and develop what is implicit there. It seems highly probable, then, that 21:2, and therefore the first Dtr account of Manasseh's reign, was written by the exilic editor of Kings, and did not form part of the pre-exilic books[60]. Since any edition of Kings which did not contain an account of Manasseh's reign is unlikely to have contained an account of Josiah's, the pre-exilic origin of 2 Kgs 22:2 is therefore put in doubt.

This doubt is intensified, secondly, by the presence in 22:2 of the phrase לא־סר ימין ושמאול. The use of ימין ושמאול with סור is found nowhere else in Kings, and occurs only occasionally, indeed, elsewhere in the OT[61]. Given that what we have in 2 Kgs 22:2 is an assessment of

---

[58] This must be maintained against Weippert, "Beurteilungen", 333-334.

[59] This point is well made by Nelson, *Redaction*, 37. Of the 15 kings of Judah from Rehoboam to Josiah, 8 are said to have done what was right (עשה הישר): Asa (1 Kgs 15:11), Jehoshaphat (22:43), Jehoash (2 Kgs 12:3), Amaziah (14:3), Azariah (15:3), Jotham (15:34), Hezekiah (18:3) and Josiah (22:2).

[60] Among scholars who accept a pre-exilic edition of Kings, and regard 2 Kgs 17:8 as exilic, it has been common to ascribe only 21:2b to the exilic redactor (so Benzinger, 188; Stade and Schwally, 53; Šanda, 2:324; Jepsen, *Quellen*, appendices). A distinction between 21:2a and 21:2b has also been made by Würthwein (440), who ascribes the former to DtrG and the latter to DtrN. This is to leave the verse, however, with no original comparative statement, which would be highly irregular. Even Jehoash (2 Kgs 12:3), who has no explicit comparative statement, is nevertheless referred to in connection with his tutor, the priest Jehoiada. A more obvious conclusion to draw from the similarity between 2 Kgs 17:8 and 21:2, since no seam is apparent between 2a and 2b, is that all of v 2 is from an exilic hand.

[61] Deut 2:27; 5:32; 17:11, 20; 28:14; Josh 1:7; 23:6; 1 Sam 6:12; and in the parallel to the present passage, 2 Chr 34:2.

the king, the most significant of these other occurrences is that in Deut 17:20, where the ideal king is said to be one that does not "turn aside from the commandment either to the right hand or to the left" (סור מן־המצוה ימין ושמאול). The author of 2 Kgs 22:2, then, seems to be claiming that Josiah is the ideal king who is referred to in Deut 17:14-20, one who behaves in accordance with the law written in the book (וכתב לו את־משנה התורה הזאת על־ספר, Deut 17:18)[62]. This theme is returned to in 2 Kgs 23:21-25, where Josiah is described as the only king ever to have kept the Passover as it is written in the "book of the covenant" (ספר הברית, 23:21-22), and to have turned to Yahweh according to all the "law of Moses" (תורת משה, 23:25). It is also the recurrent theme of the intervening material, which is centred on the "book of the law" (ספר התורה, 22:8, 11) or the "book of the covenant" (ספר הברית, 23:2), and which characterizes the period before Josiah as one of disobedience. Thus the fathers "have not obeyed the words of this book" (22:13); while the kings of Judah as a group are characterized as sanctioning the idolatry which Josiah removes (23:5, 11, 12, and, implicitly, 23:13). 2 Kgs 22:2, then, is connected to the whole account of 22:3-23:25 in its perspective that Josiah alone has done right in Yahweh's sight. It is therefore clear that, no less than 23:32 and 23:37, the verse represents a different perspective on the kings of Judah in general than that of the pre-exilic editor of Kings. Indeed, its dependence upon Deut 17:14-20, and its view of the written Dtn code as the standard of judgement, ties it closely to the conditional promise material in 1 Kgs 2:4; 8:25 and 9:4-9, suggesting that it is from the same exilic hand.

It therefore seems unlikely that Josiah was the "second David" whom the original author of Kings had in mind, and it may be noted in further support of this assertion that the figure of David does not demonstrably lie behind any element of the portrayal of Josiah in 2 Kings 22-23. It is the figure of Moses, in fact, as Friedman[63] has pointed out, which may be seen to have influenced the narrative throughout, and Josiah, it may be noted, actually leaves David behind (23:21-23) in his adherence to Moses' law. David is thus not the central character which he is in the earlier material, but has stepped into the background.

A quite different state of affairs is to be found in the case of Hezekiah. In this instance, the positive comparative reference (18:3) is associated with other material (18:7-8) which marks Hezekiah out as "like David" in ways which are not shared by his other descendants[64].

---

[62]   סור with ימין ושמאול is also linked specifically with the "book of the law" in Josh 1:7-8 and 23:6, verses which Smend ("Gesetz", 494-497, 501-504) attributes to the late Dtr redactor, DtrN.

[63]   Friedman, "Egypt", 171-173.

[64]   I can see little literary-critical reason for assigning v 7a to a different redactional layer from v 7b, as is suggested by, among others, Würthwein (406-410). I do agree with him, however, that v 3b (which I, with most scholars, attribute to the first Dtr rather than to a later editor) and v 7a must belong to the same redactional stratum, since the David theme is developed by both. The lack of literary-critical grounds for dividing vv 7a and 7b, and the presence of the David theme in both v 3b and vv 7-8, plainly implies that vv 7-8 were present in the Dtr Kings from the start, as the majority of commentators have believed (so, for example, Burney, 337; Skinner, 384; Šanda, 2:239-244; Gray, 669-671; Rehm, 2:177-179).

Thus only of David and Hezekiah among the Davidic kings is it said that "Yahweh was with him" (1 Sam 16:18; 18:12, 14; 2 Sam 5:10; 2 Kgs 18:7), and that the king prospered (השכיל) in war (1 Sam 18:5, 14, 15, as well as 18:30 with the verb in the Qal; 2 Kgs 18:7). Only David and Hezekiah, furthermore, are said to have defeated (הכה) the Philistines (1 Sam 18:27; 19:8; 2 Sam 8:1, among other references; 2 Kgs 18:8). Once more, then, it is apparent that it is Hezekiah rather than Josiah who is best seen as the "hero" of the pre-exilic edition of Kings.

4.4.2 David as a Promissory Figure

David appears as a promissory figure in the closing chapters of Kings in 2 Kgs 19:34; 20:6 and 21:7-8. Of these, 21:7-8 clearly depend on 1 Kgs 9:1-9. The promise to David is defined as the one repeated in 1 Kgs 9:1-9 to Solomon (21:7); and as in those verses it is ultimately the obedience of the whole people, and not just that of the king, upon which the continued presence of Yahweh in the Temple and Israel in the land depends, so here in 21:7-8 the emphasis is on Temple, land and the people's obedience (21:8). As the standard of obedience in the conditional material of 1 Kings 1-14 is the written תורת משה, furthermore, so here in 21:7-8 it is התורה אשר־צוה אתם עבדי משה. There can be little doubt, then, that 2 Kgs 21:7-8 derive from the same hand as the exilic 1 Kgs 2:4; 8:25 and 9:4-9, and represent the same view of the Davidic promise as is contained in this material[65]. From the reign of Manasseh on, indeed, the major theme of the books is the inevitability of Yahweh's judgement upon Israel because of her disobedience to the law of Moses, judgement which not even the righteous Josiah can avert (2 Kgs 22:8-20). Such a perspective is quite different from that represented by the ניר material earlier in the books, where the promise to the righteous David leads to the protection of Jerusalem and Judah in spite of the disobedience of certain kings, and it again implies that it is not simply a few elements of 2 Kings 21 which are late, but 2 Kings 21-25 as a whole.

If the authorship of 21:7-8 may thus be easily established, the same cannot be said of 2 Kgs 19:34 and 20:6. At first sight, it is true, both verses appear to reflect classical Zion theology, in that it is promised that Yahweh will defend Jerusalem "for my own sake and for the sake of my servant David" (למעי ולמען דוד עבדי). It might well be supposed, therefore, that they derive from the hand of the pre-exilic author of Kings, or at least that the material of which they form a part was incorporated into the books by him. However, this is unlikely

---

[65] Most of those who hold to a pre-exilic edition of Kings would ascribe 21:7-8 as a unit to an exilic redactor (so Benzinger, 188; Kittel, 294; Skinner, 406; Stade and Schwally, 53; Šanda, 2:325; Jepsen, *Quellen*, appendices; de Vaux, 17). Exceptions are Gray (705), who ascribes v 7 to the pre-exilic redactor, and Nelson (*Redaction*, 67), who ascribes v 7a to the pre-exilic redactor. Both of these attempts to divide the unit lack any support from the text.

to have been the case. We have noted thus far that the Davidic promise is referred to by this author only in the case of wicked kings, kings who were not "like David". It is usually brought into play only where there is need for an explanation as to why Yahweh's wrath did not fall, and with good kings, (those who "did what was right") there is clearly no such need. Hezekiah, of course, is pre-eminently the king who "did what was right" and was "like David" so far as our author is concerned (4.4.1 above), and an allusion to the Davidic promise with reference to this king would be unexpected in material for which he is responsible. Closer examination of 2 Kgs 19:34 and 20:6 is thus in order; and such examination in fact reveals that there is good reason, on grounds of context and language, to question whether these verses were present in the pre-exilic edition of the books.

If we may take 20:6 first of all, it is evident, as Clements[66] has pointed out, and as the dating of Hezekiah's illness fifteen years prior to his death indicates, that the author responsible for the present form of 20:1-11 wished to associate the report of the providential nature of Hezekiah's recovery from this with the earlier account of Jerusalem's escape in 18:17-19:37[67]. The one event was believed to be capable of shedding light upon the other. Since the emphasis of the illness-report is quite definitely upon Hezekiah's undisputed faithfulness to Yahweh, Clements plausibly suggests that the purpose of the story is to make a connection between such faithfulness (vv 2-3) and the divine defence of Jerusalem (v 6), hinting strongly that unless similar obedience were forthcoming from other kings, then Jerusalem could not be sure of Yahweh's protection. The narrative shows that

> ... if Judah were to continue to receive the kind of protection which the simple interpretation of the narrative of Jerusalem's deliverance in 701 attested, then this could be relied upon only if certain conditions were fulfilled[68].

If Clements' interpretation of 20:1-11 is correct, and it seems likely that it is, then it is clear that 20:6 at least cannot have been introduced to the books of Kings by the pre-exilic

---

66   R. E. Clements, *Isaiah 1-39* (NCB; Grand Rapids and London, 1980), 288-289; idem, *Isaiah and the Deliverance of Jerusalem: A Study of the Interpretation of Prophecy in the Old Testament* (JSOTSup 13; Sheffield, 1980) 63-66.

67   It seems likely that חמש עשרה in 2 Kgs 20:6 has been introduced under the influence of the dating elsewhere in the Hezekiah material as we presently find it in the MT. This tells us that Hezekiah reigned 29 years (2 Kgs 18:2), and that the Assyrian attack took place in his fourteenth year (2 Kgs 18:13). It was thus the author's intention to lead the reader to view the events of 18:17-19:37 in the light of 20:1-7, and perhaps of chap. 20 as a whole. Whether the claim of 2 Kgs 18:13 is historically accurate is, of course, another matter, and one which is not directly relevant to this study. It is disputed whether the figure there is to be emended to ארבע ועשרים (so H. H. Rowley, "Hezekiah's Reform and Rebellion", *BJRL* 44 (1961-1962) 395-431, on pp. 410-413); or retained, either on the basis that Hezekiah began to reign in 715 B.C. (W. F. Albright, "The Chronology of the Divided Monarchy of Israel", *BASOR* 100 (1945) 16-22), or on the basis that he began his *sole* reign at that time (S. H. Horn, "The Chronology of King Hezekiah's Reign", *AUSS* 2 (1964) 40-52; N. Na'aman, "Historical and Chronological Notes on the Kingdoms of Israel and Judah in the Eighth Century B.C.", *VT* 36 (1986) 71-92). A. K. Jenkins ("Hezekiah's Fourteenth Year: A New Interpretation of 2 Kings xviii 13-xix 37", *VT* 26 (1976) 284-298) retains the figure, but applies it to an earlier revolt in 714-712 B.C., the account of which has become fused with the account of Sennacherib's invasion in 701 B.C.

68   Clements, *Deliverance*, 65.

Dtr. The association of the Davidic promise with conditions which must be fulfilled is, in fact, very much the kind of thing which we find in the work of the exilic editor. The suspicion must therefore be that it is to him that we owe this verse. An exilic date for it, and indeed for the Dtr redaction and incorporation into Kings of the whole story[69], is further confirmed by the fact that the phrase למען דוד עבדי is shared by the exilic and Dtr 1 Kgs 11:13, while למעני is characteristic of Deutero-Isaiah[70]. The language of the verse thus confirms what is already evident from its context, that we have here a piece of material from an exilic hand[71].

Turning now to 2 Kgs 19:34, we find the same connection with Deutero-Isaiah, indicating exilic provenance. Indeed, the presumption must be, in view of the similarity of the verse to 20:6, that it derives from the same exilic author. The slight difference in its form supports rather than undermines this view. It is clear from the presence of להושיעה (not found in 20:6) that 19:34 refers back to 19:15-19, where Hezekiah prays: ועתה יהוה אלהינו הושיענו נא מידו (19:19). We must also take this passage into account when discussing the date of 19:34, then, as well as in discussion of the precise nuance of the verse. So far as date is concerned, it seems fairly clear that 19:15-19 is a late piece of material. Only a few examples which illustrate this need be given here. The phrase כל ממלכות הארץ (19:15, 19), for example, is found otherwise only in material written after the first fall of Jerusalem (and thus after the realization that Jerusalem was not inviolable had dawned) or later[72]; while 2 Kgs 19:18 as a whole reflects the exilic Deut 4:28[73]. More generally, the concern of the prayer is that the nations would recognize that Yahweh is the only true god. This concern is exactly that of 1

---

[69] Whatever the origins of the story (cf. Würthwein, 432-435), it is most unlikely to have been incorporated into Kings before it attained its Dtr form, and there seems little reason (*contra* Würthwein) to suppose that 20:6 was not added at this point along with 20:2b, 3a, 4-5. It is best, therefore, to view the date of the whole Dtr story as the same as that of 20:6.

[70] F. J. Gonçalves, *L'expédition de Sennachérib en Palestine dans la littérature hébraïque ancienne* (EBib n. s. 7; Paris, 1986), 470, writes of the same expression in 2 Kgs 19:34 as follows: "Du point de vue de la formulation, *II Rois* XIX, 34bα a ses parallèles stricts en *Is.* XLIII, 25; XLVIII, 11". H. Wildberger, *Jesaja* (BKAT 10; Neukirchen-Vluyn, 1972-1982), 1436, says of Isa 37:35 (par. 2 Kgs 19:34): "Der vorliegende Text hat also eine deuterojesajanische und eine deuteronomistische Formel kombiniert".

[71] A late dating for 20:6 is also confirmed if it is held that 20:1-11 were introduced by the same hand as 20:12-19. In spite of the efforts made by Nelson (*Redaction*, 129-132) to deny that 20:12-19 is a *vaticinium ex eventu*, it seems far more likely that this narrative was composed after the idea that Jerusalem was inviolable had lost its force, and thus at least after 597 B.C., when the first deportation to Babylon had taken place (so Clements, "Date"). A more plausible date for the whole complex 20:1-19, on the basis of P. R. Ackroyd's understanding of it ("An Interpretation of the Babylonian Exile: A Study of 2 Kings 20, Isaiah 38-39", *SJT* 27 (1974) 329-352, on p. 346) and on the basis of the explanation by C. T. Begg ("2 Kings 20:12-19 as an Element of the Deuteronomistic History", *CBQ* 48 (1986) 27-38) of the function of 20:12-19 in the whole exilic DH, seems to be after the events of 587 B.C. See further Begg's article "The Significance of Jehoiachin's Release: A New Proposal", *JSOT* 36 (1986) 49-56, for a discussion of 20:19 within the context of 2 Kgs 20-25 as a whole.

[72] So Jer 15:4; 24:9; 29:18; 34:1, 17, and the closely associated Deut 28:25 (cf. Deut 28:36-37, and the connection between these verses and the exilic 1 Kgs 9:6-9); Ezra 1:2; 2 Chr 36:23; and the very late Isa 23:17.

[73] This verse is also, like 2 Kgs 19:15, 19, related to Deut 28:36-37 and 1 Kgs 9:6-9.

Kgs 8:60, which shares the "recognition formula" with 2 Kgs 19:19[74], and which most scholars would agree is part of an exilic or post-exilic addition to 1 Kings 8 as a whole[75]. In all these respects, and in many others[76], 2 Kgs 19:15-19 clearly has great affinity with writings of the exile and later, and is best assigned a late date. 2 Kgs 19:34, which refers back to it, must therefore also be late.

This is confirmed if we consider the meaning of 19:34 in the context of the narrative which precedes it, and especially of the prayer. For in the same way that 2 Kgs 20:2-3 stress the piety of Hezekiah, thus causing the reader to view the promise of 20:6 in that context, so 2 Kgs 19:15-19 also bring the king's character to the fore. He is one who may himself come before Yahweh, without intercessor or any hint of the need for repentance, and make confident requests of him. As Childs notes of this prayer:

> Hezekiah has become the type of the righteous king whose heart is perfect before God[77].

The allusion to the Davidic promise in 19:34, then, is, like that in 20:6, made in the context of an emphasis on piety which may be read as conditioning the promise. This fact, coupled with the clear indications from the language that 19:34 must be late, leads one to suppose that the verse must have been added to the books of Kings by someone other than the pre-exilic author.

This is not to say, of course, that a version of the narrative in 18:17-19:37 concerning Jerusalem's deliverance could not already have been present in the pre-exilic Kings. It is only to assert that if this was the case, then it has undergone editing by an exilic Dtr hand. The whole question of whether such a story was already present, and if so, what was its extent and function, will in fact be the subject of the next section.

4.4.3 Hezekiah and the Deliverance of Jerusalem

It has been suggested in the previous section that 2 Kgs 19:34 is not from the hand of the pre-exilic author of Kings. It remains to be asked, however, whether the pre-exilic Kings

---

[74] This literary formulation was popular in the exilic and early post-exilic periods, and is particularly common in Ezekiel (וידעו כי־אני יהוה, Ezek 6:10, 14; 7:27; 12:15 *et passim*). For a discussion, see W. Zimmerli, *Erkenntnis Gottes nach dem Buche Ezekiel: Eine theologische Studie* (ATANT 27; Zürich, 1954) 48-64.

[75] Benzinger, 59, 63-64; Šanda, 1:246; Jepsen, *Quellen*, appendices; Noth, 190; Braulik, "Spuren", 25-26; Nelson, *Redaction*, 72; Würthwein, 96; Jones, 206.

[76] See the excellent detailed study of Gonçalves (*L'expédition*, 462-469), who concludes (476): "La prière est entierement construite au moyen d'expressions, d'images et de thèmes que l'on trouve dans les *Psaumes*, dans les prières deutéronomistes attribuées à David et à Salomon, dans la prière de *Jer.*, XXXII, 16-25, dans le *Deutéro-Isaïe* et dans les prières des écrits postexiliques (*II Chr.*, XX, 5-12; *Néh.*, IX, 6-37 et *Dan.*, IX, 3-19)". He dates it to the exilic period.

[77] B. S. Childs, *Isaiah and the Assyrian Crisis* (SBT 2/3; London, 1967), 100.

nevertheless contained a version of the story of the deliverance of Jerusalem of which this verse now forms part, and if it did, how extensive this version was and what its function was within the books as a whole. To these questions we shall now turn.

First of all, is there evidence which would suggest that such a story had already been incorporated[78] into Kings at a pre-exilic stage? Much here depends on the analysis of 2 Kgs 18:3-8 which is adopted. It has already been accepted above (3.8, 4.4.1) that the pre-exilic Kings included vv 3-4aα and vv 7-8. In addition, it seems more than likely, in view of the fact that both the במה theme and the comparative aspect of the David theme find their conclusion in Hezekiah's reign, that the climactic 18:5, with its ואחריו לא־היה כמהו בכל מלכי יהודה,[79] is also original. The sentiments expressed in the verse are consistent with what we know to have been the pre-exilic author's view of Hezekiah, and it is unlikely to have been composed after the reign of Josiah, of whom a similar statement is made (2 Kgs 23:25)[80]. If this analysis is correct, then it seems highly probable that some form of the story in 2 Kgs 18:17-19:37 *had* already been incorporated into Kings at the pre-exilic stage, for the points of contact between 18:3-4aα, 5, 7-8 and 2 Kgs 18:17 ff. are striking. We have already noted in 3.8 above how the removal of the במה described in 18:4 is again referred to in 18:22. It was also noted there how the theme of "trust" permeates 18:19-25, the verb בטח occurring there no fewer than six times in the space of five verses. This theme is, of course, picked up from 18:5, where we are told: ביהוה אלהי־ישראל בטח. As Gonçalves says of 18:5a:

> ... il répond à l'avance aux questions que le Rab-Shaqé pose au nom de son maître, d'entrée
> de jeu, comme une sorte d'en-tête de son discours (*II Rois*, XVIII, 19-20) ...[81]

In the same way, 18:7b, וימרד במלך־אשור ולא עבדו, evidently anticipates the following story about the events of the Assyrian expedition, and is specifically picked up in 18:20b (אל מי בטחת כי מרדת בי). As clearly as 18:3-4aα, 5, 7-8 point back in the books of Kings to previous

---

[78] We may immediately allow that, whatever else is the case, it was probably not *written* by the Dtr author of the books, but originated elsewhere, perhaps in prophetic circles interested in the life and message of Isaiah (so, for example, Gonçalves, *L'expédition*, 441-442, although the cautionary comments of Clements, *Deliverance*, 69-70, should be noted). That it was, however, incorporated into Kings first of all, and only secondarily taken up into the *book* of Isaiah, may still be accepted, since it has been argued convincingly often enough (for example, by O. Kaiser, "Die Verkündigung des Propheten Jesaja im Jahre 701", *ZAW* 81 (1969) 304-315). Whether K. A. D. Smelik's recent attempt ("Distortion of Old Testament Prophecy: The Purpose of Isaiah xxxvi and xxxvii", *OTS* 24 (1986) 70-93) to undermine the consensus at this point will succeed remains to be seen.

[79] The final phrase of the verse (ואשר היו לפניו) is probably to be regarded, with the majority of scholars and *BHS*, as a secondary addition.

[80] The same cannot be said of the less sweeping v 6, which looks very much like a duplicate comment on Hezekiah's relationship with Yahweh. The allusion to the law of Moses as the standard of behaviour suggests, in view of our discussion thus far in chap. 4, that we have here an addition from the hand of the exilic editor of Kings.

[81] Gonçalves, *L'expédition*, 338.

references to David and the במח, then, so too do these verses point forward to sections of 2 Kgs 18:17 ff. The most plausible explanation of this fact is surely that a version of this story was incorporated into the books of Kings by their pre-exilic author[82].

If this may be accepted, the next question which arises is that of the extent of this story. For it is clear that to affirm the presence of such a narrative is not to settle the issue of whether all or only some of 18:17-19:37 was included. It has been recognized by the majority of scholars since Stade[83] that 2 Kgs 18:17-19:37 is not a unity. Two accounts of Jerusalem's deliverance in 701 B.C.[84] have, in fact, been isolated, on the basis both of the close parallelism in structure and content between two different sections of the narrative, and of the historical improbability of supposing the repetition of an occurrence such as is described here[85]. Arguments from form, language and theological perspective have

---

[82] The same links cannot be demonstrated to exist between 18:3-4aα, 5, 7-8 and 18:14-16, a passage often argued to have been present in the first edition of Kings. Indeed, there is a tension between the summary of Hezekiah's reign in 18:1-8 and the narrative in 18:14-16 which has frequently been noted. The reader is surprised to find the latter following on from the former. The tension is reduced, of course, if 18:14-16 are read along with 18:17 ff., since whatever the historical realities were, the juxtaposition of the two accounts may imply that an editor wished them to be read as if the events of 18:17 ff. followed on from those of 18:14-16. It is not impossible, then, that 18:14-16 were incorporated into Kings by the pre-exilic author of the books, since the statements contained in verses like 18:5, 7 can be taken as relating to the whole story of the Assyrian invasion, Hezekiah proving himself to be worthy of the author's praise in its latter stages, if not at its beginning. This is perhaps not an entirely satisfactory solution to the problem, however, and the possibility must be allowed that 18:14-16 represent a secondary insertion into the books. It must be admitted that the absence of these verses in the parallel Isa 36:1-3 cannot speak in favour of this possibility (Kaiser, "Verkündigung", 305-306), although this passage does at least demonstrate that 18:13 can introduce 18:17 ff. quite as effectively as it does 18:14 ff. At the same time, the apparent historical reliability of the verses (stressed by Clements, *Deliverance*, 9-13, for example) cannot speak against it. The fact that the material may come from an annalistic source and approximate to what we are told in the Assyrian annals does not prove that it comprised part of the original books of Kings. It is simply a matter of judgement whether it is thought likely that the pre-exilic edition of Kings as it has been described thus far would have contained this passage. In my judgement, it is more likely that it was added later, as part of an attempt, which may also be noted in 20:12-19, to tone down the rather exaggerated picture of Hezekiah which is given by the original account.

[83] B. Stade, "Miscellen: Anmerkungen zu 2 Kö. 15-21", *ZAW* 6 (1886) 156-189.

[84] Some scholars, of course, though allowing that both accounts refer to the same events, would dispute this dating, understanding 18:17-19:37 as relating to a second campaign of Sennacherib in Palestine at a later date (J. Bright, *A History of Israel* (3rd ed.; Philadelphia, 1981) 298-309; E. W. Nicholson, "The Centralisation of the Cult in Deuteronomy", *VT* 13 (1963) 380-389; R. de Vaux, "Jérusalem et les prophètes", *RB* 73 (1966) 481-509, on pp. 498-499; S. H. Horn, "Did Sennacherib Campaign Once or Twice Against Hezekiah?", *AUSS* 4 (1966) 1-28). A quote from Rowley ("Reform", 420) seems apt, however: "... there is more here to connect the Biblical account with the known campaign of 701 B.C. than with any other campaign of which we have secure knowledge". The lack of any convincing external evidence of a second campaign by Sennacherib in Palestine remains a serious flaw in the theory, since most would agree that the slight evidence of the text in its favour may be otherwise interpreted. In this regard, it remains to be seen whether scholars will accept the new interpretation advanced by W. H. Shea ("Sennacherib's Second Palestinian Campaign", *JBL* 104 (1985) 401-418) of the recently reconstructed "letter to God" (cf. N. Na'aman, "Sennacherib's 'Letter to God' on His Campaign to Judah", *BASOR* 214 (1974) 25-39, on pp. 26-28), the Adon Papyrus, Egyptian chronology and other data, which, if correct, means that the external evidence for a second campaign is stronger than has been thought.

[85] A minority of scholars (for example, Šanda, 2:289-291; W. O. E. Oesterley and T. H. Robinson, *A History of Israel*, 1: *From the Exodus to the Fall of Jerusalem, 586 B.C.* (Oxford, 1932) 388-399, 409-410; A. Parrot, *Ninive et l'Ancien Testament* (CAB 3; Neuchâtel, 1953) 36-46; J. le Moyne, "Les deux ambassades de Sennachérib à Jérusalem", in *Mélanges bibliques rédigés en l'honneur de André Robert* (TICP 4; Paris, n.d.) 149-153; Rowley, *Reform*) have nevertheless defended the proposition that 18:17-19:37 tell us of two successive stages of the same campaign; and still others (for example, H. Winckler, *Alttestamentliche Untersuchungen* (Leipzig, 1892) 26-49; Benzinger, 177-179; A. Jeremias, *Das Alte Testament im Lichte des Alten Orients* (2nd ed.; Leipzig, 1906) 529-530; C. van Leeuwen, "Sanchérib devant Jérusalem", *OTS* 14 (1965) 245-272) that it describes two different campaigns.

additionally been brought to bear, most notably by Childs and Gonçalves[86], in order to buttress further the distinction between the accounts, which are usually referred to as B1 and B2. B1 begins with 18:17 and runs as far as 19:7, 19:8 or 19:9, with its ending perhaps in 19:36-37; while B2 begins with 19:9 and ends in 19:34, 19:35, or 19:36. Both the original beginning and the original ending of B2 are often assumed to have been lost when the accounts were combined. The manner in which this summary of the analysis of B1 and B2 has been phrased, indeed, demonstrates the degree of uncertainty which has existed, and continues to exist, among scholars as to precisely where *both* accounts end. Stade took the וישמע and וישב of 19:9 as reflecting the ושמע and ושב of 19:7, and found the ending of B1 in 19:9bα, supposing that the expected reference to Assyria had dropped out when B1 was combined with B2. The view that B1 extends as far as 19:9a has found widespread acceptance among scholars, although it has been a common modification of Stade's hypothesis to take the וישב of 19:9bα as part of B2, and to seek the end of B1 in 19:36-37 (cf. וישב וילך ויסע, 19:36)[87]. Other scholars, however, are more tentative about, or simply deny the validity of, the connection which is made between the שמעה of 19:7 and the news of Tirhakah's approach in 19:9a, and thus regard all of v 9a either as belonging to B2[88], or as part of an editorial bridge between B1 and B2[89]. On this view, the שמעה of 19:7 refers to something which is not recorded in the passage, perhaps news of difficulties in other parts of the Assyrian empire. As far as the end of chap. 19 is concerned, the major focus of disagreement apart from the place of vv 36-37 has been the attribution of v 35. Although this verse has often been seen as the natural conclusion of B2[90], it has been pointed out that it lies in some tension with 19:33[91], which appears only to be concerned with a return of Sennacherib to Assyria. As Clements notes:

> The mention of the return of Sennacherib to his homeland neither requires a previous act of
> destruction of his army, nor does it expect it[92].

---

[86] Childs, *Crisis*, 73-103; Gonçalves, *L'expédition*, 373-487.

[87] So Kittel, 280-281; Burney, 338-340; Skinner, 385-386 (tentatively); Montgomery, 514-515; de Vaux, 207; Childs, *Crisis*, 73-76; Clements, *Deliverance*, 54; Würthwein, 415-418; Jones, 568. A similar view is found among commentators on the parallel passage in Isaiah, for example O. Kaiser, *Der Prophet Jesaja, Kapitel 13-39* (ATD 18; Göttingen, 1973), 298-314, who finds B1 to include Isa 37:9a, 37aβ, 38. Gonçalves (*L'expédition*, 377-382), thinks that both וישב in 2 Kgs 19:9b and all of 19:36-37 belong to B1.

[88] So Winckler, *Untersuchungen*, 46; Benzinger, 178-179; Oesterley and Robinson, *History*, 1:409; Robinson, 2:170-172.

[89] Gray (661-662, 685-686), Rehm (2:183-186) and E. Vogt ("Sennacherib und die letzte Tätigkeit Jesajas", *Bib* 47 (1966) 427-437; *Der Aufstand Hiskias und die Belagerung Jerusalems 701 v. Chr.* (AnBib 106; Rome, 1986), 48-50) regard all of 19:8-9a as a bridge between B1 and B2. Wildberger (*Jesaja*, 1376) thinks that only Isa 37:9a (par. 2 Kgs 19:9a) is redactional, with v 8 belonging to B1.

[90] Kittel, 281; Burney, 339; Skinner, 386; Montgomery, 515; de Vaux, 207; Gray, 661-662.

[91] Childs, *Crisis*, 7 5-76; Clements, *Deliverance*, 58-61.

[92] Clements, *Deliverance*, 59. Followed by Jones (582), Clements resolves this tension by attributing v 35 to neither B1 nor B2, but to a later editor. Childs (*Crisis*, 75-76) and Gonçalves (*L'expédition*, 449-455) resolve it by removing v 33 as a secondary addition.

The precise delineation of B1 and B2, then, cannot be said to be an issue which has been settled.

It is no part of my intention here to offer a definitive solution to this problem. It would be presumptuous to attempt this in such a brief space, when so much detailed work has recently been carried out on this material. Furthermore, it is not strictly necessary to my purpose that I do so, since the argument of this section does not depend upon any precise delineation of B1 and B2, but only upon acceptance that two accounts exist which can be broadly recognized. The question which was posed above comes down to whether B1 alone, or the whole B account, was incorporated into the pre-exilic books of Kings, and this is a question which may be resolved without reference to the verses about which there is most controversy (2 Kgs 19:8-9, 35) with regard to the division between B1 and B2. Nevertheless, a few comments by way of contribution to the debate would seem to be in order.

First of all, there is in my view no convincing literary-critical evidence within 19:9 itself that 19:9b has been joined to 19:9a secondarily. The whole verse reads quite naturally as it stands, וישב וישלח being an example of verbal hendiadys, an idiom well known in biblical Hebrew. The attribution of the first part of the verse to B1 and the second to B2 has little support here, then. Thematically, too, v 9a would be a strange climax to the B1 account, since the whole thrust of the preceding narrative is that, contrary to Rabshakeh's claim, Hezekiah and the people are relying on Yahweh, not Egypt[93]. It hardly seems likely, then, that the act of God described in 19:7 is intended to be understood as involving the advance of the Egyptian army. This would be a very tame climax to B1, and one which would cut right across the distinction between Yahweh and Egypt which is earlier so important to the author[94]. This problem does not arise, of course, if all of 19:9 is assigned to B2. Such an attribution is supported, finally, if we suppose, as many scholars do, that both B1 and B2 have some connection with the historical events of 701 B.C., and thus that it is reasonable to expect a degree of harmony between these accounts and the Assyrian annals. We know from

---

[93]   So also Gonçalves, *L'expédition*, 380: "D'après ce récit, Ézéchias, contrairement aux affirmations du Rab-Shaqé, ne met pas sa confiance en l'Égypte, mais en Yahvé".

[94]   *Contra* Gonçalves, *L'expédition*, 380, who argues that since Egypt is only Yahweh's instrument in 2 Kgs 19:9, there is no tension here.

[95]   *ANET*, 287-288.

the annals[95] that the Ethiopian forces[96] were involved in the battle at Eltekeh between Egypt and Assyria, a battle which ended in an overwhelming victory for Assyria, and resulted in the wholesale capture of Egyptian and Ethiopian troops. They also suggest that this battle preceded rather than followed Sennacherib's action against Jerusalem[97]. If 19:9a belongs to B1, then the B1 account simply cannot be squared with the annalistic account, since B1 then suggests *either* that the advance of the Egyptians occurred later in the campaign than the annals suggest, and resulted in an Assyrian retreat rather than a crushing victory; or that Tirhakah advanced a second time - an advance of which there is no other record - in spite of the previous decimation of his troops. If 19:9a belongs to B2, on the other hand, then the problem disappears. B1 then does not mention the advance of the Egyptians at all (although the speech of Rabshakeh perhaps implies it, in its correct historical position)[98], while B2's reference to it as occurring at the beginning of the sequence of events in no way conflicts with the picture painted by the annals. It seems much more satisfactory to resolve the problems of 19:9a in this way, than simply to view the author of B1, as we would have to if 19:9a belonged to the B1 account, as guilty of gross historical distortion. On this understanding of B1 and B2, then, the advance of the Egyptians is the reason for the sending of the letter in B2, rather than the reason for Sennacherib's flight in B1. The present form of the whole B account may perhaps be seen as in part due to the editor's mistaken differentiation between Egypt (18:17-25) and Cush (19:9), which led him to think of the two narratives as successive rather than parallel.

---

[96] Akkadian *meluḫḫa* and Hebrew כוש are usually understood as referring to the same region to the south of Egypt, known to classical authors as Ethiopia. The mention of Tirhakah as king, and as apparently in charge of the advance, in 2 Kgs 19:9 has often been seen as a major reason why it cannot be the events of 701 B.C. which are referred to here. Tirhakah was not Pharaoh at that time, and it has been maintained that he could not even have been old enough to lead troops into battle (so W. F. Albright, "New Light from Egypt on the Chronology and History of Israel and Judah", *BASOR* 130 (1953) 4-11, on p. 9; Horn, "Sennacherib", 3-11; Bright, *History*, 299-300). The naming of Tirhakah as king is scarcely a problem, since he could well have been referred to according to his later title. The second point, if it could be definitely established as correct, would be more serious. It depends, however, on the acceptance of M. F. L. Macadam's suggestion (*The Temples of Kawa*, 1: *The Inscriptions* (London, 1949) 15) that there was a co-regency between Tirhakah and his predecessor Shebitku, and thus that the former was born in 710 B.C. This suggestion has generally been rejected by Egyptologists (for example, J. Leclant and J. Yoyotte, "Notes d'histoire et de civilisation éthiopiennes", *BIFAO* 51 (1952) 1-39; J. M. A. Janssen, "Que sait-on actuellement du Pharaon Taharqa?", *Bib* 34 (1953) 23-43; K. A. Kitchen, "Late-Egyptian Chronology and the Hebrew Monarchy: Critical Studies in Old Testament Mythology, I", *JANESCU* 5 (1973) 225-233; idem, *The Third Intermediate Period in Egypt (1100-650 B.C.)* (Warminster, 1973) 161-172; F. J. Yurco, "Sennacherib's Third Campaign and the Coregency of Shabaka and Shebitku", *Ser* 6 (1980) 221-240), and it seems clear that on a more orthodox dating, Tirhakah must have been around 20 years of age in 701 B.C. He would then have been quite old enough to accompany the Egyptian and Ethiopian troops to Palestine; and we know, indeed, that it was commonplace for royal princes to do this kind of thing (cf. Kitchen, *Period*, 157 n. 308, on the Rameses Inscriptions).

[97] It is, of course, possible that the annals do not describe the events in strict chronological order (so H. Haag, "La Campagne de Sennachérib contre Jérusalem en 701", *RB* 58 (1951) 348-359), and thus that the impression which they give is misleading.

[98] It may well be, indeed, that the reference to Pharaoh as a "broken reed" (הקנה הרצוץ, 18:21) implies that the battle of Eltekeh has already taken place.

2 Kgs 19:8, secondly, appears best understood as part of the B1 narrative[99]. On the one hand, there is no decisive argument in favour of separating 19:8 from 19:7. On the other hand, however, there is some reason to doubt that 19:8 originally preceded 19:9a. In the first place, there is a certain lack of smoothness in the transition from v 8 to v 9 which suggests a redactional break here. Translation of the two verses makes this clear:

> Rabshakeh returned and found the king of Assyria fighting against Libnah, for he had heard
> that he had departed from Lachish. And he heard concerning Tirhakah king of Cush, "He is
> coming out to fight against you", and he sent messengers once more to Hezekiah ...

The presence of שמע in v 8b leads us to expect some renewed note of the subject of וישמע in v 9a. In the absence of this, the connection between the verses is rather awkward, since it is clearly Sennacherib who is the intended subject of the second verb, and not Rabshakeh[100]. In addition, and if we may again assume that both the B1 and B2 accounts, like the Assyrian annals, have some connection with historical reality, it must be pointed out that to take v 8 with v 9a, and to identify the advance of v 9a with that of the Egyptians towards Eltekeh, necessitates that we accept a rather implausible picture of Sennacherib's campaign. Assuming that the annals give us even a general chronological picture of the campaign, we would have to assume that Sennacherib moved from the area of Joppa south through the territory of Ekron, without conquering its major cities; reduced Lachish and moved to Libnah (2 Kgs 19:8); and then returned northward to meet the Egyptians at Eltekeh and deal with Ekron[101]. If we assume, on the other hand, that the battle of Eltekeh took place before the siege of Lachish and Libnah, dividing 19:8 from 19:9a, we obtain a much more coherent picture. For reasons both literary-critical and historical, then, it seems best to take 19:8 as part of B1.

If this understanding of 19:8 and 9a is correct, then a question arises, thirdly, as to the point of reference of 19:7 - what was the news which the author believed had caused Sennacherib's return to Assyria? It is possible, of course, that this information is not present in the text, as some have suggested. Another possibility presents itself, however, which may not have been given sufficient attention in the debate so far. I refer here to the possibility that it is in v 35, a verse closely associated with vv 36-37, where the fulfilment of the other two parts of Isaiah's prophecy in 19:7 is described, that the content of the news is to be found. If this is so, then the author of B1 believed that it was the report of the decimation of

---

[99] The various attempts which have been made to separate 19:8aα from 19:8aβb (for example, K. Marti, *Das Buch Jesaja* (KHC 10; Tübingen, 1900), 253; B. Duhm, *Das Buch Jesaja* (HKAT 3/1; 3rd ed.; Göttingen, 1914), 240) have not attracted widespread support and are unconvincing (cf. Gonçalves, *L'expédition*, 377-378). The verse is best taken as a unity.

[100] Wildberger, *Jesaja*, 1376, among others, also finds the connection between vv 8 and 9 to be awkward, on the basis of the content of the two verses: "Der Übergang von 8 zu 9 (sc. Isa 37:8 and 9, par. 2 Kgs 19:8 and 9) ist hart ...". He denies any original connection.

[101] So Bright, *History*, 307).

part of his army which prompted Sennacherib to give up his campaign in Palestine, and which resulted, therefore, in the salvation of Jerusalem. Such an attribution of v 35, it is true, has been steadfastly resisted by most scholars[102]. It is difficult to escape the conclusion, however, since there appears to be little literary-critical evidence which would prevent our connection of the two[103], that this resistance has had more to do with different scholars' assessments of the relative historical worth of the B1 account and 2 Kgs 19:35, than it has with the analysis of the text. It is the case that B1 is generally regarded as much closer to the historical events than 19:35, which is either seen as a later elaboration of an original event, or as a piece of theological colouring which has no basis in fact[104]. It is not at all clear, however, that such a distinction between B1 and 19:35 can be maintained.

In the first place, we know from the comparative materials that historians throughout the ancient Near East often incorporated into their histories statements of the type found in v 35, in which the gods were described as intervening supernaturally to give their devotees victory[105]. If such statements are thus an intrinsic part of the history-writing process in the ancient world, no distinction in principle can be made between B1 as "history" and 19:35 as "legend" or "theological colouring". Indeed, B1 as a whole is itself a *theological* narrative, and not simply an account of what happened (if such were even possible). We are not justified, then, in deducing from the nature of B1 and of 19:35 that the latter is later than the former.

Secondly, with regard to the question of whether 19:35 in particular has any basis in fact, the evidence of Herodotus[106] is surely significant[107]. It is perfectly true that the Herodotean material differs markedly in its detail from the story in 2 Kings. It remains the case, nevertheless, that Egyptian tradition does seem to have known of some unusual event during

---

[102] It should be noted, however, that Stade and Schwally (52) do attribute v 35 to B1.

[103] Two pieces of evidence must be considered here. Firstly, several scholars (for example, Kaiser, *Jesaja*, 298-299; Wildberger, *Jesaja*, 1376) have suggested that the accumulation of verbs at the beginning of 2 Kgs 19:36 indicates that B2 runs as far as this verse. If this were so, then 19:35 could not easily be taken as part of B1. However, the case is not compelling. As Vogt (*Aufstand*, 36-37) points out, the text is quite translatable as it stands, and the accumulation of verbs may be understood in terms of deliberate emphasis by the author on Sennacherib's departure. There is no necessity, then, to see more than one author at work in 19:36. Secondly, 19:7 speaks of a שמועה as the cause of Sennacherib's return, while 19:35 speaks of a divine act. This is scarcely a problem, however, since 19:35 may be taken as referring to the "great army" which came to Jerusalem (18:17), about which Sennacherib (in Libnah) then hears news. It is perfectly possible, then, from a literary-critical point of view, to read 19:7(-8), 35-37 consecutively as part of one passage.

[104] So, for example, Clements, *Deliverance*, 61, who maintains that a later editor "... felt that the story of what had taken place lacked a sufficiently dramatic portrayal of how the hand of God had been at work to protect Jerusalem". He therefore composed v 35, under the influence of Isaiah's prophecies.

[105] For surveys of the evidence, see M. Weippert, "'Heiliger Krieg' in Israel und Assyrien: Kritische Anmerkungen zu Gerhard von Rads Konzept des 'Heiligen Kreises im alten Israel'", ZAW 84 (1972) 460-493; and M. Weinfeld, "Divine Intervention in War in Ancient Israel and in the Ancient Near East", in H. Tadmor, and M. Weinfeld (eds.), *History, Historiography and Interpretation: Studies in Biblical and Cuneiform Literatures* (Jerusalem, 1983) 121-147.

[106] Herodotus, 2:141, where he records an Egyptian story in which Egypt is saved by divine intervention from the army of Sennacherib.

[107] This is to be maintained in the face of continued denials, most recently from Vogt, *Aufstand*, 71-75.

the reign of Shabaka's successor[108], whom we know as Shebitku (702-690 B.C.)[109], an event
which removed the threat to Egypt from Sennacherib's army, and which was interpreted as
divine intervention. It is also the case that we have no secure knowledge from any source of
any campaign of Sennacherib in Palestine, or involving Egypt, apart from that in 701 B.C.
The fact that both Egyptian and Hebrew tradition thus seem independently to know of an
unexpected reverse suffered by the Assyrian king must therefore be taken seriously, and
remains a problem for those who would deny any historical basis behind 2 Kgs 19:35[110]. It is
surely better to regard both stories as interpretations, from different points of view, of an
occurrence, perhaps a plague[111], which was regarded by both peoples as the explanation of
the otherwise inexplicable: why Sennacherib did not conquer Egypt, although she had
severely weakened forces, and why he did not take Jerusalem.

The comparative evidence suggests, then, that there is no good reason for regarding B1 as
closer to the historical events than 19:35, and consequently no reason why the nature of
19:35 should be regarded as disqualifying it as the climax of B1. Rather, the acceptance of
19:35 as part of B1 enables us to regard B1 as more "historical" than the Stade hypothesis
and its offshoots, since it removes the necessity of postulating an advance by Tirhakah later
in the campaign than the Assyrian annals suggest, or of taking the author as intending to say
that the Egyptian advance to Eltekeh resulted in an Assyrian retreat. In addition, the verse
supplies what is otherwise completely lacking in the narrative, but which the narrative leads
us to expect: an account of an act of God, independent of any human agency, which justifies
the reliance upon Yahweh rather than men which the story emphasizes. It is not just that a
later editor felt that the story lacked drama: the story itself, in my view, demands such a
dramatic climax. For literary-critical, thematic and historical reasons, then, it seems better to
regard B1 as including 2 Kgs 18:17-37; 19:1-8, 35-37, and B2 as being contained, along with
later additions such as 19:21-31[112], in 19:9-34.

Acceptance of this precise analysis of B1 and B2 is, however, not essential to the
plausibility of the case being made out here. For the question of whether B1 alone or the

---

[108] That the tradition was solidly grounded and well-known may perhaps be indicated by the uncritical tone of
Herodotus' account, when compared with the criticism which he often applies to other traditions, and given
that he had a natural inclination to suspect superhuman and miraculous occurrences. On this, see B.
Baldwin, "How Credulous was Herodotos?", *GaR* 2/11 (1964) 167-177; and K. H. Waters, *Herodotos the
Historian: His Problems, Methods and Originality* (Beckenham, Kent, 1985), who maintains that "... though
Herodotos did not invariably use research and reason to discredit tall tales or biased accounts, he
successfully did so in the majority of cases" (p. 164).

[109] For the dating, see Kitchen, *Period*, 154-161. Herodotus calls the king Σεθων.

[110] Many scholars, indeed, do affirm that some event must lie behind the story. Thus Benzinger, 185; Kittel,
291; Skinner, 399-400; Šanda, 2:284; Montgomery, 497-498; Rowley, "Reform", 423-424; Gray, 694;
Kitchen, *Period*, 385-386; Bright, *History*, 301; A. R. Millard, "Sennacherib's Attack on Hezekiah", *TynBul*
36 (1985) 61-77. The lack of any mention of it in the Assyrian annals proves little, since we cannot be sure
that the *Assyrians* would have perceived such an event as the reason for their return from Palestine, nor, if
they had, that they would have recorded it for posterity.

[111] This has been the usual interpretation of both 2 Kgs 19:35 (cf. 2 Sam 24:15-17) and of Herodotus, 2:141.

[112] So, for example, Kaiser, *Jesaja*, 314-315.

whole B account was incorporated into the pre-exilic Kings may be settled without reference to the controversial issues surrounding 2 Kgs 19:8-9, 35. On the one hand, it seems clear that if the prayer of Hezekiah in 2 Kgs 19:15-19 is, as has been argued above (4.4.2), of late date, then so also is the B2 account of which it is an integral part[113]. On the other hand, it should be evident from the analysis above of the connections which exist between 18:3-8 and the story of Jerusalem's deliverance that these are overwhelmingly with the B1 rather than the B2 account. Indeed, nothing in the pre-exilic summary of Hezekiah's reign (18:3-4aα, 5, 7-8) presupposes the presence of the B2 account, while B1 is foreshadowed in several different ways[114]. It therefore seems most likely that it was the B1 narrative alone which was originally included in the pre-exilic edition of the books of Kings, and that the B2 narrative was only introduced at the time of the exilic editing of the books[115].

If this was so, it remains to be asked, finally, how such a narrative would have functioned within the context of the books as a whole. Clearly it would have done so very well as part of the pre-exilic Dtr's attempt to portray Hezekiah as the ideal king. Hezekiah retains great confidence in Yahweh, although facing the overwhelming might of the Assyrian army. He is thus demonstrably a man of faith in the mould of David, and to that extent, even though David is not explicitly mentioned in it[116], the story can be seen as forming part of the climax of the David theme. This is true also of the other aspect of the David theme which has been examined in this chapter, namely the use of David as a promissory figure. Nowhere in B1 is there mention of a Davidic promise. However, the narrative can be read in such a way that it provides a conclusion to this aspect of the theme. For B1 itself leaves open the question of

---

[113] This is to be maintained with the majority of scholars (for example, Vogt, *Aufstand*, 58-59, who dates B2 as a whole by the date of 2 Kgs 19:15-19) against Dietrich (*Prophetie*, 38 n. 65, 138-139 n. 115), who regards the prayer as an interpolation. As Gonçalves (*L'expédition*, 468 n. 122) says: "L'ensemble *II Rois*, XIX, 9b-19 doit être l'œuvre du même auteur". He, like Vogt, dates B2 to the exilic period.

[114] It is possible that the reference to Samaria in 18:34b represents another way in which B1 links in with the pre-exilic Kings rather better than does B2, which nowhere refers to this city (cf. 19:10-13). It has already been argued that the flow of the pre-exilic narrative depends upon the distinction between north and south, both in respect to the gods who were worshipped, and to the dynasty which ruled. Here in the B1 account, if 18:34b is original to it, this distinction is made forcibly and in its ultimate form, the fate of Samaria in 722 standing in stark contrast to the fate of Jerusalem in 701. Caution is required here, however, both because 18:32b-35 have been adjudged by some scholars (for example, Duhm, *Jesaja*, 237; Gonçalves, *L'expédition*, 385-387) to be an addition to B1 made under the influence of B2; and because, even where 18:32b-35 as a whole is accepted as original, 18:34b has often been seen as a secondary accretion (A. Rahlfs (ed.), *Septuaginta Studien* (3 vols.; Göttingen, 1904-1911), 3: *Lucians Rezension der Königsbücher* (1911), by A. Rahlfs, 278; Montgomery, 490; see, however, H. M. Orlinsky, "The Kings-Isaiah Recensions of the Hezekiah Story", *JQR* 30 (1939-1940) 33-49, on pp. 46-47, n. 30).

[115] So Gray, 668 and Vogt, *Aufstand* 50-58, both of whom regard B1 as part of the pre-exilic Kings and B2 as being added later.

[116] Gonçalves, *L'expédition*, 430-431, however, has pointed out that there are parallels between sections of B1 and the story of David and Goliath in 1 Samuel 17. There are at least allusions to David in B1, then, if not explicit references.

why Yahweh acted in the defence of Jerusalem[117], thus allowing the reader to supply his own answer. There can be little doubt that the reader of the pre-exilic edition of Kings would have regarded the basis both of Hezekiah's trust in Yahweh and of Yahweh's action on behalf of Jerusalem as the promise to David. It was this promise which guaranteed the inviolability of Jerusalem, an inviolability supremely demonstrated in the events of 701 B.C. These events underlined the difference between Judah and Israel which we have seen to have been at the heart of the pre-exilic Dtr's theology, the apostate north, which lacked Yahweh's chosen dynasty, falling before the Assyrian threat, the faithful south under the Davidides surviving. While the B1 narrative of the deliverance of Jerusalem was plainly not composed specifically for the pre-exilic books of Kings, then, it is clear that it functions well as a climactic narrative within them, and was included for this very reason.

---

[117] I cannot agree with Gonçalves (*L'expédition*, 439-440) that Hezekiah's trust in Yahweh is itself the reason for Jerusalem's deliverance in B1. The narrative itself nowhere makes a connection between the two. Thus, for example, when Yahweh's action is announced in 2 Kgs 19:6-7, no reference is made to Hezekiah's piety. The only hint of a reason for this action is to be found in 19:4, 6, where there are references to Yahweh being mocked by the Assyrians. However, 19:6bβ has often been regarded as a secondary addition to B1 (so Duhm, *Jesaja*, 239; Wildberger, *Jesaja*, 1410; Gonçalves, *op. cit.*, 387-388), and vv 3-4 seem clearly out of place. Wildberger's explanation of these two verses (*op. cit.*, 1389, 1408-1409) as a secondary insertion dependent upon B2 seems preferable to that of Gonçalves (*op. cit.*, 389), who thinks that the material is original, and only the order of 19:3-6 due to the influence of B2. When this material is removed, it is clear that no reason is given in B1 for Yahweh's intervention. It is certainly possible if one is reading the story in the light of the oracles of Isaiah, as Gonçalves is doing (*op. cit.*, 432-442) to *interpret* it in a way consistent with that prophet's message, linking "trust" and salvation in such a way as to make the latter dependent upon the former. This is, however, to introduce an idea which B1 itself does not explicitly contain, and it is not the only way to interpret the story. Interpretation here depends very much on the context in which B1 is read.

4.5 Conclusion

The examination of the David theme in Kings has been carried out on two parallel tracks. The use of David as a comparative figure is, it has been argued, an important feature of the judgement formulae of the books of Kings up until and including the reign of Hezekiah, after which it is almost completely absent, appearing only in 2 Kgs 22:2. Reasons have been advanced, arising from its immediate context in the Josiah account, and its wider context in the group of judgement formulae at the end of the books, as to why it is unlikely that the reference in 2 Kgs 22:2 is from the hand of the pre-exilic editor of the books. The use of David as a promissory figure in the ניר material, it has been maintained, suggests the view that the Davidic dynasty will continue forever, and Jerusalem remain secure, because of Yahweh's promise to David, and regardless of the wicked behaviour of any of his successors. Such a perspective is absent from some other material in the opening chapters of Kings which also refers to the Davidic promise. This material makes the promise conditional upon the obedience of the successors, and seeks to qualify the ניר material so as to lessen the force of the elements which contradict this view. The perspective of the ניר material is also absent from the material after Hezekiah's reign, where the picture is of a slide towards inevitable destruction due to the disobedience of Judah's kings. It is in the narratives about Hezekiah, it has been suggested, that the unconditional material finds its proper climax, in the B1 account of Jerusalem's deliverance. The B2 account, which seeks to reinterpret B1 in the same way as verses like 1 Kgs 11:13, 32 seek to reinterpret 11:36, is to be seen as from the same hand as those verses. The location of the climax to the pre-exilic David theme in Hezekiah's reign, and the change in attitude to David and to the Davidic promise which is apparent after this point, supports the conclusion reached in chap. 3, that the first Dtr edition of Kings only ran as far as the account of his reign.

5. THE PRE-EXILIC EDITION OF THE BOOKS OF KINGS

5.1 Introduction

The study of the David and במה themes of the books of Kings has suggested that those scholars are correct who have maintained that the books were first written in the pre-exilic period and subsequently updated during the exile. It has indicated, however, that the point in the text at which the first edition came to a conclusion, and the editor began his work, is much earlier than has usually been imagined. Hezekiah, rather than Josiah or some later king, is the "second David" whom the judgement formulae presuppose and anticipate. It is the events of his reign, specifically the centralization of Yahweh-worship and the abortive attempt by Sennacherib to take Jerusalem, which are their primary focal point. The material after 2 Kings 18-19, it has been suggested, derives in the main from one exilic hand. The present chapter will seek to provide further support for this position. First of all (5.2), three more pieces of formulaic evidence will be presented which indicate that the first edition indeed ended with Hezekiah's reign; and second (5.3), a more extensive study of 2 Kings 21-23 will confirm that chaps. 21-25 are best understood as an exilic addition. A brief discussion of the likely date and purpose of the first edition of the books of Kings (5.4) will bring the chapter to a close.

5.2 Further Evidence from the Regnal Formulae

In the course of his own analysis of the regnal formulae, Nelson argues that in general the variations among them

> ... occur quite randomly and are the natural result of the historian writing his own prose freely ...[1]

Evidence has been found in chaps. 3 and 4, however, which suggests that at least some variations in the judgement formulae are not quite so random as Nelson claims. In view of this, it would seem prudent to re-examine the accession and death/burial formulae also, in order to discover whether they can provide any further evidence which is supportive of the thesis that Hezekiah's reign marks the end-point of the first edition of Kings. Three elements of these other formulae seem to offer hope in this regard.

5.2.1 The Death/Burial Formulae Re-Examined

Of the three elements which commonly recur in relation to the death and burial of the Judaean kings, the variation with respect to one of them has long been understood as far from purposeless. The phrase וישכב עם־אבחיו is generally recognized as a device used throughout Kings to indicate that the death of the king concerned was natural rather than violent[2]. The distribution of the other two elements of the formulae suggests that random variation is not the best explanation in their case either. One of these, the notice that the king was "buried with his fathers" (קבר עם־אבחיו) appears for every king of Judah from Rehoboam to Ahaz with the exception of Abijam (1 Kgs 15:8)[3], and then never appears again. The other, that the king was buried "in the city of David" (בעיר דוד), appears for absolutely every Judaean king from Rehoboam to Ahaz, and likewise disappears completely after this point. This state of affairs is hardly likely to be the result of an author choosing phrases at random.

---

[1]   Nelson, *Redaction*, 35.

[2]   So B. Alfrink, "L'expression שכב עם אבחיו", *OTS* 2 (1943) 106-118.

[3]   Rehoboam (1 Kgs 14:31); Asa (15:24); Jehoshaphat (22:51); Jehoram (2 Kgs 8:24); Ahaziah (9:28); Jehoash (12:22); Amaziah (14:20); Jotham (15:38); Ahaz (16:20). The phrase does not appear for David or Solomon either (1 Kgs 2:10; 11:43), although in their case this is understandable, since there were no "fathers" in Jerusalem with whom they could be buried. Note that it *is* said of Solomon that he was buried in the "city of David *his father*".

Two explanations which are more plausible have been put forward. The first of these is that the difference in the description of royal burials after Ahaz reflects a difference in actual burial practice after his reign. There are different versions of this historical argument, depending upon whether the stress is laid on the first phrase, קבר עם־אבתיו, or the second, בעיר דוד, or both. Thus Yeivin, for example[4], argues that all the kings up until Hezekiah were "buried with their fathers" in the royal sepulchres, and that after this, because the royal burial-ground was full, kings were buried elsewhere. In support of this explanation, he cites 2 Chr 32:33, which he takes as indicating that Hezekiah was buried "on the ascent to the tombs of David's sons". All Judaean royal burials, however, the absence of any reference in the text to עיר דוד notwithstanding, took place within the "city of David", by which he understands the inner citadel of Jerusalem[5]. Weill and Smit[6] both make a distinction between burials within the city of David and those elsewhere. Weill, who takes עיר דוד in its widest sense as a synonym for Jerusalem, argues that one of the results of Hezekiah's reforms was that royal burials no longer took place inside the city walls, due to concern that the laws concerning ritual uncleanness should be observed[7]. A similar concern can be found in Ezek 43:7-9. Smit, who follows Yeivin in his understanding of עיר דוד and in his explanation of the reason for the change in practice, sees the later burials as outside the citadel but inside the city-walls[8]. All agree, nevertheless, that the change in phraseology does reflect a change in practice.

None of these suggestions is very convincing. A major weakness of Yeivin's case is that it does not explain why there is variation with regard to עיר דוד if the author meant only to say that the place of burial *within* the city of David had changed. Why did he not retain the reference to עיר דוד, particularly in the formulae for Hezekiah, Josiah and Jehoiakim[9], and

---

[4]   S. Yeivin, "The Sepulchers of the Kings of the House of David", *JNES* 7 (1948) 30-45.

[5]   This is also the view of J. Simons, *Jerusalem in the Old Testament: Researches and Theories* (Leiden, 1952) 194-225. S. Krauss ("Moriah-Ariel, II/5: The Sepulchres of the Davidic Dynasty", *PEQ* (1947) 102-111) seems to hold a similar view, although disagreeing that the reason for the change was that the burial-ground was full.

[6]   R. Weill, *La cité de David: Compte rendu des fouilles exécutés, à Jérusalem, sur le site de la ville primitive* (Paris, 1920) 35-44; E. J. Smit, "Death and Burial Formulas in Kings and Chronicles Relating to the Kings of Judah", in *Biblical Essays: Proceedings of the Ninth Meeting of "Die Ou-Testamentiese Werkgemeenskap in Suid-Afrika" held at the University of Stellenbosch, 26th-29th July, 1966* (Potchefstroom, 1966) 173-177.

[7]   A. Kloner, "The 'Third Wall' in Jerusalem and the 'Caves of the Kings' (Josephus War V 147)", *Levant* 18 (1986) 121-129, also thinks that the later burials took place outside the city walls.

[8]   This position has recently been adopted by G. Barkay, "לבעיית מקום קבריהם של מלכי בית דוד האחרונים", in M. Broshi (ed.), בין חרמן לסיני: יד לאמנון (Jerusalem, 1977), 75-92.

[9]   It is understandable that the phrase should be omitted in the cases of Manasseh and Amon, since the addition of בעיר דוד, with or without any reference to "burial with his fathers", would make either notice read rather awkwardly. With Hezekiah, Josiah and Jehoiakim, however, the omission of both parts of the notice is more difficult to explain, since there is no hindrance stylistically to their presence. Indeed, the addition of both phrases in these three cases would simply make the burial notices like others in the books. Those for Hezekiah and Jehoiakim would then correspond exactly to the majority, while the notice for Josiah would correspond to that for Ahaziah (2 Kgs 9:28).

merely omit ויקברהו/ויקבר עם־אבחיו? It seems far more likely, if the historical explanation is correct, that the author's intention is to tell us that the burials after the reign of Ahaz were outside the city of David. There are also problems, however, with both the alternatives which accept this. So far as Weill's case is concerned, it must be objected that it seems highly unlikely that Manasseh's house, and therefore the garden of Uzza (2 Kgs 21:18), was located outside the walls of Jerusalem, while nothing which is said of Hezekiah, Josiah and Jehoiakim implies that they were buried outside the walls either. Not only is it the case, furthermore, that there is no early evidence that the burial of kings was thought to be included within the scope of the purity laws, it may also be questioned whether even later priestly circles considered it so. P does not address the issue, while the verses cited by Weill (Ezek 43:7-9) are capable of more than one interpretation. Neiman[10] has suggested that פגר in Ezek 43:7 and 9 may, in fact, be better translated "stela" than "corpse", and that the objects of Ezekiel's attack are therefore memorial stelae to various kings rather than the kings' tombs[11]. Even if we retain the translation "corpse", it must be noted that it is the proximity of the פגרים to the Temple which seems to be the concern of the author, rather than simply their presence in Jerusalem, and that it is not clear whether it is royal burials in general, or particular royal burials, which are under attack. Given that the burials of Manasseh and Amon may have taken place in the palace garden[12], which would have adjoined the Temple, and given that their burials in particular signified the apostasy which Ezekiel so often lambasts[13], it may well have been these alone with which the prophet was concerned[14]. Certainly it is Manasseh who is most readily identifiable as the king who did "abominations" (תועבות, Ezek 43:8; cf. 2 Kgs 21:2, 11). Little can therefore be built on these verses.

Similar problems beset the hypothesis of Smit. In the first place, 2 Chr 32:33 is also capable of more than one interpretation. Most scholars, indeed, have not accepted that במעלה is intended to communicate that Hezekiah was buried elsewhere than the royal tombs, but have preferred to interpret the word as meaning that he was interred in a place of honour in

---

[10]   D. Neiman, "*Pgr*: A Canaanite Cult-Object in the Old Testament", *JBL* 67 (1948) 55-60.

[11]   This translation has been widely accepted (for example, by W. Zimmerli, *Ezechiel* (BKAT 13; 2 vols.; Neukirchen-Vluyn, 1969) 1082-1083; and *KB*, 861-862, which contains references to other literature), although it is dismissed by Vaughan (*Bāmâ*, 64-65, n. 73). It seems best in Lev 26:30, where there is a play on words between the פגרים (corpses) of the people and the פגרים (stelae) dedicated to their idols.

[12]   It is by far the most natural interpretation of בית in 2 Kgs 21:18 that it refers to the royal palace, rather than, as Yeivin ("Sepulchers", 34-35) suggests, to some other residence.

[13]   It seems likely that עזא is to be identified with the Arabian god *Al-'Uzzâ*, and that the burials were in a plot of land dedicated to this god (O. C. Whitehouse, "Uzziah", *HDB* 4:843-845; J. Gray, "The Desert God '*Attr* in the Literature and Religion of Canaan", *JNES* 8 (1949) 72-83; J. W. McKay, *Religion in Judah under the Assyrians, 732-609 BC* (SBT 2/26; London, 1973) 24-25). The alternative view, that עזא is an alternative for עוזיה, and that the land mentioned is the same as that in 2 Chr 26:23, has now largely been abandoned.

[14]   So, for example, Skinner, 409-410; Jones, 600.

the tombs, and/or in their upper section[15]. On either of these views of במעלה, Hezekiah's resting-place could not be differentiated from that of many of his predecessors in Chronicles, and it is indeed highly unlikely on other grounds that Chr intended to say that it was. Study of his burial-notices seems to indicate that "the tombs of the kings" (2 Chr 21:20; 24:25; 28:27), "the tombs of the sons of David" (2 Chr 32:33), and "the tombs of his fathers" (2 Chr 35:24) are to be thought of as the same place. If this is the case, then it is very unlikely on theological grounds, given that only apostate or deformed kings are elsewhere excluded (2 Chr 21:20; 24:25; 26:23; 28:27), that Chr would have described Hezekiah as being excluded from this place, and it is equally unlikely that historically Hezekiah would have been excluded and Josiah included, and that Chr is merely recording this fact. The relevance of 2 Chr 32:33 to the discussion about the burial-notices in Kings is therefore questionable.

Secondly, Smit's differentiation of "city of David" and "garden of Uzza" as geographically distinct parts of Jerusalem is not convincing. It is certainly true that in the Solomonic material, עיר דוד appears as an area distinct from the area in which the Temple and palace complexes lie (1 Kgs 3:1; 8:1; 9:24; 11:27). This evidence, however, is not very helpful so far as determining the meaning of the phrase later in the books is concerned. It demonstrates only that עיר דוד was a name given to the city of Jerusalem as then defined by its walls: it cannot tell us how the author used the phrase once Solomon's new city was completed. Examination of the burial formulae themselves strongly implies that a wider reference is intended in these instances. In the case of the northern kings who died a "normal" death, it is the custom of the author of the formulae to record simply that they were buried in their capital city, whether Tirzah (1 Kgs 16:6) or Samaria (1 Kgs 16:28; 2 Kgs 10:35; 13:9, 13; 14:16). In view of this, it seems more natural to understand עיר דוד in the Judaean formulae as referring to Jerusalem in general, rather than as referring to a particular part of the city. This is certainly the way in which Chr understood the formulae, as can be seen from two places where he deviates from his normal עיר דוד, describing the place of burial as בעיר יהודה (2 Chr 25:28)[16] and בעיר בירושלם (2 Chr 28:27). The notices for Manasseh and Amon in Kings are in this case simply more detailed accounts of where in the

---

15 So E. L. Curtis, *A Critical and Exegetical Commentary on the Books of Chronicles* (ICC; Edinburgh, 1910) 493-494; A. B. Ehrlich, *Randglossen zur hebräischen Bibel: Textkritisches, sprachliches und sachliches*, 7: *Hohes Lied, Ruth, Klagelieder, Koheleth, Esther, Daniel, Esra, Nehemia, Könige, Chronik, Nachträge und Gesamtregister* (Leipzig, 1914) 381; W. Rudolph, *Chronikbücher* (HAT 1/21; Tübingen, 1965) 314; J. M. Myers, *II Chronicles*, (AB 13; Garden City, 1965) 192; F. Michaeli, *Les livres des Chroniques, d'Esdras et de Néhémie* (CAT 16; Neuchâtel, 1967) 234; P. R. Ackroyd, *I and II Chronicles, Ezra, Nehemiah* (TBC; London, 1973) 196; R. J. Coggins, *The First and Second Books of the Chronicles* (CNEB; Cambridge, 1976) 284-285; H. G. M. Williamson, *1 and 2 Chronicles* (NCB; Grand Rapids and London, 1982) 388. The position adopted by Yeivin and Smit is also that of I. Benzinger (*Die Bücher der Chronik* (KHC 20; Tübingen, 1901) 128), R. Kittel (*Die Bücher der Chronik* (HKAT 1/6:1; Göttingen, 1902) 170), and Simons (*Jerusalem*, 207-208).

16 It may, of course, be that יהודה is only a scribal error for דויד, as Krauss ("Sepulchres", 103, n. 2), among others, suggests. It seems unlikely, however, that there should be a scribal error only at this point, when "city of David" occurs so frequently elsewhere in the formulae.

city of David these kings were buried, and no intention exists to communicate to the reader that a general change in the location of royal burials has occurred.

An historical explanation for the difference in the burial notices after Ahaz thus seems less likely to be correct than the alternative which has been proposed by Macy[17], namely that the notices after this point reflect a change in the scribal convention of the Dtr school. A later editor described the burials of the Judaean kings which he recorded in a slightly different way to his predecessor, omitting any reference to burial in "the city of David", and sometimes giving a few details about them. This understanding of the text is, of course, consistent with the findings of chaps. 3-4, where the judgement formulae after Hezekiah were shown to derive from a different hand to those before 2 Kings 18. Examination of the burial formulae from this point of view suggests that the first edition of Kings did indeed run, as suggested in chaps. 3-4, as far as Hezekiah's reign, but that it apparently did not contain any notice about his death and burial. On the other hand, consideration of the discussion in chap. 4 concerning the David theme in Kings may be of some help in explaining why it was that the author of the later burial formulae should have chosen to omit any reference to "the city of David". It was suggested in that chapter that whereas for the first author of Kings the unconditional promise to David was paramount, with Jerusalem being protected because of this (cf. 1 Kgs 15:4), the later editor elevated Jerusalem to the same level as David, the city's "chosenness" being in itself an important factor in determining Yahweh's dealings with Judah (cf. 1 Kgs 11:13, 32). Indeed, by 2 Kings 21 it is only the Temple and the city which are factors in the discussion about Judah's fate, David appearing merely as one of the recipients of the promise concerning these. It is thus to the original author of Kings that the fact of Jerusalem being *David's* city is so important, this fact underpinning his whole theological perspective. To the later editor, on the other hand, the most important thing about Jerusalem was not that it was David's city, but that it was Yahweh's chosen city. A large part of his editorial work is devoted, it has been argued, to the modification of the Zion theology of the first edition. It is therefore not surprising that we find עיר דוד used in the major part of Kings, but do not find it in the burial formulae of the chapters in which the work of the later editor has been identified. The change is not merely to be explained, then, in terms of style, as Macy would have it, but is also to be explained in terms of the differing theological perspectives of the editors of the books. No such theological motive can be detected in the omission of "buried with his fathers", which does seem simply to be a matter of style.

---

[17]   Macy, *Sources*, 139-142.

5.2.2 The Accession Formulae Re-Examined

The element which requires examination so far as the accession formulae are concerned is the notice about the queen-mother. It is true that in the books of Kings themselves, such variation as occurs with this part of the formulae does not seem to be explicable in terms of the redactional development of the books. The name of the queen-mother is given for all the kings of Judah from Rehoboam to Zedekiah with the exception of Jehoram and Ahaz[18], where the reason for its omission, if any exists, is not obvious[19]. We do not, therefore, find in Kings the change in formula around the time of Hezekiah which we find in the case of the death/burial formulae. It is at least a curious coincidence, however, given that much of the rest of the formulaic evidence in Kings seems to point to a Hezekian edition of the books, that we find such a change in formula at Hezekiah in Chronicles. Up until and including the account of Hezekiah's reign, with the single exception of Asa (2 Chr 14), Chr always gives a queen-mother notice where the author of Kings does so, and omits where he omits[20]. Even in the case of Asa, Chr still records the name of the queen-mother (2 Chr 15:16), showing dependence upon 1 Kgs 15:10. From Manasseh to Zedekiah, however, although the author of Kings always names the queen-mother, Chr never does. Since such a marked change in procedure is unlikely to have been accidental, there would appear to be only two possible explanations for it. In the first place, it could be the case that Chr has omitted the notices after Hezekiah for theological reasons; and secondly, it could be that the version of Kings which Chr had as his *Vorlage* did not contain any notices after this point.

---

[18] Rehoboam (1 Kgs 14:21); Abijam (15:2); Asa (15:10); Jehoshaphat (22:42); Ahaziah (2 Kgs 8:26); Jehoash (12:2); Amaziah (14:2); Azariah (15:2); Jotham (15:33); Hezekiah (18:2); Manasseh (21:1); Amon (21:19); Josiah (22:1); Jehoahaz (23:31); Jehoiakim (23:36); Jehoiachin (24:8); Zedekiah (24:18).

[19] The notice is also lacking for David (2 Sam 5:4-5), and for Solomon, although in neither case is this surprising. David is the founder of the dynasty, and the name of the queen-mother is only of significance in terms of the accession of the royal heir (so H. Donner, "Art und Herkunft des Amtes der Königinmutter im Alten Testament", in R. von Kienle *et al.* (eds.), *Festschrift: Johannes Friedrich zum 65. Geburtstag am 27. August gewidmet* (Heidelberg, 1959) 105-145; R. de Vaux, *Les institutions de l'Ancien Testament*, 1: *Le nomadisme et ses survivances; institutions familiales; institutions civiles* (Paris, 1958) 180-182); while Solomon has no proper accession formulae at all, and his mother in any case would have been well-known from the David-stories. It is possible that the omission in the case of Jehoram (2 Kgs 8:17) may be due to the presence of the reference to the daughter of Ahab in 8:18, the intention being to emphasize the influence from the north at this point, rather than the continuity in the south. The omission in the case of Ahaz (2 Kgs 16:2) is more puzzling, although it has been argued in chaps. 3-4 that 2 Kgs 16:2-4 reflects the hand of the exilic editor more than most of the formulaic sections, and it may be that the queen-mother notice has dropped out. Certainty here is beyond us, and it is not essential to attain it for the plausibility of the general argument in this section.

[20] Thus Chr includes a notice for Rehoboam (2 Chr 12:13); Abijah (13:2); Jehoshaphat (20:31); Ahaziah (22:2); Joash (24:1); Amaziah (25:1); Uzziah (26:3); Jotham (27:1) and Hezekiah (29:1); and omits, with Kings, the notices for Jehoram (2 Chronicles 21) and Ahaz (2 Chronicles 28). On occasion there is a slight difference between the works with regard to what the name was. Thus, for example, Abijam's mother is named as מעכה בת־אבישלום in 1 Kgs 15:2, but as מיכיהו בת־אוריאל in 2 Chr 13:2; and Hezekiah's mother as אבי בת־זכריה (2 Kgs 18:2) and אביה בת־זכריהו (2 Chr 29:1).

The first view is espoused by McKay[21]. He argues that the omission of the notice in the cases of Manasseh, Amon and Josiah may best be understood on the analogy of what Chr does with Asa's mother, Maacah, whose name is avoided as much as possible, either by omission (2 Chr 14:1/1 Kgs 15:10) or by rendering it in a new, Yahwistic form (2 Chr 13:2/1 Kgs 15:2). McKay thinks that Chr was ashamed to claim Maacah as the mother of the good king Asa, and that the names of the mothers of Manasseh, Amon and Josiah were likewise considered by him to be a stain on the reputation of both king and dynasty, especially since Amon's mother was clearly a foreigner, and introduced her religion to Jerusalem. The names of the mothers of the remaining kings were then omitted automatically, following the precedent set in modifying the introductions to these three kings.

Such an explanation is, however, far from satisfactory, and is unlikely to be correct. First of all, it is quite unclear why Chr would have had a problem with the mothers of Manasseh and Josiah (Hephzibah and Jedidah), whose names are no more non-Yahwistic than others in Kings which he is content to retain. Thus Azubah the daughter of Shilhi (1 Kgs 22:42; 2 Chr 20:31) is recorded in both works as the mother of the good Jehoshaphat, while Zibiah of Beersheba (2 Kgs 12:2; 2 Chr 24:1) is recorded as the mother of Jehoash, whose reign is, like Manasseh's, divided by Chr into good and bad phases. If Chr was ashamed to have Hephzibah and Jedidah in his work, why was he content to have Azubah and Zibiah[22]? Furthermore, if he was so ashamed that Maacah was the mother of Asa, why did he retain her name at all in the account of Asa's reign (2 Chr 15:16), rather than simply referring to "his mother", and leaving her nameless[23]? The argument does not seem to work.

Secondly, it is not at all clear why, on McKay's view, Chr would have omitted the name of the queen-mother in the case of Amon, who receives an unreservedly negative judgement from him. Even in the case of Rehoboam, who has his positive features (2 Chronicles 11), Chr is quite prepared to name the king's foreign mother (2 Chr 12:13). Why, then, should he be so concerned to omit the name of Amon's mother, when its presence could damage neither the reputation of the king, nor that of the dynasty, any more than it is damaged by Chr's own comments? There is simply no motive for omission in this case, nor, as McKay acknowledges, in the cases of the kings who follow Josiah. It is most unlikely, then, that his explanation for the change in procedure in Chronicles after Hezekiah is correct, and it is very

---

[21] McKay, *Religion*, 23-25.

[22] It certainly cannot have been because the last two are natives and the first two foreigners. Kings give no more information about Hephzibah's origins than about Azubah's, while both Beersheba and Bozkath (cf. Josh 15:39) are clearly Judaean.

[23] This is a major problem for those who wish to claim that the queen-mother notice at this point is omitted for theological reasons. Nor can it be said that the name given by Chr for Abijah's mother in 2 Chr 13:2 is evidence in favour of this, since Abijah's mother *is* named as Maacah in 2 Chr 11:22.

difficult in general to imagine, if the version of Kings which Chr possessed contained queen-mother notices after this point, what other reason he might have had for not including them[24].

The alternative explanation therefore seems more plausible. Chr did not follow Kings in naming the queen-mother after Hezekiah because in the version of Kings known to him no notices occurred after this point. This means either that Chr knew of an edition of Kings which only reached as far as Hezekiah[25], or, at least, that the edition of Kings which he knew itself contained no such notices after Hezekiah. The precise relationship between Kings and Chronicles is, of course, a very complex issue, and one to which no space can be devoted here. I shall therefore offer no comment on which of these alternatives is more likely to be correct. On either view, the evidence from the accession formulae of Chronicles offers some support for the idea being propounded in the present study. If the first is correct, we have explicit evidence that there once existed an edition of Kings which only ran as far as Hezekiah. If the second is right, then we have evidence that at a particular point in the evolution of the books of Kings, the pattern for the queen-mother notices was exactly the same as that which exists in our present books of Kings for the notices in the death/burial formulae discussed above. In this reconstructed Kings, the queen-mother notice would be almost always present up to and including the formulae for Hezekiah, and completely absent in the formulae after this point. Since no reason appears to exist why a single author of Kings would suddenly have altered his style in this way at Manasseh's reign, it is likely that the change is to be explained, as it was in the case of the death/burial formulae, in terms of a change in authorship. Whatever the general relationship between Kings and Chronicles, then, the pattern of the accession formulae in Chronicles provides us with supportive evidence that the original edition of Kings ran only as far as Hezekiah, and that the remaining chapters of 2 Kings were added at a later date.

5.2.3 Conclusion

In the examination of three further elements of the regnal formulae, it has been discovered that such variation as exists can hardly be described as "random". It is true that slight variation, some of which cannot be adequately explained in the present state of our knowledge about the texts, does occur in these elements of the formulae before Hezekiah. However, the overwhelming impression given by the two elements of the death/burial material discussed in relation to the kings of Judah is of two quite distinct blocks of material.

---

[24]   It is worth noting here that T. Willi (*Die Chronik als Auslegung: Untersuchungen zur literarischen Gestaltung der historischen Überlieferung Israels* (FRLANT 106; Göttingen, 1972) 98) is clearly unable to explain the problem.

[25]   This is essentially the position adopted by Halpern ("Source"), although he also allows that Chr knew Kings in a fuller form as well. See also McKenzie, *Use*, 175.

One reaches from Rehoboam to Ahaz, the other from Hezekiah to the end of Kings, and there is a marked difference between them. It seems more than coincidental that in the case of the text of Kings upon which Chr apparently depended, if he depended upon any after the account of Hezekiah's reign, the same pattern should be detected for the queen-mother notices of the accession formulae. Here, in a block from Rehoboam to Hezekiah, the queen-mother is almost always named, while in a block from Manasseh to Zedekiah, she is never named. The cumulative force of all this evidence should be readily seen from the following diagrammatic summary. Col. 1 lists the occasions upon which the queen-mother of the Judaean king is named in Kings; col. 2, the same in Chronicles; col. 3, the occasions upon which it is noted in Kings that he was "buried with his fathers"; and col. 4, the occasions upon which it is noted in Kings that he was buried "in the city of David":

	1	2	3	4
Rehoboam	yes	yes	yes	yes
Abijam	yes	yes	no	yes
Asa	yes	(yes)	yes	yes
Jehoshaphat	yes	yes	yes	yes
Jehoram	no	no	yes	yes
Ahaziah	yes	yes	yes	yes
Jehoash	yes	yes	yes	yes
Amaziah	yes	yes	yes	yes
Azariah	yes	yes	yes	yes
Jotham	yes	yes	yes	yes
Ahaz	no	no	yes	yes
Hezekiah	yes	yes		
			no	no
Manasseh	yes	no	no	no
Amon	yes	no	no	no
Josiah	yes	no	no	no
Jehoahaz	yes	no	no	no
Jehoiakim	yes	no	no	no
Jehoiachin	yes	no	no	no
Zedekiah	yes	no	no	no

The isolated variations which exist before Hezekiah cannot diminish the significance of the fact that in all three elements a change of style occurs at his reign. There is, therefore, some evidence from the other regnal formulae which can be said to support the conclusion reached in chaps. 3-4 as a result of the study of the judgement formulae, namely that the first edition of Kings only ran as far as Hezekiah's reign.

5.3 2 Kings 21-23 and the Exilic Redaction

Examination of the accession and death/burial formulae has confirmed that a decisive break in the regnal formulae of the books of Kings, with regard both to their theology and to their style, occurs at Hezekiah's reign. The existence of a pre-exilic edition of the books which ended with Hezekiah is thus established. It remains now to provide further support for the second conclusion which was drawn from study of the David and במה themes in chaps. 3-4, that the material in 2 Kings 21-25 was only added to the books during the exile, in the main by a single redactor. The analysis in 5.2 above has, indeed, already indirectly provided additional evidence which points in this direction, since it is noticeable that after the definite change in the accession and death/burial formulae at 2 Kings 18, there is no further change which might be taken as indicating another editorial hand. If, as this suggests, only one main editor is at work in 2 Kings 21-25, he must, of course, have worked during the exile, since it is clear enough that the present form of these chapters is thoroughly exilic. Most scholars who have accepted that there was a pre-exilic Kings have argued, however, that pre-exilic and exilic material can be differentiated in chaps. 21-23, indicating that accounts of the reigns of Manasseh, Amon and Josiah at least had already been included in the books in the pre-exilic period. If this position could convincingly be maintained, then we should have to reckon with a pre-exilic redaction of the original Dtr Kings in addition to the exilic one which has been proposed above. Whether it can be so maintained is doubtful, however, as the following analysis of 2 Kgs 21:1-18 and 22:1-23:30, the passages upon which the debate has focussed[26], will demonstrate.

---

[26] Friedman ("Egypt") and Vanoni ("Terminologie"), of course, have recently drawn 2 Kings 24-25 into the debate as well, using arguments other than those from the style of the judgement formulae in these chapters (cf. Weippert, Nelson) which have been rejected in chap. 2 above. Neither the comparative lack of Dtr terminology and themes in these chapters, however, nor the differences between some of the terminology which is present and Dtr language elsewhere in the books, constitutes independent evidence that the position under discussion here is correct. The absence of Dtr terminology and themes may only prove that the editor to whom the account of Josiah's reign was the climax of the books had less interest in the history of the kingdom after this point, and so did not provide much theological commentary. The differences in language discussed in Vanoni's article only demonstrate that a redactor has been at work in these chapters: they do not prove that a redactional break exists at Josiah's reign in particular. It is clear, then, that priority must be given to the analysis of 2 Kgs 21:1-23:30, some of which (for example, 23:25-27) Vanoni and Friedman do indeed discuss. If the case cannot be made here, it cannot be made in chaps. 24-25.

5.3.1 The Reign of Manasseh (2 Kings 21:1-18)

It is evident that if there once existed a pre-exilic version of the books of Kings which extended as far as Josiah, then some version of 2 Kings 21 must have been present in this edition. Proponents of the view that the chapter had a pre-exilic form, however, have found it remarkably difficult to agree on what that form was. All agree that 21:1, 17-18 are pre-exilic; and most also accept that 21:2a and 16 are as well[27]. These verses alone, however, can scarcely have formed the "original" material on Manasseh[28]; and it is when the discussion turns to the question of which other verses might have been included that we find widespread disagreement. There is a consensus only that 21:10-15 could not have been included, but must derive from an exilic hand. Burney and McKenzie[29] take the exilic addition no further back into the chapter than these verses, while Gray and Friedman[30] include vv 8 and 9. Most of the older commentators regarded 21:7-15 as an exilic unit, and also found later material in vv 2b-6[31]. Thus Benzinger[32] assigned 21:2b, 3b, 5 to the same editor as 21:7-15, and took 21:3a, 4, 6 as still later additions; Stade and Schwally[33] gave 21:2b, 3b to the editor of vv 7-15 and 3a, 4-6 to later hands; and Šanda[34], 21:2b, 3bβ, 4, 6 to the author of vv 7-15. Skinner did not commit himself on vv 2b-6, affirming that in these verses

> ... it is quite impossible to discriminate between the two editors[35].

Nelson[36] takes the exilic addition right back to 21:3, although he is prepared to allow that the pre-exilic form of the chapter (basically 21:1-3bα, 16-18) already had

---

[27]   The exceptions here are Cross (*Myth*, 285-286), who apparently includes 21:2a in the work of his second editor; and McKenzie (*Use*, 192-193), who takes 21:16 as from the exilic hand.

[28]   Benzinger (188) and Stade and Schwally (53-54) limit the pre-exilic contribution to 21:1-2a, 16-18 alone. This would mean, however, that the material on Manasseh would be much briefer than that for any of the other kings. Furthermore, 21:16 seems to demand some prior account of the way in which Manasseh led Israel astray, and there is no literary-critical evidence in favour of dividing 21:2a from 21:2b. It therefore seems unlikely that 21:1-2a, 16-18 alone ever formed a pre-exilic version of the account of Manasseh's reign.

[29]   Burney, 352-353; McKenzie, *Use*, 191-193.

[30]   Gray, 704-705; Friedman, "Egypt", 176-178.

[31]   The exception here is Kittel (294), who attributes none of 21:2b-6 to the exilic editor of 21:7-15.

[32]   Benzinger, 188.

[33]   Stade and Schwally, 53-54.

[34]   Šanda, 2:324-325.

[35]   Skinner, 406.

[36]   Nelson, *Redaction*, 65-67.

... the annalistic notices 4a, 6a, and perhaps 7a, floating somewhere in between[37].

The obvious difficulty which scholars have had in pinning down the supposed pre-exilic text hardly inspires confidence in its actual existence. Confidence is further undermined when it is realised that the ground upon which the division between pre-exilic and exilic material is usually made in these analyses is not the presence of literary-critical indicators in the text. Rather, it is simply assumed that since there existed a pre-exilic edition of Kings which reached at least as far as Josiah, some parts of this chapter *must* be pre-exilic. Verses and part-verses which do not explicitly reflect exilic language and interests must therefore derive from this earlier period, whether or not there is any evidence that they can be separated from their present exilic context. Thus there are absolutely no literary-critical grounds for separating 21:2a from 21:2b, as has been argued in chap. 4, but a distinction is, nevertheless, often made between them because 21:2a is very like the other pre-exilic formulae, whereas 21:2b is considered to be from an exilic hand (cf. 2 Kgs 17:8). In the same way, there is no justification from the text for separating 21:3bβ from 21:3bα (Šanda, Nelson). Nor is it necessary, given that both verses reflect 1 Kgs 9:1-9, to distinguish 21:7 and 21:8 (Gray, Friedman)[38], or to divide 21:9 from 21:10 (Burney, McKenzie). Only in the case of 21:4, 6, which both begin with waw-copulatives and contain elements which appear to duplicate other material in the section[39], and perhaps in the case of 21:16[40], is there really any reason to suspect interference in the text. It is significant that it is only at these points that there is anything approaching a majority of scholars in favour of division[41]. All the other distinctions which have been made rest, not so much on the evidence of the text of 2 Kgs 21:1-18 itself, but on a general presumption that a pre-exilic version must have existed. Analysis of a particular text on the basis of a general theory of redaction which has been built up from the evidence of other texts is, of course, quite legitimate, if the general theory is strong. It cannot be expected that a redactor will always leave traces of his work at all points where he has been active. If the evidence in general for a pre-exilic edition of Kings which ran further

---

[37] Ibid., 67.

[38] Friedman ("Egypt", 176-178) presents one of the few arguments from the text itself to be offered in defence of a division when he maintains that a shift of theme, which occurs "... amidst some syntactical awkwardness", is to be found in 21:7-8. The syntax seems to me to be perfectly straightforward, and has caused most scholars no problem, while the shift of theme from "house" to "land" is already a feature of 1 Kgs 9:4-9, which were attributed above to a single author, and on which 2 Kgs 21:7-8 clearly depend. The same shift in theme in the latter verses can therefore hardly be taken as signifying that redaction has taken place there, particularly when the close connection between Temple and land is quite natural.

[39] These verses have already been referred to in the discussion on the use of the waw-copulative in chap. 3, and need not be further examined here.

[40] 2 Kgs 21:16, introduced by בם, has the appearance of an afterthought to the whole section, and may well be a later addition.

[41] The overwhelming majority of those who favour the idea of a pre-exilic version of the chapter regard 21:16 as secondarily attached to 21:15, although most, surprisingly, take the view that the verse was part of the pre-exilic text and has been displaced by the exilic insertion(s). The majority also separate v 5 from vv 4 and 6, although not always explaining the development of the text in the same way (Benzinger, 188; Kittel, 294; Stade and Schwally, 53; Šanda, 2:324-325; Gray, 705-707; Nelson, *Redaction*, 67).

than Hezekiah were strong, therefore, and if it were possible to demonstrate affinities of language and style between 2 Kgs 21:1-18 and both pre-exilic and exilic sections elsewhere in the books, then the division of the text in this way might be acceptable. However, if the features which have previously been taken to indicate the existence of a pre-exilic edition of Kings have now been satisfactorily explained in terms of an edition which ended with Hezekiah, and if in addition the accession and death/burial formulae indicate continuity of authorship from Manasseh to Zedekiah, then the general case for a pre-exilic version of 2 Kings 21 is considerably weakened. There is then no compelling reason, except in the case of vv 4 and 6, and perhaps v 16, to divide the text up at all, since it reads perfectly well as a unity. As such, it is clearly an exilic unity with two sections. The first section, which describes the sins of Manasseh in detail, is framed by two references to the native peoples of Canaan which make clear the context in which these sins are to be viewed. As Manasseh and the people have behaved like these nations, so it is implied that they will, like them, be driven out of the land if they persist in disobeying the law (21:8). The statement that "they did not listen" to this threat then leads into the second section of the Manasseh account (vv 10-15), in which Yahweh's response to their behaviour is described. Yahweh will bring evil upon Judah and Jerusalem and cast off his people, because this phase of their history is the last in a long series of others throughout which Israel has disobeyed and provoked him. Such a reading is entirely natural, and at no point ignores or distorts the textual evidence. The thesis of an edition of Kings which ended with Hezekiah may thus be seen to carry with it the implication that 2 Kgs 21:1-18 derives from an exilic hand.

5.3.2 The Reign and Reform of Josiah (2 Kings 22:1-23:30)

On any understanding of the books of Kings, it must be accepted that the reign and reform of Josiah form the high point of the history of the monarchy as it now stands. Josiah is the only king, in the view of these chapters, fully to have kept the law of Moses in his religious policy (22:2; 23:21-25). The question which must be addressed here is whether there is any compelling evidence that Josiah was the hero of a pre-exilic, rather than an exilic edition of the books.

The present form of 2 Kgs 22:1-23:30 is accepted by all as dating from no earlier than the exile. This is certainly indicated by 23:26-27, which know of the exile and of the destruction of both city and Temple[42]. Most scholars also regard at least the present form of the oracle of

---

[42] These verses are unanimously ascribed to an exilic hand by supporters of the idea of a pre-exilic edition: Benzinger, 189; Kittel, 297; Burney, 355-356; Skinner, 423; Stade and Schwally, 56; Šanda, 2:361; Gray, 715; Cross, *Myth*, 286; Nelson, *Redaction*, 85; Friedman, "Egypt", 186; McKenzie, *Use*, 191.

Huldah (22:15-20) as exilic[43]. Any attempt to argue for a pre-exilic version of Kings in these chapters must, therefore, be able convincingly to demonstrate that pre-exilic and exilic elements can be separated from one another. As far as the story about the discovery of the law-book (*Auffindungsbericht*)[44] is concerned, however, such convincing demonstration has been entirely lacking among scholars who support the idea of a pre-exilic Kings. Many have assumed, certainly, that the oracle of Huldah must have had a pre-exilic form, often on the ground that the promise to Josiah of a peaceful death (22:20a) could not have been written after his violent death at Megiddo (23:29-30)[45]. It has proved quite impossible, however, to reconstruct the "weal oracle" of which 22:20a is supposed to form a part. Thus Gray says

> Some response of Huldah is certainly to be expected here in the pre-exilic compilation, but this is so much worked over by the exilic redactor that earlier and later matter is impossible to distinguish[46].

Nelson, who argues that vv 18-20a form the original oracle, is nevertheless forced to admit:

> ... vv.16,17,19, and 20 are all connected by the *Leitmotif* of "this place". In other words, all these verses received some of their present form from the exilic editor[47].

Friedman opines that

> ... both the Josianic and Exilic hands may be present here in an editorial combination which is too complex to unravel[48].

McKenzie accepts that

> ... there are no good literary criteria for distinguishing two different oracles or levels here[49].

---

[43] Benzinger, 189; Kittel, 297; Burney, 355-356; Skinner, 414-416; Gray, 713-715; Cross, *Myth*, 286; J. Priest, "Huldah's Oracle", *VT* 30 (1980) 366-368; Nelson, *Redaction*, 76-79; Friedman, *Exile*, 25; Mayes, *Story*, 128-130; McKenzie, *Use*, 199. An exception here is Šanda, 2:360.

[44] I shall for the sake of brevity use the German term for the story from this point on, as I shall later use *Reformbericht* for the account of the reform in 2 Kgs 23:4-20. The use of *Auffindungsbericht* for the material in 2 Kgs 22:3-20; 23:1-3, 21-23 is merely for convenience, however, and does not imply acceptance of the distinction made by T. Oestreicher (*Das deuteronomische Grundgesetz* (BFT 27/4; Gütersloh, 1923)) between this material and that of 23:4-20, nor of N. Lohfink's view ("Die Bundesurkunde des Königs Josias (Eine Frage an die Deuteronomiumsforschung)", *Bib* 44 (1963) 261-288, 461-498) of the nature and date of the material.

[45] Those who explicitly state this include Bentzen (*Introduction*, 2:99-100) and Fohrer (*Einleitung*, 256).

[46] Gray, 713.

[47] Nelson, *Redaction*, 79.

[48] Friedman, *Exile*, 25.

[49] McKenzie, *Use*, 198.

It may well be asked, then, why it is that scholars have persisted with the view that 2 Kgs 22:15-20 had a pre-exilic form. After all, even if it were accepted that 22:20a itself is a saying originally uttered before Josiah's death, this would not prove, in the absence of literary-critical indications within the text[50], that there was ever a pre-exilic *Auffindungsbericht*, but only that the author of the whole had incorporated an early oracle. As it happens, however, there is not even any compelling reason to take 22:20a as dating from Josiah's reign. The whole case for this rests on the assumption that בשלום in the verse refers to the manner of Josiah's death, and therefore that the verse is in tension with 23:29-30. The evidence of the death/burial formulae discussed above, however, should make us cautious here. In these, the phrases "he slept with his fathers" and "he was buried with his fathers" refer to two different things, the first describing the circumstances of the king's death and the second the circumstances of his burial[51]. It seems probable, since otherwise the second phrase of 20a is tautologous, that Hoffman and Mayes[52] are right when they argue that a similar distinction is intended here, v 20aα referring to Josiah's death and v 20aβ to his burial. If this is the case, it is notable that v 20aα conspicuously avoids any reference to the manner of Josiah's death[53], and that בשלום is only predicated of his burial. That is to say, what is being promised here is not that Josiah will die a natural death, but that he will be buried "in time of peace", before the events of which the prophecy speaks come to pass[54]. All the comments which have been made by scholars as to the meaning of the phrase "to die in peace" in the OT are therefore irrelevant. On this interpretation of the verse, it does not conflict in any way with 23:29-30. Indeed, it should be pointed out that 23:30 seems concerned to stress that 22:20a was fulfilled, Josiah being brought back to Jerusalem and buried "in his tomb" (בקברתו, cf. 22:20, אל־קברתיך)[55]. The evidence that the oracle of Huldah, and thus the *Auffindungsbericht*, ever had a pre-exilic form is therefore extremely weak.

---

[50] Nelson (*Redaction*, 77) suggests that the end of v 18 has been broken off, indicating a literary seam, but admits that the words הדברים אשר שמעת can be construed with v 19 as an extended *nomen pendens*: "concerning the words which you have heard, because ...".

[51] Both phrases occur in 1 Kgs 14:31; 15:24; 22:51; 2 Kgs 15:7, 38; 16:20.

[52] Hoffman, *Reform*, 181-189; Mayes, *Story*, 129-130.

[53] The phrase אסף על־אבות occurs elsewhere in Dtr literature only in Judg 2:10 (with אל instead of על), and it cannot be shown to be anything other than a general euphemism for death, which carries no connotation as to its manner (*contra* M. Rose, "Bemerkungen zum historischen Fundament des Josia-Bildes in II Reg 22f.", *ZAW* 89 (1977) 50-63, on p. 59). When it is considered that the author of 2 Kgs 22:20 had at his disposal the phrase שכב עם־אבות, which is always used in the burial notices for peaceful death, and is also found in Yahweh's address to Moses in Deuteronomy 31 (31:16, cf. also 2 Sam 7:12, שכב את־אבות), his choice of this neutral term instead seems significant. Nothing about 22:20aα implies a peaceful death for Josiah.

[54] It is interesting that this interpretation of the verse is already found in the Talmud (cf. *b. Mo'ed Qat.* 28b).

[55] קברחיך (22:20) is universally emended to קברחך by scholars. It seems highly likely that the precise choice of the phrase in 23:30 is influenced by such a concern for the fulfilment of prophecy, since Josiah is the only king of Judah apart from Ahaziah (2 Kgs 9:28) of which it is said that he was buried "in his tomb". It seems too much of a coincidence that the prophecy and the burial notice should happen to match up in this way.

The fact that the present context of the account of Josiah's reform (the *Reformbericht*, 23:4-20) cannot be demonstrated to have a pre-exilic basis does not necessarily mean, of course, that the account itself only became part of the books of Kings during the exile. It has been the common view since at least the time of Oestreicher[56] that the *Auffindungsbericht* and the *Reformbericht* are to be distinguished as to their origin precisely because the latter does not explicitly presuppose the former. It contains no reference to any "book of the law", and differs markedly from it in style. The possibility remains, therefore, that it is in all or part of this section of 2 Kings 22-23 that the pre-exilic form of the Josiah account is to be found. Such a view has recently been taken by Mayes[57], who finds the introduction to the reform in the story of the Temple-repairs in 22:3-7, 9[58], the original account of the reform in 23:4-20 and the conclusion of the whole in 23:25. This analysis, however, is not very convincing.

In the first place, it is difficult to see the force of Mayes' division between 22:3-7, 9 and 22:8, 10-20. He maintains that v 10 cannot be the original continuation of v 9, since it constitutes a new beginning. However, since Shaphan is first of all responding to the king's own command (22:4-7)[59], and then to the discovery of the book, this "new beginning" is satisfactorily explained by the change of subject[60]. There hardly seems enough evidence here to justify the attribution of the two sections to different redactors, and it seems much better to regard 22:3-20, with the majority, as from one hand.

Secondly, the evaluative statement at the beginning of the Josiah account (22:2) indicates that the *Auffindungsbericht* was present in the account from the beginning. 2 Kgs 22:2 has been discussed in some detail in chap. 4, where it was shown how closely it is linked to the "book of the law" theme which runs throughout 2 Kings 22-23. Josiah did not turn to the right or the left from obeying this law. This "judgement formula" for Josiah is hardly likely ever to have been present in Kings without the *Auffindungsbericht*, then, and since it is equally unlikely that there could have been a Dtr account of Josiah's reign which contained *no* formulae, the *Auffindungsbericht* must have formed part of this account from the beginning. No plausible pre-exilic context in Kings for the *Reformbericht* alone can therefore be found.

---

[56]   Oestreicher, *Grundgesetz*.

[57]   Mayes, *Story*, 128-131.

[58]   Mayes here follows the analysis of Dietrich ("Josia"), though rejecting his opinion that two originally separate stories are combined in 22:3-11.

[59]   The integrity of these verses, too, has not always been accepted (Benzinger, 189-190; Šanda, 2:360-361; Hölscher, "Könige", 198; Montgomery, 524). Dietrich ("Josia", 21, n. 37), however, rightly regards attempts to differentiate primary and secondary material within 22:4-7 as arbitrary. The narrative reads quite naturally as a unit.

[60]   It is true that the repetition of Shaphan's name in vv 9-10 is somewhat awkward. Such repetition is a feature of the whole section 22:8-10, however, and the awkwardness is little eased by the removal of v 9.

Finally, it is not even clear that anything in 2 Kgs 23:4-20 demands a pre-exilic date. On the contrary, the passage depends to a large extent upon 2 Kgs 21:1-9[61], and there are good reasons for thinking that 21:1-9 are exilic. Furthermore, similar ideology to that found in the *Auffindungsbericht* is apparent in 23:5, 11-12. The entire history of the monarchy is viewed as one of rebellion against Yahweh, with Josiah the only king to have acted properly. Positive evidence that the *Reformbericht* alone ever formed part of a pre-exilic edition of Kings is thus lacking, whatever might be surmised about the origin of some of its individual elements.

Study of 2 Kgs 22:1-23:30 in the light of the thesis of an edition of Kings which ended with Hezekiah, therefore, leads to the same conclusion as in the case of 2 Kings 21. The evidence of the text itself is not strong enough to enable us to reconstruct any version of the Josiah account which might plausibly be taken to have been part of a pre-exilic Kings. It is unlikely that the *Reformbericht* was ever present in Kings without the *Auffindungsbericht*, and the *Auffindungsbericht* is an exilic entity which shares the same perspective as 23:26-27 on the inevitability of the judgement on Judah[62]. There is little reason to suppose from the evidence of 2 Kgs 22:1-23:30, then, that the original edition of Kings was revised and updated in the pre-exilic period[63].

5.3.3 Conclusion

While the thesis that the original edition of Kings ended with Hezekiah is not incompatible in principle with the thesis that accounts of the reigns of Manasseh, Amon and Josiah were included in these books in the pre-exilic period, more detailed study of 2 Kings 21-23 has confirmed the impression that once the first thesis is accepted, no good case can be made for the second. The textual evidence does not seem strong enough to support the reconstruction of a pre-exilic text, and there is no compelling reason on thematic grounds to

---

[61] Josiah is portrayed in 2 Kgs 23:4-20 as reversing the apostasy of Manasseh described in 21:1-9 (21:3/23:4-5, 8; 21:5/23:12; 21:6a/23:10; 21:7/23:6).

[62] The fact that 23:26-27 share the same perspective as the *Auffindungsbericht* does not necessarily imply that they are from the same author. It has usually been held that these verses, introduced as they are by אך, are from a different hand to those preceding them, and it must be said that they do appear to have a slightly different perspective from both 21:1-18 and 22:1-23:30. In both the latter passages, the focus is not only on Manasseh, but also on the sinfulness of the people throughout history and up until the present (21:9-10, 14-15; 22:13, 17). In both 23:26-27 and 24:3-4 (also introduced by אך), however, it is specifically the sins of Manasseh which are singled out for attention. Of course, this may simply be shorthand for "the sins of Manasseh in which the people participated". On the other hand, it is possible that a later exilic author has added both passages in order to put the blame firmly on Manasseh himself.

[63] It is often implied or stated by scholars that the enthusiasm for reform shown in 2 Kings 23 demonstrates that the account was composed during or shortly after Josiah's reign. Thus Burney (356) writes of 2 Kgs 23:26-27 that they strike a note "... strangely alien to the enthusiasm of the pre-exilic author in view of Josiah's reformation ...". It must be objected, however, that the fact that the author sees Josiah and his reforms as paradigms does not mean that he could not also have recognized that, in the past, reform came too late. The message of 2 Kings 22-23 in its present form is quite clear: Yahweh demands righteousness of the type exhibited by Josiah at all times.

make the attempt. The impression given by all the evidence which has been considered in chaps. 3-5 is that the first edition of Kings was the only pre-exilic edition of the books; that it was first revised during the exile; and that thereafter it attracted isolated additions.

5.4 The Pre-Exilic Edition of the Books of Kings

The question which must finally be addressed in connection with the first edition of the books of Kings is that of its date and purpose. So far as date is concerned, the formulaic material in the books would be consistent with a date as early as the latter part of Hezekiah's own reign. It has been argued above (chaps. 3-5) that the regnal formulae show evidence of a decisive break at this point, indicating that the books ended with Hezekiah. Indeed, the absence of any death/burial formulae for this king in the primary material (5.2.1 above) could be taken as a positive indication that they were completed before his death. However, this is not the only possible explanation of the omission; nor is it safe to assume that because the original work ended with Hezekiah it must be dated to his reign. Other factors than simply the date of composition may have influenced when and how it came to a conclusion. Before assessing the significance of the formulae, therefore, it is necessary to consider the books of Kings more generally, to see if there are other indications of date within them.

Two pieces of evidence seem decisive. In the first place, the reference in the B1 narrative of the deliverance of Jerusalem to the death of Sennacherib (2 Kgs 19:37) dates the composition of this narrative to a point after 681 B.C., perhaps shortly before[64] or during[65] the reign of Josiah. If the arguments in 4.4.3 above are correct, and B1 was incorporated into the pre-exilic edition of Kings, then the composition of Kings must be placed no earlier than the same period. Secondly, although 2 Kgs 18:5, with its ואחריו לא־היה בכל מלכי יהודה, is unlikely to have been written after the reign of Josiah[66], it is also unlikely to have been written before it. Clearly the reigns of Manasseh and Amon must already have passed for this expression, with its plural מלכי, to have made any sense. The most plausible date for this verse is, in fact, early in Josiah's reign, before this king's achievements began to match those of Hezekiah and he came to be regarded in a similar light. 2 Kgs 18:5 and 19:37 taken together, then, suggest a date early in Josiah's reign for the composition of the first edition of Kings.

If this is correct, then the author's lack of reference to Hezekiah's death, as indeed to the reigns of Manasseh and Amon, requires an explanation. It is, however, not difficult to see why he might have omitted such reference. The pre-exilic edition as it has been described in chaps. 3-5 finishes on a high note. Hezekiah is portrayed as the ideal king, the figure towards

---

64   So, for example, Goncalves, *L'expédition*, 441-442.

65   So, for example, Clements, *Deliverance*, 91-97.

66   See 4.4.3 above.

whom the whole work points. The fate of this king, whom Yahweh helped (2 Kgs 18:7) and who survives the Assyrian threat with life and kingdom intact, is in stark contrast to that of Sennacherib, whom Yahweh opposed (19:6-7) and who is finally killed by his own sons (19:37). There can be little doubt that the addition after 19:37 of material concerning Hezekiah's death and the reigns of Manasseh and Amon would have done nothing to heighten this sense of climax and much to diminish it. The presence of a death/burial notice for Hezekiah would diminish the force of the distinction which is made between him and Sennacherib, while an account of the reigns of Manasseh and Amon, given the structure of the books as a whole, would simply be superfluous. If, indeed, the author's purpose was to appeal to precedent, as will be argued below, descriptions of the activities of Manasseh and Amon, both of whom pursued very different policies to Hezekiah[67], would have somewhat weakened his case. The absence of any material after 2 Kgs 19:37, then, can be satisfactorily explained, and need not be taken as significant in regard to the dating of the pre-exilic edition of the books, which may with confidence be assigned to a period early in the reign of Josiah.

Recent scholarship has, of course, highlighted Josiah's reign as one of great literary activity[68], some of which, it has been maintained, was carried out in the service of the state and to further the designs of those in power. Is the pre-exilic edition of the books of Kings to be understood in this way? We are necessarily in the realm of conjecture here, of course, since we have no way of knowing what was in the mind of the author when he wrote. Nevertheless, it does seem reasonable to assume, with Lemaire[69] and others, that it was produced at the royal court. It seems likely, furthermore, that the purpose of such a work was not simply to inform its readers about the past, but to influence their attitudes and behaviour in the present. The author praises particular religious and political policies, presumably hoping that the reader will adopt, or at least support, these same policies. He refers back to the behaviour of Hezekiah as a precedent for the behaviour of the present king. This does not, of course, help us to settle the precise question of for whom the books were written. Were they intended as educational material for the royal functionaries of the future[70], or perhaps, more generally, as propaganda for Josiah's centralist and nationalist policies? Or, given that the books were apparently composed early in Josiah's reign, were they perhaps

---

[67] Bright, *History*, 310-312, 315.

[68] The composition of an edition of all or parts of the DH is now commonly attributed to the Josianic era (for example, Cross, *Myth*; Lohfink, "Kerygmata"; see further 1.3.1 above), while the idea that there was a Josianic redaction of the prophecies of Isaiah (H. Barth, *Die Jesaja-Worte in der Josiazeit: Israel und Assur als Thema einer produktiven Neuinterpretation der Jesajaüberlieferung* (WMANT 48; Neukirchen-Vluyn, 1977); Clements, *Isaiah*; idem, *Deliverance*; Goncalves, *L'expédition*, 291-327) is steadily gaining ground. It is also possible that editions of the oracles of other eighth century prophets were published at this time (see J. Blenkinsopp, *A History of Prophecy in Israel from the Settlement in the Land to the Hellenistic Period* (London, 1984) 80-125 for a recent discussion, with bibliography).

[69] Lemaire, "Rédaction", 233-234.

[70] Lemaire, "Rédaction", 233-234, and further his *Les écoles et la formation de la Bible dans l'ancien Israël* (OBO 39; Göttingen, 1981), esp. 67-68, 78-81.

commissioned by an influential group at court, with a view to educating Josiah himself? We lack any means of deciding this question. A general statement of purpose may now be framed, however, which allows for the various possibilities. The original books of Kings were composed, it may be suggested, as part of the attempt by a nationalist and proto-Dtr group at the royal court to justify their religious and political position and persuade others of its correctness. If Josiah was not allied to this group at the time of the books' composition, he certainly appears to have become so at a later date, as the history of his reign illustrates.

6. THE BOOKS OF KINGS AND THE DEUTERONOMISTIC HISTORY

6.1 Introduction

Fresh analysis of the books of Kings has suggested that their first edition ended with Hezekiah, and was written early in Josiah's reign, and that they were substantially revised during the exile, with minor adjustments being made at a still later date. A question which then arises is how the books in the main stages of their development were related to the other books which have been understood to comprise the DH. Were the pre-exilic books of Kings part of a larger history dating from that period, or a separate pre-exilic document which was incorporated into an exilic whole? If the former, is the pre-exilic history to be regarded as reaching back as far as Deuteronomy, as most who have argued the case for such a history have maintained, or is it perhaps to be more narrowly defined? Such issues obviously cannot be confronted in any detail within the confines of this study. The best that can be hoped for here is that a few observations about selected parts of the work might provide the outline of a more extensive theory which could then be filled out and refined by further research. The present chapter will therefore limit itself in the main to some broader observations about the relationship between Samuel and Kings (6.2) and between Judges and Samuel-Kings (6.3), concentrating on the thematic and linguistic links between different parts of these books and their possible significance for our understanding of the development of the DH. The relationship between Deuteronomy-Joshua and Kings will only be very briefly touched upon (6.4). For reasons of space, I shall not generally enter into detailed discussion of the text, nor annotate fully, and majority positions on a variety of matters will be adopted without much discussion. Any suggestions which may be offered about the DH are offered tentatively, and as starting points for further discussion rather than as definite conclusions.

It has generally been accepted by scholars that the books of Kings were not intended by their author to be a self-contained, independent work, but were rather designed as the concluding section of a history which must have included much of the books of Samuel. That this is the case is indicated by the complete lack of any passage in the opening chapters of Kings which might be taken as a fresh beginning. Thus 1 Kings 3, which has been attributed above to the earliest edition of the books, opens abruptly with a reference to Solomon which requires the introduction to him contained in 1 Kings 1-2; while it has always been recognized that even the earliest material of these two chapters is closely linked to that of 2 Samuel, and presupposes the reader's acquaintance with it[1]. It seems clear from this that Kings must always have been preceded by at least those parts of 2 Samuel ascribed by scholars to the "Court" or "Succession Narrative" (SN)[2]. In addition, it seems likely that the History of David's Rise (HDR) which precedes this narrative was also already present in the original history[3]. The David theme in Kings, as well as requiring some such prior mention of Yahweh's promise to David as is found in 2 Samuel 7, also requires as background some account of David's life in which he is demonstrated to be the pious king *par excellence* to whom constant reference is made in the judgement formulae. David's piety is something which is continually stressed in the HDR[4], but which is overshadowed in the

---

[1]   Thus the story about the succession in 1 Kings 1, for example, assumes familiarity with various of the characters introduced in the earlier narratives, including Absalom (1 Kgs 1:5-8).

[2]   Thus we must suppose that at least the bulk of 2 Samuel 9-20 was included; and given the universal acknowledgement that 2 Sam 9:1 is unlikely to have constituted a beginning, we must probably include more. There has been some support for Rost's suggestion (*Thronnachfolge*, 104-107) that some form of the prophecy of Nathan was present (Mettinger, *King*, 31, 56-62); while others have found the opening scenes in 2 Samuel 2-4 (so M. H. Segal, "The Composition of the Books of Samuel", *JQR* 55 (1964-1965) 318-339, on pp. 322-324; Schulte, *Geschichtsschreibung*, 138-178; D. M. Gunn, *The Story of King David: Genre and Interpretation* (JSOTSup 6; Sheffield, 1978) 65-84). The question is very complex, and no resolution of it will be attempted here.

[3]   The HDR is generally agreed to extend from at least 1 Sam 16:14 to 2 Samuel 5 (so, for example, F. Crüsemann, *Der Widerstand gegen das Königtum: Die antiköniglichen Texte des Alten Testamentes und der Kampf um den frühen israelitischen Staat* (WMANT 49; Neukirchen-Vluyn, 1978) 128-142). Here too, however, there is disagreement as to the precise limits of the work. Some support exists for the inclusion of 1 Sam 16:1-13 (A. Weiser, "Die Legitimation des Königs David: Zur Eigenart und Entstehung der sogen. Geschichte von Davids Aufstieg", *VT* 16 (1966) 325-354, on pp. 325-327; J. H. Grønbaek, *Die Geschichte vom Aufstieg Davids (1. Sam 15-2. Sam 5): Tradition und Komposition* (AThD 10; Copenhagen, 1971) 25-29; Mettinger, *King*, 33-35, while Grønbaek (*Aufstieg*, 25-29) and Mettinger (*King*, 33-35) include most of 1 Samuel 15 as well. At the other end of the work, it has been argued by some that an early version of 2 Samuel 7 was included (Weiser, "Legitimation", 342-349; Mettinger, *King*, 41-45).

[4]   Thus David is the man of faith who takes on Goliath when everyone else is afraid to do so (1 Samuel 17); is blameless with regard to Saul, even when unjustly persecuted by him (1 Sam 19:4-5; 20:1, 8, 32; 24:1-23; 26:1-25); is a man who is dependent upon Yahweh's guidance (1 Sam 23:2, 4, 10-12; 2 Sam 2:1); and is generally blameless in his dealings with his fellow-man (1 Sam 25:32-34, 39; 29:6-9; 30:23-25; 2 Samuel 1; 3:26-39; 4:9-12). See further P. K. McCarter, Jnr., "The Apology of David", *JBL* 99 (1980) 489-504.

SN by his grave sin in respect of Bathsheba and her husband (2 Samuel 11)[5]. His piety could hardly have been so emphatically maintained in Kings, then, if the SN alone originally preceded these books. The presence of the HDR is essential to the credibility of the David theme, and indeed is suggested by the parallels noted in chap. 4 between David and Hezekiah. It is also probable that at least some of the Samuel and Saul stories contained in the opening chapters of Samuel were already in place, since the HDR itself demands narratives like those of 1 Sam 1:1-28 and 1 Sam 9:1-10:16 in which they first appear[6]. Indeed, given that this latter passage already presupposes knowledge of the Philistine crisis (9:16)[7], 1 Sam 1:1-28 is really the only passage which can realistically be argued to be the beginning of the work. Here the reader is introduced to entirely new characters in a most general way (ויהי איש אחד, 1 Sam 1:1), and no continuity with earlier episodes is suggested. It therefore seems most likely that the version of the books of Samuel which preceded the first edition of Kings was much the same in its extent as our present books, reaching back as far as the Samuel and Saul stories contained in 1 Samuel 1-14, and including the accounts of David's rise to power and the succession.

The fact that the pre-exilic edition of the books of Samuel was probably similar in extent to the present books does not necessarily mean, of course, that it was exactly the same in terms of its content. The possibility exists that some of the material to be found within them derives, like some in Kings, from the hand of the exilic editor of the history rather than from the initial author. A detailed analysis of the redactional development of Samuel along these lines is obviously outside the brief of this chapter. One particular section of the Samuel/Saul

---

5   See especially L. Delekat, "Tendenz und Theologie der David-Salomo-Erzählung", in F. Maass (ed.), *Das ferne und nahe Wort: Festschrift Leonhard Rost zur Vollendung seines 70. Lebensjahres am 30. November 1966 gewidmet* (BZAW 105; Berlin, 1967) 26-36. This is true even in the present form of the text, which some scholars (so Würthwein, *Thronfolge*; Veijola, *Dynastie*; F. Langlamet, "Salomon"; "Absalom et les concubines de son père: Recherches sur II Sam., xvi, 21-22", *RB* 84 (1977) 161-209; "David et la maison de Saül: Les épisodes 'Benjaminites' de II Sam., ix; xvi, 1-14; xix, 17-31; I Rois, ii, 36-46", *RB* 86 (1979) 194-213, 385-436, 481-513; *RB* 87 (1980) 161-210; *RB* 88 (1981) 321-332; "Affinités sacerdotales, deutéronomiques, élohistes dans l'Histoire de la succession (2 S 9-20; 1 R 1-2)", in A. Caquot and M. Delcor (eds.), *Mélanges bibliques et orientaux en l'honneur de M. Henri Cazelles* (AOAT 212; Neukirchen-Vluyn, 1981) 233-246) understand as having undergone pro-Davidic/pro-Solomonic editing.

6   Whichever of the passages mentioned in n. 3 is seen as the first extant part of the HDR, it is clear that the narrative begins very abruptly, and presupposes that the reader is already familiar with the characters. Thus 1 Samuel 15 opens with a speech of Samuel to Saul; 1 Samuel 16 with a speech of Yahweh to Samuel; and 1 Sam 16:14 begins a story about Saul. All of these passages require a prologue of some kind. Campbell (*Prophets*, 125-138) therefore suggests that the beginning of the HDR is to be found in 1 Sam 9:1. Whether this is correct or not, there is certainly no evidence that the HDR, as usually reconstructed, ever began any edition of Samuel-Kings.

7   The fact that 9:16 and the material concerning the secret anointing of Saul generally may comprise part of the expansion of an original story about Saul in 1 Samuel 9-10 (so, among others, H. J. Stoebe, "Noch einmal die Eselinnen des Ḳîš (1 Sam. ix)", *VT* 7 (1957) 362-370; W. Richter, *Die sogenannten vorprophetischen Berufungsberichte* (FRLANT 101; Göttingen, 1970) 13-56; L. Schmidt, *Menschlicher Erfolg und Jahwes Initiative* (WMANT 38; Neukirchen-Vluyn, 1970) 58-102; B. C. Birch, "The Development of the Tradition on the Anointing of Saul in I Sam 9:1-10:16", *JBL* 90 (1971) 55-68; J. M. Miller, "Saul's Rise to Power: Some Observations Concerning 1 Sam 9:1-10:16; 10:26-11:15 and 13:2-14:46", *CBQ* 36 (1974) 157-174, on pp. 157-161; Mettinger, *King*, 64-79; Campbell, *Prophets*, 18-21) does not affect this point, since it is clear that both the HDR and the Dtr Kings presuppose the story in its fuller form (see especially Mettinger, *King*, 74-78). We may further note that 10:14-16, if, as seems likely, they form part of the same redactional level as the נציב material, presuppose knowledge of Samuel as a renowned prophet, and thus also assume the earlier stories (cf. 3:20-21).

complex requires some discussion, however, since it is of importance in terms of the wider question as to the full extent of the original DH. I refer here to the account of the rise of the monarchy in 1 Samuel 7-12. It has long been recognized by scholars that these chapters are replete with inconsistencies and thematic tensions which make it extremely unlikely that they are from one hand. As with so many issues in OT scholarship, it is the attempt made by Wellhausen[8] to find coherent strands within them which has been the most widely influential. Wellhausen divided the material into two literary strands. The earlier of the two included 9:1-10:16 and 11:1-11, 15, and was a pre-exilic narrative which was positive about the monarchy. The later, which was post-exilic, influenced by D, and antagonistic to the monarchy, included 7:2-8:22, 10:17-27 and 12:1-25. It was this analysis of the text which was accepted by Noth[9], albeit within the new framework of the DH which he was proposing. For Noth, 9:1-10:16 and 10:27b-11:15 represented material from an old Saul tradition, while 7:2-8:22; 10:17-27a and 12:1-25 were Dtr insertions, being either original pieces from Dtr himself (8:1-22; 12:1-25), or thorough revisions of older traditions from a Dtr viewpoint (7:2-17; 10:17-27a).

The general division of the text into the two strands proposed by Wellhausen and adopted by Noth is very plausible, has been assumed by most scholars as the starting point for research on 1 Samuel 7-12[10] and is accepted here. It seems quite clear that 9:1-10:16, while representing Samuel as a prophet who is well-known in Israel (9:5-10; 10:14-16), and thus probably reflecting awareness of 1 Samuel 3, has no knowledge of him as a national leader, as he is in 7:3-8:22. Nor does 9:1-10:16 seem to be aware of the great victory won by Israel in 7:3-17, and of the time of peace which is reported to have followed it (7:12-14). 1 Sam 9:16 rather assumes that the situation is as it is described in 1 Sam 4:1-7:2, with Israel in

---

[8]   Wellhausen, *Composition*, 241-246; *Prolegomena*, 244-253.

[9]   Noth, *Studien*, 54-60.

[10] The most important recent exception is the work of B. C. Birch (*The Rise of the Israelite Monarchy: The Growth and Development of 1 Samuel 7-15*, (SBLDS 27; Missoula, 1976)). Birch argues in detail that originally independent traditions were first collected by a pre-Dtr prophetic editor, whose work already contained the conflicting views of the monarchy now apparent in our books of Samuel, while having an antimonarchical emphasis. Dtr is responsible for only a few additions, being for the most part sympathetic to the tone of the prophetic edition. It may well be true, as Noth accepted, that Dtr used older narratives as the basis for his antimonarchical material: the case for differentiating prophetic and Dtr *editors*, however, and thus for denying the two-strand theory, does not seem very strong (so also R. E. Clements, in his review of Birch in *JTS* 29 (1978) 507-508).

great distress, and "lamenting after Yahweh" (7:2)[11]. In 9:1-10:16, furthermore, the initiative in the matter of the kingship is taken by Yahweh, not the people, and there is no hint of any prior request for a king, nor any notion, as there is in 8:4-22, that human kingship and divine kingship are antithetical to one another. Kingship is rather portrayed in this narrative as Yahweh's way of dealing with the Philistines, in the same way as judgeship is portrayed as such in 7:3-8:22. The grounds for regarding 7:3-8:22 as a secondary insertion into a pre-existing narrative therefore seem strong. The "rejection" theme is then continued in 10:17-19, where it is attached to an account of the public anointing of Saul at Mizpah for which the preceding 9:1-10:16 does not prepare, and which 1 Sam 11:1-11 does not appear to presuppose[12]; and is finally expounded in detail in the Dtr speech of 1 Samuel 12. This speech reviews the previous history of Israel, emphasizing the ideal nature of Yahweh's government through his judges (including Samuel), in the context of which the request for a king is seen to demonstrate lack of faith in and rejection of Yahweh. It also describes the terms under which the monarchy will succeed or fail.

The basic distinction between pro-monarchical, foundational narrative and antimonarchical (at least in the sense that kingship is not Yahweh's preferred choice of government), pro-judicial editorial additions thus seems likely to be correct. What is more doubtful, however, is whether Noth's assertion that both strands belong to the same Dtr level of the text is also correct. Noth, of course, assumed a single Dtr throughout the DH, and was therefore compelled to argue that thematic tensions in all the books which comprise the history, including Kings, were merely the result of the incorporation of sources which had a different perspective to that of the editor. It has been argued in chaps. 3-5, however, that the books of Kings at least are the product of more than one Dtr hand, the major tensions there reflecting redactional activity in the text. The possibility therefore arises that the tension in 1 Samuel 7-12 with regard to the monarchy is also to be explained in terms of the pre-exilic and exilic

---

[11] 1 Sam 7:2 is the natural referent of 1 Sam 9:16, and should on this ground surely be included with the early material, with the possible exception of the phrase וַיְהִי עֶשְׂרִים שָׁנָה, rather than with the later, as in Wellhausen and Noth. The connection between 9:16 and 1 Sam 4:1-7:2, the latter setting the scene for the former, is evidence against Noth's claim that the author of the intervening section was the first to gather the individual pericopes into a coherent narrative. The omission of 1 Sam 7:3-8:22 still leaves us with a continuous story. It is also evidence that the Ark Narrative, however it is precisely defined (cf. Rost, *Thronnachfolge*, 4-47; F. Schicklberger, *Die Ladeerzählungen des ersten Samuel-Buches: Eine literaturwissenschaftliche und theologiegeschichtliche Untersuchung* (FzB 7; Würzburg, 1973); A. F. Campbell, *The Ark Narrative (1 Sam 4-6; 2 Sam 6): A Form-Critical and Traditio-Historical Study* (SBLDS 16; Missoula, Montana, 1975); P. D. Miller, Jnr., and J. J. M. Roberts, *The Hand of the Lord: A Reassessment of the "Ark Narrative" of 1 Samuel* (JHNES; Baltimore, 1977); A. F. Campbell, "Yahweh and the Ark: A Case Study in Narrative", *JBL* 98 (1979) 31-43) was, if originally a separate entity (something questioned by J. T. Willis, "Samuel Versus Eli: I Sam. 1-7", *TZ* 35 (1979) 201-212), certainly present in the earliest edition of Samuel-Kings. It is interesting within the context of this study to note that Schicklberger (*Ladeerzählungen*, 211-234) argues that the Ark Narrative was given its present setting during the reign of Hezekiah or Manasseh, and under the influence of the events of Hezekiah's reign.

[12] 9:1-10:16 already contains an anointing of Saul (10:1), and seems to imagine that the next meeting between Saul and Samuel will be after some definite action by Saul (10:7), and at Gilgal rather than Mizpah (10:8). 11:1-11 seems to envisage the sending of messengers to all parts of Israel (11:3), this and the reaction of the people in 11:4 implying no public awareness of Saul's kingship.

versions of the history in Samuel[13]. That this is indeed the best way to understand the chapters is suggested by links both ideological and linguistic between the antimonarchical strand in Samuel and material attributed above to the exilic editor of Kings.

In the first place, it should be noted that there is not a hint of any negative sentiment with regard to the monarchy in general in the material assigned to the first edition of Kings. There are certainly bad kings and good kings as far as the author of this material is concerned, but there is no idea that, overall, the monarchy has been a harmful influence on Israel, at least insofar as the Davidic dynasty is concerned. Nor is there any mention of the period of the judges as one in which the ideal form of government was in operation. We do find such elements, however, at certain points within the exilic additions to Kings. In 2 Kgs 23:5, 11, 12, the kings of Judah in general are condemned for their idolatrous practices, while in 23:21-23 it is specifically stated that the Passover had not been kept by any of the kings of Israel and Judah before Josiah, but had last been celebrated in the days of the judges. The monarchy in general in 2 Kings 23, then, seems to be viewed as having failed to rule the people in accordance with Yahweh's will. King Josiah is excepted only because he is the first king ever to have governed as the judges did, "according to all the law of Moses" (23:25). The links between this perspective and that of the antimonarchical strand of 1 Samuel 7-12 are evident. The latter material is also linked to the exilic sections of Kings by its insistence that if king and people are to survive, they must obey Yahweh's commandments (1 Sam 12:14-15, 24-25; 1 Kgs 9:4-9; 2 Kgs 21:7-8). Such an idea is very far removed from that of the pre-exilic edition of Kings, where the divine promise to David acts as a safeguard against such an end to people and dynasty[14]. The vocabulary and style of the material should, finally, be noted. Arguments from vocabulary and style, of course, must be used with caution. If the evidence is regarded cumulatively, however, it is doubtless of some value, and it is the case that at several points the language used in the antimonarchical strand of 1 Samuel 7-12 is found in Kings only in sections of the books which were ascribed above to the exilic editor, or which may now plausibly be so ascribed. Thus the expression שוב אל־יהוה בכל־לבב (1 Sam 7:3) is found only in 1 Kgs 8:48, of the people during the exile, and in 2 Kgs 23:25 of Josiah. The apparent use of the term האמרי for the pre-Israelite

---

[13]   The absence of Dtr language in the early material of 1 Samuel 7-12 does not of itself mean, of course, that this material could not have been part of a Dtr edition of Samuel-Kings, since no matter which view is taken of the DH, it is clear that the Dtr author(s) often incorporated earlier materials into the work without adding to them at all. The question must therefore rather be settled positively with regard to the Dtr language which we do find in the later parts of 1 Sam 7-12: to which Dtr edition of Kings do these sections show the greater affinity?

[14]   It could, of course, be argued that we should not in any case expect the same idea in 1 Sam 12:25 as in the pre-exilic edition of Kings, since Yahweh made Saul no promise of the type found in 2 Samuel 7. It is certainly true that a threat against Saul or his dynasty would not be out of place here, even in the pre-exilic work. However, the threat against the people which is linked to the threat against the king is of such finality (cf. the verb ספה in 1 Sam 26:10; 27:1 and elsewhere) as to suggest an exilic date for the verse, and thus to suggest that it is kingship in general which is under consideration, and not just the kingship of Saul.

inhabitants of Canaan in general (7:14)[15] is paralleled only in 1 Kgs 21:26[16] and 2 Kgs 21:11; while the claim that the Israelites had sinned מיום העלחי אותם ממצרים ועד־היום הזה (1 Sam 8:8) is only paralleled in 2 Kgs 21:15, in very similar language: מר־היום אשר יצאו אבותם ממצרים ועד היום הזה. The phrase עבד אלהים אחרים in the same verse (8:8)[17] is directly paralleled only in 1 Kgs 9:6, 9 and 2 Kgs 17:35. Moving into 1 Samuel 12, we find that מרה את־פי יהוה (12:14, 15) occurs only in 1 Kgs 13:21, 26, in the former case without the את. The verb נטש (12:22) is found in Kings only in 1 Kgs 8:57 and 2 Kgs 21:14; the phrase שם גדול in relation to Yahweh (12:22) only in 1 Kgs 8:42; and the phrase הדרך הטובה with ירה (12:23) only in 1 Kgs 8:36. If we now include two other phrases which are mainly, but not exclusively found in the exilic material of Kings, namely עזב את־יהוה (1 Sam 8:8; 12:10, cf. 1 Kgs 9:9; 2 Kgs 21:22; 22:17, with 1 Kgs 11:33 the exception) and ירא את־יהוה (1 Sam 12:14, 18, 24, cf. 1 Kgs 8:40, 43; 2 Kgs 17:25, 28, 36, 39, with 1 Kgs 18:12 the exception; see also 2 Sam 6:9), it can be seen that the case for attributing the insertion of the antimonarchical strand of 1 Samuel 7-12 to the exilic editor of Kings is strong. If this is the case, then his method is similar in Samuel to that which we discovered it to be in Kings. In order to lead the reader to view the story in a different way than was originally intended, he has inserted material both before and after the account of the rise of the monarchy as it lay before him in the original history. In the first edition, the monarchy was Yahweh's response to the Philistine crisis. In the edited version, however, Yahweh had already dealt with the Philistine crisis through the judge Samuel, so that no need for a king existed. Kingship is thus explained as arising from a sinful request from the people, one incident in the whole history of Israel's rebelliousness which the editor knew had resulted in the exile.

A plausible case may therefore be made in support of the view that the original edition of Kings was preceded by a version of Samuel which was similar in extent to the present books, although not necessarily exactly the same in content. I have examined here by way of example one part of the books which seems more likely to have come from an editor's hand than to have formed part of the original work. The significance of this discussion for the question of the full extent of the original DH will become clear in the following section.

---

[15] For this use of the term, see Driver, *Deuteronomy*, 11. It occurs otherwise in Samuel only in 2 Sam 21:2, where it is clearly part of an insertion into the story which interrupts the connection between ויאמר אליהם in 21:2 and the question of 21:3.

[16] 1 Kgs 21:25-26 are evidently an insertion into the context (so, for example, Šanda, 1:469; Gray, 443; S. Timm, *Die Dynastie Omri: Quellen und Untersuchungen zur Geschichte Israels im 9. Jahrhundert vor Christus* (FRLANT 124; Göttingen, 1982) 130) from the hand of the exilic editor of Kings (cf. הזכבר, 21:20, 25; 2 Kgs 17:17; אשר הוריש יהוה מפני בני ישראל, 21:26, 1 Kgs 14:24; 2 Kgs 16:3; 17:8; 21:2).

[17] This phrase is also found in a pre-Dtr context in 1 Sam 26:19.

6.3 The Books of Judges and Samuel-Kings

If the case for including the books of Samuel as an integral part of the pre-exilic history which ended with the account of Hezekiah's reign is a strong one, the situation is quite different where the book of Judges is concerned. Whereas in the case of Samuel and the pre-exilic Kings a continuity of narrative was apparent which implied that the books belonged together from the start, no such continuity is evident between Judges and the pre-exilic Samuel-Kings. On the one hand, 1 Sam 1:1 constitutes a most satisfactory beginning[18], certainly *allowing* that there may be a still earlier beginning to be found in Deuteronomy, Joshua or Judges, but removing any necessity to look for one. On the other hand, there is no passage in Samuel-Kings which indubitably belonged to the first edition and which may be said to presuppose that Judges preceded these books. The antimonarchical sections of 1 Samuel 7-12, where the book of Judges is assumed (1 Sam 12:9-11)[19], and 2 Kgs 23:21-23 have already been argued to be from the exilic hand. The only other points at which familiarity with the period of the judges seems to be assumed are 1 Sam 4:18 and 2 Sam 7:11. והוא שפט את־ישראל ארבעים שנה in the former, however, which portrays Eli as a national leader, in contrast to the portrayal of him in the preceding stories as simply עלי הכהן (1:9), is from a later hand than those stories, and has been introduced to account for the *interregnum* between the previous judge and Samuel[20]. In the case of 2 Sam 7:11, there is also good

---

[18] For an interesting article of some relevance here, see A. van Selms, "How Do Books of the Bible Commence?", in *Biblical Essays: Proceedings of the Ninth Meeting of "Die Ou-Testamentiese Werkgemeenskap in Suid-Afrika"* held at the University of Stellenbosch, 26th-29th July, 1966 (Potchefstroom, 1966) 132-141.

[19] These verses reflect both the cyclical pattern found in Judges (apostasy, oppression, cry to Yahweh, deliverance) and the particular stories which appear there. The only difficulty lies in the word בדן in 1 Sam 12:11, which seems to be intended as the name of one of the judges. No such name appears in the book of Judges. Most Greek witnesses have Βαραχ at this point, which has prompted the suggestion that ברק was the original Hebrew reading. The MT certainly has the *lectio difficilior*, however, and must be retained. No simple solution to the problem exists, although it seems likely that בדן was an alternative name for one of the judges, as in the case of Gideon/Jerubaal, but that the name was lost from the judges stories in the course of their editing (so Y. Zakovitch, "בדן = יפתח", *VT* 22 (1972) 123-125).

[20] So Noth, *Studien*, 23.

evidence that the reference to judges is a secondary addition to the pre-exilic context[21]. The connection between Judges and Samuel-Kings in general, then, is in no way as strong as that between Samuel and Kings, where the latter presupposed the former at many different points, and in such a way as to suggest a primary link between them. The links between Judges and Samuel-Kings rather seem to be secondary, opening up the possibility that the original DH did not contain any account of the period of the judges[22].

In view of this, it is worth recalling that one of the main objections advanced by some scholars against Noth's view of the DH has been that the Dtr Judges and the Dtr Kings are unlikely to have been composed by the same author. In the first place, it has been argued[23] that in Kings we find nothing of the cycles of apostasy, oppression, repentance and deliverance which are so characteristic of Judges. The history is presented in Kings in a more linear fashion, with judgement against sin reserved until the end. Given that the author of Kings had copious extant literary material dealing with political successes and reverses, why, it is asked, did he not structure both in the same way? In spite of attempts on the basis of the work of Richter[24] to explain the difference in structure in terms of a pre-Dtr book of

---

[21]   2 Sam 7:10b-11aα reads as follows: ולא יסיפו בני־עולה לענותו כאשר בראשונה ולמן־היום אשר צויתי שפטים על־עמי ישראל. Many scholars, however, have felt the awkwardness of this. As S. R. Driver (*Notes on the Hebrew Text and the Topography of the Books of Samuel* (2nd ed.; Oxford, 1913) 275) says: "As the text stands, the reference in 10b will be to the sufferings of Egypt; but this is a thought alien to the context ...". This is indeed so, and it seems much more likely that v 10b is to be taken as a reference to the time of wandering *in* the land, when the building of a house was a practical option, although one spurned by Yahweh (7:6-7). This being the case, most scholars emend ולמן in v 11a to למן, following LXX[B], and read the sentence as "Wicked men will no longer oppress them as formerly, from the days when I appointed judges over my people Israel". However, there is little justification for accepting the LXX[B] reading in this instance, since it is supported by only two Hebrew MSS and, among the Greek MSS, only LXX[A] and a few other witnesses, whereas Chr, LXX[L(-O)MN] and other witnesses all read the ו. The omission in the case of LXX[AB] can be explained as an attempt to smooth out the text in view of exactly the problem under discussion here. A better solution is to take 7:11aα as a secondary addition (so Noth, "David", 125; Veijola, *Dynastie*, 72-73). Further evidence in favour of this proposal may be found if we enquire into the identity of the בני־עולה of 2 Sam 7:10. This phrase occurs nowhere in the traditions about the oppression in Egypt, nor anywhere in the DH except in 2 Sam 3:34 and 7:10. In the former verse, it is said of Abner that he fell before בני־עולה. Since the whole thrust of the pre-exilic Dtr version of 2 Samuel 7 is to make clear that the Temple could only be built in time of peace and stability (i.e. in Solomon's reign), it seems likely that the בני־עולה of 2 Sam 7:10 is meant to refer back to the incident mentioned in 3:34. In the future, the Davidic king will not be troubled by strife *within* Israel of the kind found in 2 Samuel 2-4 (cf. 2 Sam 15-20), nor by pressure from outside (2 Sam 7:11aβ, cf. 2 Samuel 8, 10-11). If this is the most likely interpretation of בני־עולה in 2 Sam 7:10b, then it is even more clear how awkward 7:11aα is, since the mention of the judges is unexpected in the context, and interrupts the flow of thought from 7:10b to 7:11aβ.

[22]   That is not to say, of course, that stories similar to those incorporated into the Dtr Judges are not to be found in the first edition of Samuel-Kings. 1 Samuel 11 obviously has something in common with the "deliverer" stories found there. I am concerned here with the extent of the original Dtr work, rather than with the sources used in composing it.

[23]   So von Rad, *Theologie*, 1:343-344; Fohrer, *Einleitung*, 211.

[24]   Richter (*Richterbuch*, 319-343; *Retterbuch*) sought to distinguish a "framework" influenced by Dtn law from later "introductions" which were from the hand of Dtr himself. In spite of the continuing influence of Richter's work on Judges studies (cf. most recently A. D. H. Mayes, *Judges* (OTG; Sheffield, 1985) 9-34), his arguments seem to me to be far from convincing. Solid evidence that the framework and introductory sections represent different redactional layers is lacking; and if, indeed, Noth (in his review of *Richterbuch* in *VT* 15 (1965) 126-128) is right to object that the Jephthah stories must have formed part of the original *Retterbuch*, then the introduction in Judg 10:6-16 simply must have been present at the first level of Dtn or Dtr redaction. Noth's view (*Studien*, 47-54), that a single author combined the "deliverer" stories and the list of minor judges, and supplied the whole with a framework which included the sections characterized by Richter as "introductions", still seems best. Such Dtr redaction as may have taken place later appears to be of a minor nature.

Judges, this argument against an original Dtr linking of Judges and Kings remains, in my view, a strong one. The arguments in favour of secondary linking, on the other hand, derive further support from the fact that the sole passage in Kings which does reflect the cyclical patterning found in Judges (2 Kgs 13:3-7) almost certainly has such a form as the result of secondary editing of the pre-exilic Dtr account[25]. This is, of course, consistent with the fact that the only other passage to reflect such patterning in Samuel-Kings is 1 Sam 7:3-17, which has been assigned to the exilic editor.

Another argument which has been advanced[26] against the common authorship of Judges and Kings is the difference in perspective which exists between them with regard to the relationship between ruler and people. In Judges it is the people who are the main focus of attention, and who are characterised as "doing what was evil in Yahweh's sight" (2:11; 3:7, 12; 4:1; 6:1; 10:6; 13:1). The judges are distinguished from the people, and are not involved in any evaluative judgement which may be made of them. Indeed, the people are criticized for failing to heed their words (Judg 2:17). In Kings, on the other hand, the king is in the forefront of the picture. It is he who is assessed as having done good or evil, with the people very much in the background. Von Rad undoubtedly goes too far when he moves on from this observation to suggest that in Kings the guilt of the people is loaded on the king, since it is clear that even in the pre-exilic Kings, the people are held responsible for their sins (2 Kgs 17:21-23). It cannot be denied, however, that in the pre-exilic Kings it *is* the ruler who is the main focus of attention, as the one who is responsible for the direction taken by the people. The people only occupy a prominent position in their own right in sections of Kings, like 2 Kgs 17:7aβ-17, which have been assigned to the exilic editor. By the same token, it is noteworthy that the distinction between people and ruler in Judges is quite consistent with the idealized picture of the judges contained in the exilic sections of Samuel and Kings. The difference between Judges and the pre-exilic Kings in this matter, and the similarity between Judges and the exilic additions to Kings, is not decisive of itself, but is nevertheless useful as part of a cumulative argument.

A final indication that the book of Judges was probably not part of the original DH is that the linguistic affinities of its framework are not generally with the material so far identified as from the hand of the pre-exilic editor of Samuel-Kings. They are rather with sections of these books already argued to be from a later hand. If we begin with those phrases which

---

[25]   כי לא חטאיר (2 Kgs 13:7) most naturally refers back to ויתנם ביד in 13:3, while כל-הימים in v 3 is in some tension with the content of vv 4-5. 13:4-6 have thus usually been taken as secondary to 13:3, 7 (Benzinger, 162; Kittel, 257; Skinner, 347-348; Stade and Schwally, 43; Šanda, 2:153; Montgomery, 433-434; de Vaux, 182; D. J. McCarthy, "2 Kings 13,4-6", *Bib* 54 (1973) 409-410; Gray, 594-596; Robinson, 2:121; Würthwein, 360-362; Rehm, 2:128-130; Jones, 499), the insertion having been prompted, it may be suggested, by the occurrence of ויחר-אף יהוה בישׂראל in 13:3, a phrase which introduces the characteristic Judges cycle in Judg 3:8 and 10:7 (cf. also 2:20).

[26]   So von Rad, *Theologie*, 1:332, 343-344.

Richter understood to have been already present in the earliest framework of the book, we discover that although עשה הרע בעיני יהוה is shared by both Judges and Kings, three of the others are found in Samuel-Kings only in the antimonarchical sections of 1 Samuel 7-12. Thus מכר ביד of Yahweh's initiation of oppression (Judg 2:14; 3:8; 4:2; 10:7) is found only in 1 Sam 12:9[27]; זעק אל־יהוה of the people's cry to Yahweh (Judg 3:9, 15; 6:6, 7; 10:10) only in 1 Sam 12:8, 10[28]; and נכנע (cf. the Hiphil of the same verb in Judg 4:23) of the subjugation of Israel's enemies (Judg 3:30; 8:28; 11:33) only in 1 Sam 7:13. Taking the framework in the older, wider sense as including passages like Judg 2:11 ff. and 10:6 ff., we find that the occasions upon which Judges and the exilic sections of Samuel-Kings share language which is not found elsewhere in Samuel-Kings are numerous. The phrase יהוה אלהי אבותם (Judg 2:12) occurs in Samuel-Kings only in 2 Kgs 21:22, and הלך אחרי אלהים אחרים (2:12, 19) only in 1 Kgs 11:10. השתחוה לאלהים אחרים (Judg 2:12, 17, 19) is found only in 1 Kgs 9:6, 9 and 2 Kgs 17:35. The couplet הבעלים והעשתרות (Judg 10:6, cf. also 2:13; 3:7) occurs only in 1 Sam 7:4; 12:10, the full phrase עבד את־הבעלים ואת־העשתרות being shared by Judg 10:6 and 1 Sam 12:10. ויתנם ביד־שסים (Judg 2:14) is found only in 2 Kgs 17:20. Use of the root קשה of Israel's attitude to Yahweh (Judg 2:19) is confined in Samuel-Kings to 2 Kgs 17:14. שכח את־יהוה (Judg 3:7) is only otherwise found in 1 Sam 12:9, and the participle משיע used as a noun ("saviour") (Judg 3:9, 15) only in 2 Kgs 13:5. The close linguistic affinity between Judg 6:8b-9a and 1 Sam 10:18 is evident[29]. The verb רצץ in the sense of "oppress" (Judg 10:8) occurs only in 1 Sam 12:3-4; and the phrase הסיר את־אלהי הנכר (Judg 10:16) only in 1 Sam 7:3. To these may be added phrases in Judges which do not only occur in exilic contexts in Samuel-Kings, but mainly do so. Thus עזב את־יהוה and עבד אלהים אחרים, discussed above with regard to the relationship between Samuel and Kings, are found also in Judges in 2:12, 13; 10:6, 10, 13, and 2:19; 10:13 respectively. The phrase היה יד־יהוה ב (Judg 2:15) occurs only in the Ark Narrative (1 Sam 5:9) and in the Dtr 1 Sam 7:13; 12:15. The phrase עבד את־יהוה (Judg 2:7; 10:6, 16) is found, apart from the pre-Dtr 2 Sam 15:8, only in 1 Sam 7:3, 4; 12:10, 14, 20, 24, while the verb לחץ of action against Israel (Judg 4:3; 6:9; 10:12)

---

[27]   The synonymous phrase נתן ביד in the framework (6:1; 13:1, cf. also 2:23) is found more widely in Samuel-Kings (2 Sam 16:8; 1 Kgs 22:6, 12, 15; 2 Kgs 3:10, 13; 13:3; 17:20; 18:30; 19:10; 21:14).

[28]   We may also note within the Judges framework צעק אל־יהוה (4:3, cf. 10:12), and, in Samuel, the phrase זעק אל־יהוה of Samuel's appeal on Israel's behalf (1 Sam 7:9). The same phrase also occurs in 1 Sam 15:11, in a passage which has often been understood as part of the antimonarchical strand represented in 1 Samuel 7-12 (thus, for example, H. P. Smith, *A Critical and Exegetical Commentary on the Books of Samuel* (ICC; Edinburgh, 1912) xv-xxii), though not universally so.

[29]   Thus 1 Sam 10:18 runs: ויאמר אל־בני ישראל כה־אמר יהוה אלהי ישראל אנכי העליתי את־ישראל ממצרים ואציל אתכם מיד ויאמר להם כה־אמר יהוה אלהי ישראל אנכי העליתי אתכם ממצרים; and Judg 6:8b-9a: מצרים ומיד כל־הממלכת הלוצים אתכם ואציא אתכם מבית עבדים ואצל אתכם מיד מצרים ומיד כל־לחציכם. We may further note in relation to Judg 6:10 the use of the term האמרי for the pre-Israelite inhabitants of Canaan, which usage has been discussed above. Many scholars, of course, regard Judg 6:7-10 as a later insertion into the Dtr Judges, but this does not affect the argument here. The passage is still connected to the exilic rather than the pre-exilic Samuel-Kings.

appears in 1 Sam 10:18; 2 Kgs 13:4, 22[30]. On the basis even of this brief analysis of the linguistic affinities of the Dtr framework of Judges, then, it would seem that a strong case can be made for attributing the composition of this book to the exilic editor of Samuel-Kings.

In summary, it may be said that the points of contact between Judges and Samuel-Kings outside of 1 Samuel 7-12 are very few, and of an apparently secondary nature; that there are certain differences of presentation between Judges and Kings which create doubt that they were composed or edited by the same author; and that the linguistic evidence suggests that the Dtr Judges was composed by the exilic editor identified in Samuel-Kings. It therefore seems probable that the original DH did not contain any account of the period of the judges[31].

---

[30] It is likely, since the impression given by it is of constant oppression, that 2 Kgs 13:22 is not from the same hand as the exilic addition in 2 Kgs 13:4-6. It may well be part of the original text, and has perhaps been displaced from its original position, as A. Jepsen ("Israel und Damaskus", *AfO* 14 (1941-1944) 153-172, on p. 159) suggests, by those verses.

[31] It is just possible, however, although this must remain speculation within the context of this study, that Judges 17-21 did form part of the original. Thematically, they provide the perfect prologue to the pre-exilic edition, demonstrating that the kingship was necessary (17:6; 21:25) because of the cultic and social corruption of the pre-monarchical period; and like the other two introductory scenes of the history (1 Samuel 1, 9), they are introduced (Judg 17:1) by ויהי־איש (although it must be admitted that this is also true of the Samson stories, cf. Judg 13:2). They have, on the other hand, nothing to do with the preceding history of the judges, nor with the exilic sections of Kings, which express the view that kingship was unnecessary, and the period of the judges generally one of cultic and social rectitude (1 Sam 7:15-16; 12:1-5; 2 Kgs 23:21-23).

6.4 The Books of Kings and the Deuteronomistic History

Study of the books of Judges, Samuel and Kings has suggested that there is good reason to suppose that the first edition of Kings was preceded by an early version of Samuel, but that it is probable that Judges was joined secondarily to Samuel-Kings to form a history of greater extent. Since Judges provides the link between Deuteronomy-Joshua and Samuel-Kings, the implication of this is that the former books must also have been added at a secondary, exilic stage. In their present form, at least, there are indeed close links between Deuteronomy-Joshua and the exilic Samuel-Kings. The relationship of Deuteronomy to this edition of the books has already been touched upon at various points in chaps. 3-5 above. With regard to Joshua, we may note, among others, the studies by Porter[32], who notes the close connection between David's speech to Solomon in 1 Kings 2 and the Dtr presentation of the succession of Joshua; and by Nelson[33], who sees the portrayal of Joshua throughout the book as having been influenced by the author's "ideal" in king Josiah. Even a cursory review of the Dtr language of the last two chapters of Joshua would confirm the book's connection with the later material. That is not to say, of course, that the first edition of Samuel-Kings was not influenced by laws which are now found in Deuteronomy. As was briefly mentioned in chap. 4, the author of the Solomonic material seems clearly to have known an early version of the law of the king in Deut 17:14-20; while it is likely that an early version of the law of centralization in Deuteronomy 12 provided the foundation for the במה theme described in chap. 3[34]. What is being maintained is rather that the first DH, although influenced by Dtn laws, probably did not contain the books of Deuteronomy and Joshua. It was simply a history of the monarchy from Saul to Hezekiah, with its necessary prologue in 1 Samuel 1-8, and perhaps in Judges 17-21. Deuteronomy and Joshua were added, along with Judges, at a later time. Whether they were first composed by a Dtr author

---

32 J. R. Porter, "The Succession of Joshua", in J. I. Durham and J. R. Porter (eds.), *Proclamation and Presence: Old Testament Essays in Honour of Gwynne Henton Davies* (London, 1970) 102-132.

33 Nelson, "Josiah". See further C. T. Begg, "The Function of Josh 7,1-8,29 in the Deuteronomistic History", *Bib* 67 (1986) 320-334.

34 The connection between Deuteronomy 12 and Kings with regard to the centralization of worship has long been understood. As the repetitions and variations indicate, however, the chapter is not a unity; and the elements which are most closely related to the exilic material of Samuel-Kings (12:1-5, 29-31) are also those generally recognized by scholars to be among the latest additions to it (see H. D. Preuss, *Deuteronomium* (EF 164; Darmstadt, 1982) 26-45, 51-52). While this material evidently regards the issue as between worship of Yahweh at the central sanctuary and worship of other gods at the provincial shrines, this perspective is not apparent in the remainder of the material. Mayes (*Deuteronomy*, 220-222) takes 12:13-19 to be the original Dtn law of the central sanctuary, and this would function well as the background to the pre-exilic במה theme.

at this stage, as Noth[35] argued, or whether the exilic editor was dependent upon a more extensive narrative for his account of the settlement period[36], is a question which cannot be entered into here, and which requires further study. Whatever is the case, Noth's DH seems best understood as an exilic expansion of an early work so as to include an account of the giving of the law, the conquest of the land, the period of the judges and the exile.

---

[35] Noth, *Studien*, 27-47.

[36] This would be the case if Lohfink ("Kerygmata") is correct in his understanding of DtrL; or if those scholars are correct who have continued to believe that Pentateuchal sources are to be found in Joshua. The latter view has retained a degree of popularity in the post-Noth period. Apart from the scholars mentioned in chap. 1, we may note, among many others, S. Mowinckel, *Zur Frage nach dokumentarischen Quellen in Josua 13-19* (ANVAOH; Oslo, 1946); idem, *Erwägungen zur Pentateuch Quellenfrage* (Oslo, 1964); idem, *Tetrateuch-Pentateuch-Hexateuch: Die Berichte über die Landnahme in den drei altisraelitischen Geschichtswerken* (BZAW 90; Berlin, 1964); C. A. Simpson, *The Early Traditions of Israel: a Critical Analysis of the Pre-Deuteronomic Narrative of the Hexateuch* (Oxford, 1948); Soggin, *Josué*; F. Langlamet, "Josué, II, et les traditions de l'Hexateuque", *RB* 78 (1971) 5-17, 161-183, 321-354; idem, "La traversée du Jourdain et les documents de l'Hexateuque", *RB* 79 (1972) 7-38; W. Beltz, *Die Kaleb-Traditionen im Alten Testament* (BWANT 98; Stuttgart, 1974); E. Otto, *Das Mazzotfest in Gilgal* (BWANT 107; Stuttgart, 1975); S. Tengström, *Die Hexateucherzählung: Eine literaturgeschichtliche Studie* (ConBOT 7; Lund, 1976). For a recent discussion of the issues involved, see A. G. Auld, *Joshua, Moses and the Land: Tetrateuch-Pentateuch-Hexateuch in a Generation since 1938* (Edinburgh, 1980).

7. CONCLUSION

This monograph has sought, in the context of the current widespread disagreement as to the date and nature of the DH, and of the weaknesses of each of the major positions currently adopted with regard to it (chap. 1), to advance the discussion by means of a re-examination of its final part, the books of Kings. Analysis of the judgement formulae, which form part of the framework around which these books are constructed, has been thought to be a useful way in which to approach the question. Because they are Dtr compositions rather than extracts from a source, variation in these formulae cannot be explained as resulting from the incorporation of different sources, but must be accounted for in terms of the Dtr redactor(s). They should therefore yield solid evidence as to the way in which the books were composed. Weaknesses in the recent work carried out in this area (chap. 2), however, have necessitated an entirely fresh analysis here.

Two different views regarding the במות have been found in the judgement formulae and in their related materials throughout the books of Kings (chap. 3). On the one hand, they seem to have been regarded as Yahwistic places of worship (3.2, 3.3, 3.4); and on the other, as idolatrous places of worship (3.5, 3.6, 3.7). Correspondingly, the concern of the author in each case was different. On the one hand, he was concerned with the centralization of Yahweh-worship, and on the other, with the removal of idolatry from Israel. The first theme is the major of the two for most of the books, and finds its natural conclusion in the account of Hezekiah's reign in 2 Kings 18; while the second is very much a sub-theme in the material before 2 Kings 21-23, where it becomes dominant (3.8). It has been suggested that we are dealing here with a pre-exilic Dtr layer which has been supplemented by later editors.

With regard to the David theme in Kings, it has also been suggested that a pre-exilic Dtr layer has been expanded, both in the formulae proper and in other parts of the books (chap. 4). In the primary material (4.2, 4.3.1, 4.3.2.1, 4.3.2.3), David functions as the standard of comparison by which each Judaean king is judged, and the unconditional promise of a dynasty to David is regarded as the crucial factor which made the course of Judah's history different from that of Israel. The David theme so described also comes to a natural conclusion in the account of Hezekiah's reign in 2 Kings 18-19 (4.4.1, 4.4.3), where Hezekiah is presented as the second David, and the Zion theology is portrayed as vindicated by the miraculous reversal of Assyria's fortunes recorded in 2 Kgs 18:17-19:37. Another view of the Davidic covenant, however, may be found in Kings (4.3, 4.4), according to which the disobedience of Judah's kings to the law of Moses is the crucial factor in Judah's history. This new standard of comparison subsumes, and to some extent renders insignificant, the standard of likeness to David. It has been argued that passages with such a perspective represent secondary additions to the original Dtr Kings.

Close examination of the two main themes of the judgement formulae has thus suggested that the first Dtr edition of Kings was composed before the exile. It has also suggested, however, that this edition ran no further than the account of Hezekiah's reign. Such a conclusion is supported by changes in the burial formulae at Hezekiah's reign in Kings (5.2.1). It is also supported by changes in the accession formulae at the same reign in the books of Chronicles, which at this point almost certainly reflect an earlier edition of Kings than our present MT (5.2.2). Taken together, all the evidence points to an original edition of Kings written early in the reign of Josiah, but not yet including any material on Manasseh, Amon or Josiah himself (5.4). While it is possible that this edition was then revised before the exile to include accounts of the reigns of at least these three kings, positive evidence that this is what actually happened is difficult to find (5.3). The hypothesis which best accounts for all the evidence without going beyond it is that the first edition of Kings underwent a major revision during the exile, and thereafter attracted isolated additions.

If we may now set these results in the context of the debate about the DH as it was described in chap. 1, and specifically as it relates to the books of Kings, it is clear that they support those scholars, like Cross and Nelson, who have argued for pre-exilic composition of the books with exilic redaction, rather than those, like Noth and Dietrich, who have argued for exilic composition with exilic redaction. Within the former group, they support those who have thought in terms of two main editions of Kings (for example, Cross and Nelson) rather than those who have argued for three or more (Weippert, Lemaire). Finally, they to some extent support both those who have seen the reign of Hezekiah as the original climax of the first edition (for example, Barrick, McKenzie and Halpern) and those who have dated it to the reign of Josiah. The first idea has been worked out much more fully and precisely than before, however; while the claim that Hezekiah is the hero, and his reign the climax, of the work composed in Josiah's reign, as well as its dating *early* in that reign, makes the position adopted in this study quite different from that of past proponents of a "Josianic edition". The first edition of Kings as it has been described in chaps. 3-5 above is "Josianic" only in the sense that it dates from Josiah's reign and had a function with regard to the religion and politics of that time. With regard to its themes and their climax it is "Hezekian". Such an analysis, of course, removes the major problem which has particularly afflicted all redactional hypotheses about Kings which have been based on the Cross model - that of finding a suitable climax for the themes in 2 Kings 22-23. The thesis that the first edition of Kings was a pre-exilic edition has thus, I believe, been given a firmer basis than it has had hitherto, and consequently must be taken more seriously in the future than it has been by some in the past when the question of the composition of the DH is discussed.

It cannot be assumed, of course, although it often seems to have been in the course of the four and a half decades which have passed since the publication of Noth's *Studien*, that the adoption of a view of the composition of Kings which is at variance with his view affects only the question of the date and purpose of the DH, and that other aspects of his hypothesis need not be revised. The question of the *extent* of the original DH must also be re-examined when a new position on Kings is accepted. In chap. 6, I have tentatively and briefly examined how the theory that the Dtr Kings originally concluded with the reign of Hezekiah affects one's understanding of the redactional development of the DH as a whole. Such an edition of Kings seems to require the books of Samuel in much their present form as its prologue, and may also have included the stories in Judges 17-21. The linguistic and thematic affinities of the Dtr framework of Judges and of the "antimonarchical" sections of 1 Samuel 7-12, however, are with passages which did not form part of the pre-exilic Kings. This implies that those same sections of Samuel were introduced to Samuel-Kings, and Judges added to these books, as part of the exilic revision of the history. This in turn implies that the original DH did not contain Deuteronomy-Joshua, since Judges provides the link between these books and Samuel-Kings. The new thesis about Kings, then, seems to entail a view of the DH which, although having something in common with the earlier theories of Jepsen, Steck and Schüpphaus (1.3.2, 1.4 above), is itself new. It would seem that the original DH, as well as being earlier and of different purpose, was also much shorter than envisaged by Noth. It is also clear that Noth's exilic Dtr had before him a far larger and more coherent block of material relating to the monarchy than Noth himself imagined. Whether this editor also used a larger narrative for the account of the entry into and conquest of the land, as would be implied if Pentateuchal sources are to be found in Joshua, or if Lohfink's views about Deuteronomy-Joshua are correct, must remain, within the context of this study, an open question. Whatever is the case, study of the David and במות themes of the books of Kings has led in the end to a theory about the DH which is quite different from any which has hitherto been formulated. The detailed examination of Deuteronomy, Joshua and Judges which will be necessary in order fully to establish this theory must be left until another time.

BIBLIOGRAPHY

INDEX OF BIBLICAL REFERENCES

BIBLIOGRAPHY

Primary Sources

Hebrew Old Testament

Elliger, K., and W. Rudolph (eds.) *Biblica Hebraica Stuttgartensia* (Stuttgart, 1967-1977).

Herodotus

Goold, G. P. (ed.), *Herodotus*, 1: *Books I and II* (trans. A. D. Godley; LCL; Cambridge, Massachusetts, 1981).

Septuagint

Brooke, A. E., N. McLean and H. St. John Thackeray (eds.), *The Old Testament in Greek*, 2: *The Later Historical Books* (London, 1927-1930).

Babylonian Talmud

Goldschmidt, L. (ed.), *Der babylonische Talmud mit Einschluss der vollstaendigen Mišnah*, 3: *Sukkah, Jom-Ṭob, Roš-Hašanah, Tânith, Megilla, Moêd-Qaṭan, Ḥagiga, Šeqalim* (Berlin, 1899).

Ras Shamra Texts

Herder, A., *Corpus des tablettes en cunéiformes alphabétiques découvertes à Ras Shamra-Ugarit de 1929 à 1939* (MRS 10; 2 vols.; Paris, 1963).

Secondary Literature

Ackroyd, P. R.,

I and II Chronicles, Ezra, Nehemiah (TBC; London, 1973).

"An Interpretation of the Babylonian Exile: A Study of 2 Kings 20, Isaiah 38-39", *SJT* 27 (1974) 329-352.

Albright, W. F.,

"The Chronology of the Divided Monarchy of Israel", *BASOR* 100 (1945) 16-22.

"The Biblical Period", in L. Finkelstein (ed.), *The Jews: Their History, Culture, and Religion* (2 vols.; New York, 1949), 1:3-69.

"New Light from Egypt on the Chronology and History of Israel and Judah", *BASOR* 130 (1953) 4-11.

Alfrink, B.,   "L'expression שכב עם אבוחיו", *OTS* 2 (1943) 106-118.

Alt, A.,   "Judas Gaue unter Josia", *PJ* 21 (1925) 100-116.

"Das System der Stammesgrenzen im Buche Josua", in A. Jirku (ed.), *Sellin-Festschrift: Beiträge zur Religionsgeschichte und Archäologie Palästinas* (Leipzig, 1927) 13-24.

"Josua", in P. Volz, F. Stummer and J. Hempel (eds.), *Werden und Wesen des Alten Testaments: Vorträge gehalten auf der internationalen Tagung alttestamentlicher Forscher zu Göttingen vom 4.-10. September 1935* (BZAW 66; Berlin, 1936) 13-29.

Amsler, S.,   *David, roi et messie: La tradition davidique dans l'Ancien Testament* (CT 49; Neuchâtel, 1963).

Auld, A. G.,   *Joshua, Moses and the Land: Tetrateuch-Pentateuch-Hexateuch in a Generation since 1938* (Edinburgh, 1980).

Baldwin, B.,   "How Credulous was Herodotos?" *GaR* 2/11 (1964) 167-177.

Barkay, G.,   "לבעיית מקם קברים של מלכי ביח דוד האחרונים", in M. Broshi (ed.), בין חרמן לסיני: יד לאמנת (Jerusalem, 1977), 75-92.

Barrick, W. B.,   "On the 'Removal of the High Places' in 1-2 Kings ", *Bib* 55 (1974) 257-259.

"What Do We Really Know about 'High Places'?", *SEÅ* 45 (1980) 50-57.

Barth, H.,   *Die Jesaja-Worte in der Josiazeit: Israel und Assur als Thema einer produktiven Neuinterpretation der*

Jesajaüberlieferung (WMANT 48; Neukirchen-Vluyn, 1977).

Begg, C. T., "2 Kings 20:12-19 as an Element of the Deuteronomistic History", *CBQ* 48 (1986) 27-38.

"The Function of Josh 7,1-8,29 in the Deuteronomistic History", *Bib* 67 (1986) 320-334.

"The Significance of Jehoiachin's Release: A New Proposal", *JSOT* 36 (1986) 49-56.

Begrich, J., *Die Chronologie der Könige von Israel und Juda und die Quellen des Rahmens der Königsbücher* (BHT 3; Tübingen, 1929).

Beltz, W., *Die Kaleb-Traditionen im Alten Testament* (BWANT 98; Stuttgart, 1974).

Bentzen, A., *Introduction to the Old Testament*, 2: *The Books of the Old Testament* (Copenhagen, 1948).

Benzinger, I., *Die Bücher der Könige* (KHC 9; Freiburg, 1899).

Die Bücher der Chronik (KHC 20; Tübingen, 1901).

Jahvist und Elohist in den Königsbüchern (BWANT 27; Berlin, 1921).

Bickert, R., "Die Geschichte und das Handeln Jahwes: Zur Eigenart einer deuteronomistischen Offenbarungsauffassung in den Samuelbüchern", in A. H. J. Gunneweg and O. Kaiser (eds.), *Textgemäss: Aufsätze und Beiträge zur Hermeneutik des Alten Testaments* (FS Würthwein; Göttingen, 1979) 9-27.

"Die List Joabs und der Sinneswandel Davids: Eine dtr bearbeitete Einschaltung in die Thronfolgeerzählung - 2 Sam. xiv 2-22", in J. A. Emerton (ed.), *Studies in the Historical Books of the Old Testament* (VTSup 30; Leiden, 1979) 30-51.

Bibliography

Bin-Nun, S. R.,   "Formulas from Royal Records of Israel and of Judah", *VT* 18 (1968) 414-432.

Birch, B. C.,   "The Development of the Tradition on the Anointing of Saul in I Sam 9:1-10:16", *JBL* 90 (1971) 55-68.

The Rise of the Israelite Monarchy: The Growth and Development of I Samuel 7-15 (SBLDS 27; Missoula, Montana, 1976).

Blenkinsopp, J.,   *A History of Prophecy in Israel from the Settlement in the Land to the Hellenistic Period* (London, 1984).

Boecker, H.-J.,   *Die Beurteilung der Anfänge des Königtums in den deuteronomistischen Abschnitten des I. Samuelbuches: Ein Beitrag zum Problem des 'deuteronomistischen Geschichtswerks'* (WMANT 31; Neukirchen-Vluyn, 1969).

Boling, R. G.,   *Judges* (AB 6A; Garden City, 1975).

"Levitical History and the Role of Joshua", in C. L. Meyers and M. O'Connor (eds.), *The Word of the Lord Shall Go Forth: Essays in Honor of David Noel Freedman in Celebration of His Sixtieth Birthday* (ASORSVS 1; Winona Lake, Indiana, 1983) 241-261.

Boling, R. G.,
  and G. E. Wright,   *Joshua* (AB 6; Garden City, 1982).

Braulik, G.,   "Spuren einer Neubearbeitung des deuteronomistischen Geschichtswerkes in I Kön 8,52-53.59-60", *Bib* 52 (1971) 20-33.

Bright, J.,   "The Book of Joshua: Introduction", *IB* 2: 541-550.

A History of Israel (3rd ed.; Philadelphia, 1981).

Brown, F.,
  S. R. Driver and
    C. A. Briggs (eds.)   *A Hebrew and English Lexicon of the Old Testament, with an Appendix Containing the Biblical Aramaic* (Oxford, 1906).

Budde, K.,   *Die Bücher Richter und Samuel, ihre Quellen und ihr*
                              Aufbau (Giessen, 1890).

                              Die Bücher Samuel (KHC 8; Tübingen, 1902).

Burney, C. F.,   *Notes on the Hebrew Text of the Books of Kings* (Oxford,
                              1903).

Campbell, A. F.,   *The Ark Narrative (1 Sam 4-6; 2 Sam 6): A Form-Critical*
                              and Traditio-Historical Study (SBLDS 16; Missoula,
                              Montana, 1975).

                              "Yahweh and the Ark: A Case Study in Narrative", *JBL*
                              98 (1979) 31-43.

                              Of Prophets and Kings: A Late Ninth-Century Document
                              (1 Samuel 1-2 Kings 10) (CBQMS 17; Washington,
                              1986).

Carlson, R. A.,   *David, the Chosen King: A Traditio-Historical Approach*
                              to the Second Book of Samuel (trans. E. J. Sharpe and S.
                              Rudman; Uppsala, 1964).

Cheyne, T. K.,
J. Sutherland Black
    (eds.),   *Encyclopaedia Biblica: A Critical Dictionary of the*
                              Literary, Political and Religious History, the
                              Archaeology, Geography and Natural History of the
                              Bible (4 vols.; London, 1899-1903).

Childs, B. S.,   *Isaiah and the Assyrian Crisis* (SBT 2/3; London, 1967).

Clements, R. E.,   *God and Temple* (Oxford, 1965).

                              "The Deuteronomistic Interpretation of the Founding of
                              the Monarchy in I Sam. viii", *VT* 24 (1974) 398-410.

                              "Review of B. C. Birch, *The Rise of the Israelite*
                              Monarchy: The Growth and Development of 1 Samuel
                              7-15", *JTS* 29 (1978) 507-508.

                              Isaiah 1-39 (NCB; Grand Rapids and London, 1980).

Isaiah and the Deliverance of Jerusalem: A Study of the
Interpretation of Prophecy in the Old Testament
(JSOTSup 13; Sheffield, 1980).

"The Isaiah Narrative of 2 Kings 20:12-19 and the Date
of the Deuteronomic History", in A. Rofé, and Y.
Zakovitch (eds.), *Isac Leo Seeligmann Volume: Essays on*
the Bible and the Ancient World (3 vols.; Jerusalem,
1983), 3:209-220.

Coggins, R. J.,   *The First and Second Books of the Chronicles* (CNEB;
                               Cambridge, 1976).

Cohn, R. L.,   "Convention and Creativity in the Book of Kings: The
                               Case of the Dying Monarch", *CBQ* 47 (1985) 603-616.

                               "Literary Technique in the Jeroboam Narrative", *ZAW* 97
                               (1985) 23-35.

Cornill, C. H.,   *Einleitung in das Alte Testament* (GTW 2/1; 2nd ed.;
                               Freiburg, 1892).

Cortese, E.,   "Lo schema deuteronomistico per i re di Guida e
                               d'Israele", *Bib* 56 (1975) 37-52.

                               "Problemi attuali circa l'opera deuteronomistica", *RivB*
                               26 (1978) 341-352.

Cross, F. M.,   "The Structure of the Deuteronomic History", in J. M.
                               Rosenthal (ed.), *Perspectives in Jewish Learning, 3*
                               (Chicago, 1967) 9-24.

                               Canaanite Myth and Hebrew Epic: Essays in the History
                               of the Religion of Israel (Cambridge, Massachusetts,
                               1973).

Crüsemann, F.,   *Der Widerstand gegen das Königtum: Die antiköniglichen*
                               Texte des Alten Testamentes und der Kampf um den
                               frühen israelitischen Staat (WMANT 49; Neukirchen-
                               Vluyn, 1978).

Curtis, E. L.,   *A Critical and Exegetical Commentary on the Books of*
                               Chronicles (ICC; Edinburgh, 1910).

Danielus, E.,   "The Sins of Jeroboam Ben-Nabat", *JQR* 58 (1967-1968)
                         95-114, 204-223.

Debus, J.,   *Die Sünde Jerobeams: Studien zur Darstellung Jerobeams
                         und der Geschichte des Nordreichs in der
                         deuteronomistischen Geschichtsschreibung* (FRLANT 93;
                         Göttingen, 1967).

Delekat, L.,   "Tendenz und Theologie der David-Salomo-Erzählung", in
                         F. Maass (ed.), *Das ferne und nahe Wort: Festschrift
                         Leonhard Rost zur Vollendung seines 70. Lebensjahres
                         am 30. November 1966 gewidmet* (BZAW 105; Berlin,
                         1967) 26-36.

DeVries, S. J.,   *Prophet against Prophet: The Role of the Micaiah
                         Narrative (I Kings 22) in the Development of Early
                         Prophetic Tradition* (Grand Rapids, 1978).

                         1 Kings (WBC 12; Waco, Texas, 1985).

Diepold, P.,   *Israels Land* (BWANT 95; Stuttgart, 1972).

Dietrich, W.,   *Prophetie und Geschichte: Eine redaktionsgeschichtliche
                         Untersuchung zum deuteronomistischen Geschichtswerk*
                         (FRLANT 108; Göttingen, 1972).

                         "Josia und das Gesetzbuch (2 Reg. xxii)", *VT* 27 (1977)
                         13-35.

Donner, H.,   "Art und Herkunft des Amtes der Königinmutter im Alten
                         Testament", in R. von Kienle, A. Moortgat, H. Otten, E.
                         von Schuler and W. Zaumseil (eds.), *Festschrift:
                         Johannes Friedrich zum 65. Geburtstag am 27. August
                         gewidmet* (Heidelberg, 1959) 105-145.

                         "Hier sind deine Götter, Israel!", in H. Gese and H. P.
                         Rüger (eds.), *Wort und Geschichte: Festschrift für Karl
                         Elliger zum 70. Geburtstag* (AOAT 18; Neukirchen-
                         Vluyn, 1973) 45-50.

Driver, S. R.,   *A Critical and Exegetical Commentary on Deuteronomy*
                         (ICC; Edinburgh, 1902).

	Notes on the Hebrew Text and the Topography of the Books of Samuel (2nd ed.; Oxford, 1913).
	An Introduction to the Literature of the Old Testament (ITL; 9th ed. revd.; Edinburgh, 1913).
Duhm, B.,	*Das Buch Jesaja* (HKAT 3/1; 3rd ed.; Göttingen, 1914).
Eben-Shoshan, A. (ed.),	קונקורדנציה חדשה לתורה נביאים וכתובים (3 vols.; Jerusalem, 1977-1980).
Ehrlich, A. B.,	*Randglossen zur hebräischen Bibel: Textkritisches, sprachliches und sachliches, 7: Hohes Lied, Ruth, Klagelieder, Koheleth, Esther, Daniel, Esra, Nehemia, Könige, Chronik, Nachträge und Gesamtregister* (Leipzig, 1914).
Eichhorn, J. G.,	*Einleitung in das Alte Testament* (3rd ed.; 3 vols.; Leipzig, 1803).
Eissfeldt, O.,	*Einleitung in das Alte Testament* (NTG; Tübingen, 1934).
	"Die Geschichtswerke im Alten Testament", *TLZ* 72 (1947) 71-76.
	Geschichtsschreibung im Alten Testament: Ein kritischer Bericht über die neueste Literatur dazu (Berlin, 1948).
	"Lade und Stierbild", *ZAW* 58 (1940-1941) 190-215.
	"Deuteronomium und Hexateuch" in R. Sellheim and F. Maass (eds.), *Kleine Schriften* (6 vols.; Tübingen, 1962-1979), 4:238-258.
Fewell, D. N.,	"Sennacherib's Defeat: Words at War in 2 Kings 18.13-19.37", *JSOT* 34 (1986) 79-90.
Fichtner, J.,	*Das erste Buch von den Königen* (BAT 12/1; Stuttgart, 1964).
Fohrer, G.,	*Einleitung in das Alte Testament* (10th ed.; Heidelberg, 1965).

Foresti, F.,

The Rejection of Saul in the Perspective of the
Deuteronomistic School: A Study of 1 Sm 15 and Related
Texts (SThT 5; Rome, 1984).

Fowler, M. D.,

"The Israelite Bāmâ: A Question of Interpretation", ZAW
94 (1982) 203-213.

Fretheim, T. E.,

Deuteronomic History (ITB; Nashville, 1983).

Friedman, R. E.,

"From Egypt to Egypt: Dtr^1 and Dtr^2", in B. Halpern and
J. D. Levenson (eds.), Traditions in Transformation:
Turning Points in Biblical Faith (Winona Lake, Indiana,
1981) 167-192.

The Exile and Biblical Narrative: The Formation of the
Deuteronomistic and Priestly Works (HSM 22; Chico,
California, 1981).

Galling, K.,

"Das Königsgesetz im Deuteronomium", TLZ 76 (1951)
133-138.

Garbini, G.,

"Le fonti citate nel 'Libro dei Re' (a proposito degli 'Atti
di Salomone', degli 'Annali dei re di Guida' e degli
'Annali dei re d'Israele')", Hen 3 (1981) 26-46.

Gerbrandt, G. E.,

Kingship According to the Deuteronomistic History
(SBLDS 87; Atlanta, 1986).

Gonçalves, F. J.,

L'expédition de Sennachérib en Palestine dans la
littérature hébraïque ancienne (EBib n. s. 7; Paris, 1986).

Gooding, D. W.,

"Pedantic Timetabling in 3rd Book of Reigns", VT 15
(1965) 153-166.

"The Septuagint's Version of Solomon's Misconduct",
VT 15 (1965) 325-335.

"Temple Specifications: A Dispute in Logical
Arrangement between the MT and the LXX", VT 17
(1967) 143-172.

Görg, M.,

Gott-König-Reden in Israel und Ägypten (BWANT 105;
Stuttgart, 1975).

"Ein 'Machtzeichen' Davids 1 Könige xi 36", *VT* 35 (1985) 363-368.

Gray, J.,

"The Desert God *'Attr* in the Literature and Religion of Canaan", *JNES* 8 (1949) 72-83.

I and II Kings (OTL; London, 1964).

Joshua, Judges and Ruth (NCB; London, 1967).

I and II Kings (OTL; 3rd ed.; London, 1977).

Gressmann, H.,

Die älteste Geschichtsschreibung und Prophetie Israels (von Samuel bis Amos und Hosea) (SAT 2/1; Göttingen, 1910).

Grønbaek, J. H.,

Die Geschichte vom Aufstieg Davids (1. Sam. 15-2. Sam. 5): Tradition und Komposition (AThD 10; Copenhagen, 1971).

Gunn, D. M,

The Story of King David: Genre and Interpretation (JSOTSup 6; Sheffield, 1978).

Gunneweg, A. H. J.,

Leviten und Priester: Hauptlinien der Traditionsbildung und Geschichte des israelitisch-jüdischen Kultpersonals (FRLANT 89; Göttingen, 1965).

Haag, H.,

"La Campagne de Sennachérib contre Jérusalem en 701", *RB* 58 (1951) 348-359.

Habgood, J.,

"Paradigm", *NDCT* 427.

Hahn, J.,

Das "Goldene Kalb": Die Jahwe-Verehrung bei Stierbildern in der Geschichte Israels (EHS 23/154; Frankfurt-am-Main, 1981).

Halpern, B.,

"Levitic Participation in the Reform Cult of Jeroboam I", *JBL* 95 (1976) 31-42.

"Sacred History and Ideology: Chronicles' Thematic Structure - Indications of an Earlier Source", in R. E. Friedman (ed.), *The Creation of Sacred Literature: Composition and Redaction of the Biblical Text* (UCNES 22; Berkeley, 1981) 35-54.

	The Constitution of the Monarchy in Israel (HSM 25; Chico, California, 1981).
Hanson, P.,	"The Song of Heshbon and David's *Nîr*", *HTR* 61 (1968) 297-320.
Hastings, J. (ed.),	*A Dictionary of the Bible, Dealing with its Language, Literature and Contents* (5 vols.; Edinburgh, 1898-1904).
Heider, G. C.,	*The Cult of Molek: A Reassessment* (JSOTSup 43; Sheffield, 1985).
Hillers, D. R.,	*Treaty-Curses and the Old Testament Prophets* (BibOr 16; Rome, 1964).
Hobbs, T. R.,	*2 Kings* (WBC 13; Waco, Texas, 1985).
Hoffman, G.,	"Kleinigkeiten", *ZAW* 2 (1882) 175.
Hoffman, H.-D.,	*Reform und Reformen: Untersuchungen zu einem Grundthema der deuteronomistischen Geschichtsschreibung* (ATANT 66; Zürich, 1980).
Holder, J. W. D.,	*Models of Kingship in the Books of Samuel and Kings: A Literary and Theological Study of Kingship in the Books of Samuel and Kings* (Ph.D thesis; University of London, 1985).
Holladay, W. L.,	"On Every High Hill and under Every Green Tree", *VT* 11 (1961) 170-176.
Hollenstein, H.,	"Literarkritische Erwägungen zum Bericht über die Reformmassnahmen Josias 2 Kön. xxiii 4ff.", *VT* 27 (1977) 321-336.
Hölscher, G.,	*Geschichtsschreibung in Israel: Untersuchungen zum Jahvisten und Elohisten* (SHVL 50; Lund, 1952).
	"Das Buch der Könige, seine Quellen und seine Redaktion" in *EYXAPIΣTHPION: Studien zur Religion und Literatur des Alten und Neuen Testaments* (FS Gunkel; FRLANT 36; Göttingen, 1923), 1: *Zur Religion und Literatur des Alten Testaments*, 158-213.

Honor, L. L.,   *Sennacherib's Invasion of Palestine: A Critical Source Study* (COHP 12; New York, 1926).

Hoppe, L. J.,   "The Meaning of Deuteronomy", *BTB* 10 (1980) 111-117.

Horn, S. H.,   "The Chronology of King Hezekiah's Reign", *AUSS* 2 (1964) 40-52.

"Did Sennacherib Campaign Once or Twice against Hezekiah?", *AUSS* 4 (1966) 1-28.

Hossfeld, F.-L.,
and I. Meyer,   *Prophet gegen Prophet: Eine Analyse der alttestamentlichen Texte zum Thema "wahre und falsche Propheten"* (BibB 9; Fribourg, 1973).

Humbert, P.,   "Le substantif *to'ēbā* et le verbe *t'b* dans l'Ancien Testament", *ZAW* 72 (1960) 217-237.

Hylander, I.,   *Der literarische Samuel-Saul-Komplex (1. Sam. 1-15) traditionsgeschichtlich untersucht* (Uppsala, 1932).

Janssen, E.,   *Juda in der Exilszeit: Ein Beitrag zur Frage der Entstehung des Judentums* (FRLANT 69; Göttingen, 1956).

Janssen, J. M. A.,   "Que sait-on actuellement du Pharaon Taharqa?", *Bib* 34 (1953) 23-43.

Jenkins, A. K.,   "Hezekiah's Fourteenth Year: A New Interpretation of 2 Kings xviii 13-xix 37", *VT* 26 (1976) 284-298.

Jenni, E.,   "Zwei Jahrzehnte Forschung an den Büchern Josua bis Könige", *TRu* N.F. 27 (1961) 1-32, 97-146.

Jepsen, A.,   "Israel und Damaskus", *AfO* 14 (1941-1944) 153-172.

Die Quellen des Königsbuches (2nd ed.; Halle, 1956).

"Die Reform des Josia", in L. Rost (ed.), *Festschrift: Friedrich Baumgärtel zum 70. Geburtstag, 14. Januar 1958* (ErF A/10; Erlangen, 1959) 97-108.

Jeremias, A., Das Alte Testament im Lichte des Alten Orients (2nd ed.; Leipzig, 1906).

Jones, G. H., 1 and 2 Kings (NCB; 2 vols.; Grand Rapids and London, 1984).

Jongeling, B., "La particule רק", OTS 18 (1973) 97-107.

Kaiser, O., "Die Verkündigung des Propheten Jesaja im Jahre 701", ZAW 81 (1969) 304-315).

Der Prophet Jesaja, Kapitel 13-39 (ATD 18; Göttingen, 1973).

Kapelrud, A. S., The Violent Goddess: Anat in the Ras Shamra Texts (Oslo, 1969).

Kautzsch, E. (ed.), Gesenius' Hebrew Grammar (2nd ed.; trans. A. E. Cowley; Oxford, 1910).

Kenik, H. A., Design for Kingship: The Deuteronomistic Narrative Technique in 1 Kings 3:4-15 (SBLDS 69; Chico, California, 1983).

Kitchen, K. A., The Third Intermediate Period in Egypt (1100-650 B.C.) (Warminster, 1973).

"Late-Egyptian Chronology and the Hebrew Monarchy: Critical Studies in Old Testament Mythology, I", JANESCU 5 (1973) 225-233.

Kittel, R., Die Bücher der Könige (HKAT 1/5; Göttingen, 1900).

Die Bücher der Chronik (HKAT 1/6:1; Göttingen, 1902).

Koehler, L., and
W. Baumgartner, Hebräisches und aramäisches Lexikon zum Alten Testament (3rd ed.; Leiden, 1967-).

Kloner, A., "The 'Third Wall' in Jerusalem and the 'Caves of the Kings' (Josephus War V 147)", Levant 18 (1986) 121-129.

Krause, G.,
  and G. Müller (eds.),   *Theologische Realenzyklopädie* (Berlin, 1977-).

Krauss, S.,   "Moriah-Ariel, II/5: The Sepulchres of the Davidic
                                Dynasty", *PEQ* (1947) 102-111.

Kruse, H.,   "David's Covenant", *VT* 35 (1985) 139-164.

Kuenen, A.,   *Historisch-kritisch onderzoek naar het ontstaan en de
                                verzameling van de boeken des Ouden Verbonds*, 1: *Het
                                ontstaan van de Historische Boeken des Ouden Verbonds*
                                (Leiden, 1861).

Kuhl, C.,   "Die 'Wiederaufnahme' - ein literarkritisches Prinzip?",
                                ZAW 64 (1952) 1-11.

Kuhn, T. S.,   *The Structure of Scientific Revolutions* (IEUS 2/2; Chicago,
                                1962).

Kumaki, F. K.,   "The Deuteronomistic Theology of the Temple - as
                                Crystallized in 2 Sam 7, 1 Kgs 8", *AJBI* 7 (1981) 16-52.

Kutsch, E.,   "Die Dynastie von Gottes Gnaden: Probleme der
                                Nathanweissagung in 2. Sam 7.", *ZTK* 58 (1961) 137-
                                153.

Langlamet, F.,   "Josué, II, et les traditions de l'Hexateuque", *RB* 78 (1971)
                                5-17, 161-183, 321-354.

                                "La traversée du Jourdain et les documents de
                                l'Hexateuque", *RB* 79 (1972) 7-38.

                                "Review of W. Dietrich, *Prophetie und Geschichte: Eine
                                redaktionsgeschichtliche Untersuchung zum
                                deuteronomistischen Geschichtswerk*", *RB* 81 (1974) 601-
                                606.

                                "Pour ou contre Salomon? La rédaction prosalomonienne
                                de I Rois, I-II", *RB* 83 (1976) 321-379, 481-528.

                                "Absalom et les concubines de son père: Recherches sur
                                II Sam., xvi, 21-22", *RB* 84 (1977) 161-209.

"David et la maison de Saül: Les épisodes 'Benjaminites' de II Sam., ix; xvi, 1-14; xix, 17-31; I Rois, ii, 36-46", *RB* 86 (1979) 194-213, 385-436, 481-513; *RB* 87 (1980) 161-210; *RB* 88 (1981) 321-332.

"Affinités sacerdotales, deutéronomiques, élohistes dans l'Histoire de la succession (2 S 9-20; 1 R 1-2)", in A. Caquot and M. Delcor (eds.), *Mélanges bibliques et orientaux en l'honneur de M. Henri Cazelles* (AOAT 212; Neukirchen-Vluyn, 1981) 233-246.

le Moyne, J.,
"Les deux ambassades de Sennachérib à Jérusalem", in *Mélanges bibliques rédigés en l'honneur de André Robert* (TICP 4; Paris, n.d.) 149-153.

Leclant, J.,
and J. Yoyotte,
"Notes d'histoire et de civilisation éthiopiennes", *BIFAO* 51 (1952) 1-39.

van Leeuwen, C.,
"Sanchérib devant Jérusalem", *OTS* 14 (1965) 245-272.

Lemaire, A.,
Les écoles et la formation de la Bible dans l'ancien Israël (OBO 39; Göttingen, 1981).

"Vers l'histoire de la rédaction des livres des Rois", *ZAW* 98 (1986) 221-236.

Lemke, W. E.,
"The Way of Obedience: I Kings 13 and the Structure of the Deuteronomistic History", in F. M. Cross, W. E. Lemke and P. D. Miller, Jnr. (eds.), *Magnalia Dei: The Mighty Acts of God* (FS Wright; Garden City, 1976) 301-326.

Levenson, J. D.,
"Who Inserted the Book of the Torah?", *HTR* 68 (1975) 203-233.

"From Temple to Synagogue: 1 Kings 8", in B. Halpern and J. D. Levenson (eds.), *Traditions in Transformation: Turning Points in Biblical Faith* (Winona Lake, Indiana, 1981) 143-166.

"The Last Four Verses in Kings", *JBL* 103 (1984) 353-361.

Levin, C.,   Der Sturz der Königin Atalja: Ein Kapitel zur Geschichte Judas im 9. Jahrhundert v. Chr. (SBS 105; Stuttgart, 1982).

"Joschija im deuteronomistischen Geschichtswerk", *ZAW* 96 (1984) 351-371.

Lindblom, J.,   Erwägungen zur Herkunft der josianischen Tempelurkunde (SMVHL; Lund, 1971).

Lohfink, N.,   "Die Bundesurkunde des Königs Josias (Eine Frage an die Deuteronomiumsforschung)", *Bib* 44 (1963) 261-288, 461-498.

"Kerygmata des deuteronomistischen Geschichtswerks", in J. Jeremias and L. Perlitt (eds.), *Die Botschaft und die Boten: Festschrift für Hans Walter Wolff zum 70. Geburtstag* (Neukirchen-Vluyn, 1981) 87-100.

"Zur neueren Diskussion über 2 Kön 22-23", in N. Lohfink (ed.), *Das Deuteronomium: Entstehung, Gestalt und Botschaft* (BETL 68; Leuven, 1985) 24-48.

Macadam, M. F. L.,   *The Temples of Kawa*, 1: *The Inscriptions* (London, 1949).

McCarter, P. K., Jnr.,   "The Apology of David", *JBL* 99 (1980) 489-504.

I Samuel (AB 8; Garden City, 1980).

II Samuel (AB 9; Garden City, 1984).

McCarthy, D. J.,   "II Samuel 7 and the Structure of the Deuteronomic History", *JBL* 84 (1965) 131-138.

"The Inauguration of Monarchy in Israel: A Form-Critical Study of I Samuel 8-12", *Int* 27 (1973) 401-412.

"2 Kings 13,4-6", *Bib* 54 (1973) 409-410.

McKay, J. W.,   Religion in Judah under the Assyrians, 732-609 BC (SBT 2/26; London, 1973).

McKenzie, S. L.,
The Chronicler's Use of the Deuteronomistic History (HSM 33; Atlanta, 1985).

Macy, H. R.,
The Sources of the Books of Chronicles: A Reassessment (Ph.D thesis; Harvard University, 1975).

Maisler, B.,
"Ancient Israelite Historiography", *IEJ* 2 (1952) 82-88.

Marti, K.,
Das Buch Jesaja (KHC 10; Tübingen, 1900).

Mayes, A. D. H.,
"The Rise of the Israelite Monarchy", *ZAW* 90 (1978) 1-19.

Deuteronomy (NCB; London, 1979).

The Story of Israel between Settlement and Exile: A Redactional Study of the Deuteronomistic History (London, 1983).

Judges (OTG; Sheffield, 1985).

Mettinger, T. N. D.,
King and Messiah: The Civil and Sacral Legitimation of the Israelite Kings (ConBOT 8; Lund, 1976).

Meyer, R.,
"Auffallender Erzählungsstil in einem angeblichen Auszug aus der 'Chronik der Könige von Juda'", in L. Rost (ed.), *Festschrift: Friedrich Baumgärtel zum 70. Geburtstag, 14. Januar 1958* (ErF A/10; Erlangen, 1959) 114-123.

Michaeli, F.,
Les livres des Chroniques, d'Esdras et de Néhémie (CAT 16; Neuchâtel, 1967).

Millard, A. R.,
"Sennacherib's Attack on Hezekiah", *TynBul* 36 (1985) 61-77.

Miller, J. M.,
"Saul's Rise to Power: Some Observations Concerning 1 Sam 9:1-10:16; 10:26-11:15 and 13:2-14:46", *CBQ* 36 (1974) 157-174.

Miller, P. D., Jnr., and J. J. M. Roberts,
The Hand of the Lord: A Reassessment of the "Ark Narrative" of 1 Samuel (JHNES; Baltimore, 1977).

Montgomery, J. A.,   "Archival Data in the Book of Kings", *JBL* 53 (1934) 46-
                                   52.

Montgomery, J. A.,
  and H. S. Gehman,   *A Critical and Exegetical Commentary on the Books of
                                   Kings* (ICC; Edinburgh, 1951).

Motzki, H.,   "Ein Beitrag zum Problem des Stierkultes in der
                                   Religionsgeschichte Israels", *VT* 25 (1975) 470-485.

Mowinckel, S.,   *Zur Frage nach dokumentarischen Quellen in Josua 13-19*
                                   (ANVAOH; Oslo, 1946).

                                   Erwägungen zur Pentateuch Quellenfrage (Oslo, 1964).

                                   *Tetrateuch-Pentateuch-Hexateuch: Die Berichte über die
                                   Landnahme in den drei altisraelitischen
                                   Geschichtswerken* (BZAW 90; Berlin, 1964).

Myers, J. M.,   *II Chronicles* (AB 13; Garden City, 1965).

Na'aman, N.,   "Sennacherib's 'Letter to God' on His Campaign to
                                   Judah", *BASOR* 214 (1974) 25-39.

                                   "Historical and Chronological Notes on the Kingdoms of
                                   Israel and Judah in the Eighth Century B.C.", *VT* 36
                                   (1986) 71-92.

Neiman, D.,   "*Pgr*: A Canaanite Cult-Object in the Old Testament", *JBL*
                                   67 (1948) 55-60.

Nelson, R. D.,   *The Double Redaction of the Deuteronomistic History*
                                   (JSOTSup 18; Sheffield, 1981).

                                   "Josiah in the Book of Joshua", *JBL* 100 (1981) 531-540.

Nicholson, E. W.,   "The Centralisation of the Cult in Deuteronomy", *VT* 13
                                   (1963) 380-389.

                                   Deuteronomy and Tradition (Oxford, 1967).

Nielsen, E.,   *Shechem: A Traditio-Historical Investigation* (Copenhagen,
                                   1955).

Noth, M.,   *Das Buch Josua* (HAT 1/7; Tübingen, 1938).

                                  Überlieferungsgeschichtliche Studien, 1: *Die sammelnden
                                  und bearbeitenden Geschichtswerke im Alten Testament*
                                  (SKGG 2; Halle, 1943).

                                  "David und Israel in II Samuel, 7", in *Mélanges
                                  bibliques rédigés en l'honneur de André Robert* (TICP 4;
                                  Paris, n.d.) 122-130.

                                  "Review of W. Richter, *Traditionsgeschichtliche
                                  Untersuchungen zum Richterbuch*", *VT* 15 (1965) 126-
                                  128.

                                  Könige (BKAT 9/1; Neukirchen-Vluyn, 1968).

Obbink, H. T.,   "Jahwebilder", *ZAW* 47 (1929) 264-274.

Oesterley, W. O. E.,
and T. H. Robinson,   *A History of Israel*, 1: *From the Exodus to the Fall of
                                  Jerusalem, 586 B.C.* (Oxford, 1932).

                                  An Introduction to the Books of the Old Testament
                                  (London, 1934).

Oestreicher, T.,   *Das deuteronomische Grundgesetz* (BFT 27/4; Gütersloh,
                                  1923).

Ogden, G. S.,   "The Northern Extent of Josiah's Reforms", *AusBR* 26
                                  (1978) 26-34.

Orlinsky, H. M.,   "The Kings-Isaiah Recensions of the Hezekiah Story",
                                  JQR 30 (1939-1940) 33-49.

Otto, E.,   *Das Mazzotfest in Gilgal* (BWANT 107; Stuttgart, 1975).

Parrot, A.,   *Ninive et l'Ancien Testament* (CAB 3; Neuchâtel, 1953).

Peckham, B.,   "The Composition of Deuteronomy 5-11", in C. L. Meyers
                                  and M. O'Connor (eds.), *The Word of the Lord Shall Go
                                  Forth: Essays in Honor of David Noel Freedman in
                                  Celebration of His Sixtieth Birthday* (ASORSVS 1;
                                  Winona Lake, Indiana, 1983) 217-240.

"The Composition of Joshua 3-4", *CBQ* 46 (1984) 413-431.

"The Deuteronomistic History of Saul and David", *ZAW* 97 (1985) 190-209.

The Composition of the Deuteronomistic History (HSM 35; Atlanta, 1985).

Pfeiffer, R. H.,   *Introduction to the Old Testament* (revd. ed.; New York, 1948).

Plein, I.,   "Erwägungen zur Überlieferung von I Reg 11,26-14,20", *ZAW* 78 (1966) 8-24.

Polzin, R.,   *Moses and the Deuteronomist: A Literary Study of the Deuteronomic History*, 1: *Deuteronomy, Joshua, Judges* (New York, 1980).

Porter, J. R.,   "The Succession of Joshua", in J. I. Durham and J. R. Porter (eds.), *Proclamation and Presence: Old Testament Essays in Honour of Gwynne Henton Davies* (London, 1970) 102-132.

                            "Old Testament Historiography" in G. W. Anderson (ed.), *Tradition and Interpretation: Essays by Members of the Society for Old Testament Study* (Oxford, 1979) 125-162.

Preuss, H. D.,   *Deuteronomium* (EF 164; Darmstadt, 1982).

Priest, J.,   "Huldah's Oracle", *VT* 30 (1980) 366-368.

Pritchard, J. B.,
   (ed.),   *Ancient Near Eastern Texts Relating to the Old Testament* (3rd ed.; Princeton, 1969).

von Rad, G.,   *Das formgeschichtliche Problem des Hexateuchs* (BWANT 78; Stuttgart, 1938).

                            Deuteronomium-Studien (FRLANT 58; Göttingen, 1947).

                            Theologie des Alten Testaments, 1: *Die Theologie der geschichtlichen Überlieferungen Israels* (EET 1; 2nd ed.;

Munich, 1958).

Das fünfte Buch Mose: Deuteronomium (ATD 8; Göttingen, 1964).

Radjawane, A. N., "Das deuteronomistische Geschichtswerk: Ein Forschungsbericht" *TRu* N.F. 38 (1974) 177-216.

Rahlfs, A. (ed.), *Septuaginta Studien* (3 vols.; Göttingen, 1904-1911), 3: *Lucians Rezension der Königsbücher* (1911), by A. Rahlfs.

Rehm, M., *Das erste Buch der Könige* (Eichstätt, 1979).

Das zweite Buch der Könige (Eichstätt, 1982).

Richardson, A., and J. Bowden (eds.), *A New Dictionary of Christian Theology* (London, 1983).

Richter, W., *Traditionsgeschichtliche Untersuchungen zum Richterbuch* (BBB 18; Bonn, 1963).

Die Bearbeitungen des 'Retterbuches' in der deuteronomischen Epoche (BBB 21; Bonn, 1964).

Die sogenannten vorprophetischen Berufungsberichte: Eine literaturwissenschaftliche Studie zu 1 Sam 9,1-10, 16, Ex 3f. und Ri 6,11b-17 (FRLANT 101; Göttingen, 1970).

Robinson, J., *The First Book of Kings* (CNEB; London, 1972).

The Second Book of Kings (CNEB; Cambridge, 1976).

Rose, M., "Bemerkungen zum historischen Fundament des Josia-Bildes in II Reg 22f.", *ZAW* 89 (1977) 50-63.

Rosenbaum, J., "Hezekiah's Reform and the Deuteronomistic Tradition", *HTR* 72 (1979) 23-43.

Rost, L., *Die Überlieferung von der Thronnachfolge Davids* (BWANT 42; Stuttgart, 1926).

Roth, W.,   "The Deuteronomic Rest Theology: A Redaction-Critical
                             Study", *BR* 21 (1976) 5-14.

                             "Deuteronomium/Deuteronomistisches
                             Geschichtswerk/Deuteronomistische Schule", in *TRE*
                             8:530-552.

Rowley, H. H.,   "Hezekiah's Reform and Rebellion", *BJRL* 44 (1961-1962)
                             395-431.

Rubinstein, A.,   "The Anomalous Perfect with *Waw*-Conjunctive in Biblical
                             Hebrew", *Bib* 44 (1963) 62-69.

Rudolph, W.,   *Der "Elohist" von Exodus bis Josua* (BZAW 68; Berlin,
                             1938).

                             Chronikbücher (HAT 1/21; Tübingen, 1955).

Šanda, A.,   *Die Bücher der Könige* (EHAT 9; 2 vols.; Münster, 1911-
                             1912).

Schicklberger, F.,   *Die Ladeerzählungen des ersten Samuel-Buches: Eine
                             literaturwissenschaftliche und theologiegeschichtliche
                             Untersuchung* (FzB 7; Würzburg, 1973).

Schmidt, L.,   *Menschlicher Erfolg und Jahwes Initiative* (WMANT 38;
                             Neukirchen-Vluyn, 1970).

Schulte, H.,   *Die Entstehung der Geschichtsschreibung im Alten Israel*
                             (BZAW 128; Berlin, 1972).

Schunck, K.-D.,   *Benjamin: Untersuchungen zur Entstehung und Geschichte
                             eines israelitischen Stammes* (BZAW 86; Berlin, 1963).

Schüpphaus, J.,   *Richter- und Prophetengeschichten als Glieder der
                             Geschichtsdarstellung der Richter- und Königszeit* (Diss.
                             theol.; University of Bonn, 1967).

Seebass, H.,   "Die Vorgeschichte der Königserhebung Sauls", *ZAW* 79
                             (1967) 155-171.

                             "Zur Teilung der Herrschaft Salomos nach I Reg 11,29-
                             39", *ZAW* 88 (1976) 363-376.

Segal, M. H.,   "The Composition of the Books of Samuel", *JQR* 55 (1964-1965) 318-339.

van Selms, A.,   "How Do Books of the Bible Commence?", in *Biblical Essays: Proceedings of the Ninth Meeting of "Die Ou-Testamentiese Werkgemeenskap in Suid-Afrika" held at the University of Stellenbosch, 26th-29th July, 1966* (Potchefstroom, 1966) 132-141.

Sellin, E.,   *Einleitung in das Alte Testament* (ETB 2; Leipzig, 1910).

van Seters, J.,   "Histories and Historians of the Ancient Near East: The Israelites", *Or* N.S. 50 (1981) 137-185.

Shea, W. H.,   "Sennacherib's Second Palestinian Campaign", *JBL* 104 (1985) 401-418.

Simons, J.,   *Jerusalem in the Old Testament: Researches and Theories* (Leiden, 1952).

Simpson, C. A.,   *The Early Traditions of Israel: A Critical Analysis of the Pre-Deuteronomic Narrative of the Hexateuch* (Oxford, 1948).

Skinner, J.,   *Kings* (CenB; Edinburgh, n.d.).

Smelik, K. A. D.,   "Distortion of Old Testament Prophecy: The Purpose of Isaiah xxxvi and xxxvii", *OTS* 24 (1986) 70-93.

Smend, R., Snr.,   "JE in den geschichtlichen Büchern des AT." *ZAW* 39 (1921) 181-217.

Smend, R.,   "Das Gesetz und die Völker: Ein Beitrag zur deuteronomistischen Redaktionsgeschichte", in H. W. Wolff (ed.), *Probleme biblischer Theologie: Gerhard von Rad zum 70. Geburtstag* (Munich, 1971) 494-509.

     Die Entstehung des Alten Testaments (TW 1; Stuttgart, 1978).

Smit, E. J.,   "Death and Burial Formulas in Kings and Chronicles Relating to the Kings of Judah", in *Biblical Essays: Proceedings of the Ninth Meeting of "Die Ou-*

Testamentiese Werkgemeenskap in Suid-Afrika" held at
the *University of Stellenbosch, 26th-29th July, 1966*
(Potchefstroom, 1966) 173-177.

Smith, H. P.,   *A Critical and Exegetical Commentary on the Books of
                                 Samuel* (ICC; Edinburgh, 1912).

Snaith, N. H.,   "The Historical Books", in H. H. Rowley (ed.), *The Old
                                 Testament and Modern Study: A Generation of Discovery
                                 and Research* (Oxford, 1951) 84-114.

                                 "The First and Second Books of Kings: Introduction and
                                 Exegesis", *IB* 3:3-338.

Soggin, J. A.,   *Le livre de Josué* (CAT 5A; Neuchâtel, 1970).

                                 Introduction to the Old Testament (revd. ed.; London,
                                 1980).

                                 Judges (OTL; London, 1981).

                                 "Problemi de storia e de storiografia nell'antico Israele",
                                 Hen 4 (1982) 1-16.

Speiser, E. A.,   "Background and Function of the Biblical *Nāśī'*", *CBQ* 25
                                 (1963) 111-117.

Spieckermann, H.,   *Juda unter Assur in der Sargonidenzeit* (FRLANT 129;
                                 Göttingen, 1982).

Stade, B.,   "Miscellen: Anmerkungen zu 2 Kö. 15-21", *ZAW* 6 (1886)
                                 156-189.

Stade, B.,
  and F. Schwally,   *The Book of Kings* (SBOT 9; Leipzig, 1904).

Stahl, R.,   *Aspekte der Geschichte deuteronomistischer Theologie: Zur
                                 Traditionsgeschichte der Terminologie und zur
                                 Redaktionsgeschichte der Redekompositionen* (Diss. B;
                                 Jena, 1982).

Steck, O. H.,   *Israel und das gewaltsame Geschick der Propheten:
                                 Untersuchungen zur Überlieferung des
                                 deuteronomistischen Geschichtsbildes im Alten Testament,*

	Spätjudentum und Urchristentum (WMANT 23; Neukirchen-Vluyn, 1967).
Stoębe, H. J.,	"Noch einmal die Eselinnen des *Kîš* (1 Sam. ix)", *VT* 7 (1957) 362-370.
	"Review of W. Dietrich, *Prophetie und Geschichte: Eine redaktionsgeschichtliche Untersuchung zum deuteronomistischen Geschichtswerk*", *TLZ* 99 (1974) 181-183.
Talmon, S.,	"Polemics and Apology in Biblical Historiography - 2 Kings 17:24-41", in R. E. Friedman (ed.), *The Creation of Sacred Literature: Composition and Redaction of the Biblical Text* (UCNES 22; Berkeley, 1981) 57-68.
Tengström, S.,	*Die Hexateucherzählung: Eine literaturgeschichtliche Studie* (ConBOT 7; Lund, 1976).
Timm, H.,	"Die Ladeerzählung (1. Sam. 4-6; 2. Sam. 6) und das Kerygma des deuteronomistischen Geschichtswerks", *EvT* 26 (1966) 509-526.
Timm, S.,	*Die Dynastie Omri: Quellen und Untersuchungen zur Geschichte Israels im 9. Jahrhundert vor Christus* (FRLANT 124; Göttingen, 1982).
Trompf, G. W.,	"Notions of Historical Recurrence in Classical Hebrew Historiography" in J. A. Emerton (ed.), *Studies in the Historical Books of the Old Testament* (VTSup 30; Leiden, 1979) 213-229.
Vanoni, G.,	*Literarkritik und Grammatik: Untersuchung der Wiederholungen und Spannungen in 1 Kön 11-12* (ATSAT 21; St. Ottilien, 1984).
	"Beobachtungen zur deuteronomistischen Terminologie in 2 Kön 23,25-25,30", in N. Lohfink (ed.), *Das Deuteronomium: Entstehung, Gestalt und Botschaft* (BETL 68; Leuven, 1985) 357-362.

Vaughan, P. H.,   *The Meaning of 'Bāmâ' in the Old Testament: A Study of*
                           Etymological, Textual and Archaeological Evidence
                           (SOTSMS 3; London, 1974).

de Vaux, R.,   *Les livres de Samuel* (SBJ; Paris, 1953).

                           Les livres des Rois (SBJ; 2nd ed.; Paris, 1958).

                           Les institutions de l'Ancien Testament, 1: Le nomadisme
                           et ses survivances; institutions familiales; institutions
                           civiles (Paris, 1958).

                           "Jérusalem et les prophètes", *RB* 73 (1966) 481-509.

Veijola, T.,   *Die ewige Dynastie: David und die Entstehung seiner*
                           Dynastie nach der deuteronomistischen Darstellung
                           (AASF B/193; Helsinki, 1975).

                           Das Königtum in der Beurteilung der
                           deuteronomistischen Historiographie: Eine
                           redaktionsgeschichtliche Untersuchung (AASF B/198;
                           Helsinki, 1977).

                           Verheissung in der Krise: Studien zur Literatur und
                           Theologie der Exilszeit anhand des 89. Psalms (AASF
                           B/220; Helsinki, 1982).

                           "Remarks of an Outsider Concerning Scandinavian
                           Tradition History with Emphasis on the Davidic
                           Traditions", in K. Jeppesen and B. Otzen (eds.), *The*
                           Productions of Time: Tradition History in Old Testament
                           Scholarship (trans. F. H. Cryer; Sheffield, 1984) 29-51.

Vogt, E.,   "Sennacherib und die letzte Tätigkeit Jesajas", *Bib* 47
                           (1966) 427-437.

                           Der Aufstand Hiskias und die Belagerung Jerusalems 701
                           v. Chr. (AnBib 106; Rome, 1986).

Waters, K. H.,   *Herodotos the Historian: His Problems, Methods and*
                           Originality (Beckenham, Kent, 1985).

Weill, R.,   *La cité de David: Compte rendu des fouilles exécutés, à Jérusalem, sur le site de la ville primitive* (Paris, 1920).

Weinfeld, M.,   *Deuteronomy and the Deuteronomic School* (Oxford, 1972).

"Divine Intervention in War in Ancient Israel and in the Ancient Near East", in H. Tadmor and M. Weinfeld (eds.), *History, Historiography and Interpretation: Studies in Biblical and Cuneiform Literatures* (Jerusalem, 1983) 121-147.

"The Emergence of the Deuteronomic Movement: The Historical Antecedents", in N. Lohfink (ed.), *Das Deuteronomium: Entstehung, Gestalt und Botschaft* (BETL 68; Leuven, 1985) 76-98.

Weippert, H.,   "Die 'deuteronomistischen' Beurteilungen der Könige von Israel und Juda und das Problem der Redaktion der Königsbücher", *Bib* 53 (1972) 301-339.

"Die Ätiologie des Nordreiches und seines Königshauses (I Reg 11,29-40)", *ZAW* 95 (1983) 344-375.

"Das deuteronomistische Geschichtswerk: Sein Ziel und Ende in der neueren Forschung", *TRu* N.F. 50 (1985) 213-249.

Weippert, M.,   "Gott und Stier: Bemerkungen zu einer Terrakotte aus *jāfa*", *ZDPV* 77 (1961) 93-117.

"'Heiliger Kreig' in Israel und Assyrien: Kritische Anmerkungen zu Gerhard von Rads Konzept des 'Heiligen Kreiges im alten Israel'", *ZAW* 84 (1972) 460-493.

"Fragen des israelitischen Geschichtsbewusstseins", *VT* 23 (1973) 415-442.

Weiser, A.,   *Samuel: Seine geschichtliche Aufgabe und religiöse Bedeutung* (FRLANT 81; Göttingen, 1962).

"Die Tempelbaukrise unter David", *ZAW* 77 (1965) 153-168.

"Die Legitimation des Königs David: Zur Eigenart und Entstehung der sogen. Geschichte von Davids Aufstieg", *VT* 16 (1966) 325-354.

Einleitung in das Alte Testament (6th ed.; Göttingen, 1966).

Wellhausen, J.,   *Die Composition des Hexateuchs und der historischen Bücher des Alten Testaments* (2nd ed.; Berlin, 1889).

Prolegomena zur Geschichte Israels (6th ed.; Berlin, 1905).

Skizzen und Vorarbeiten, 2: *Die Composition des Hexateuchs* (Berlin, 1885).

Wevers, J. W.,   "Exegetical Principles Underlying the Septuagint Text of 1 Kings ii 12-xxi 43", *OTS* 8 (1950) 300-322.

Whitehouse, O. C.,   "Uzziah", *HDB* 4:843-845.

Whitney, J. T.,   "'Bamoth' in the Old Testament", *TynBul* 30 (1979) 125-147.

Wiener, H. M.,   *The Composition of Judges II 11 to I Kings II 46* (Leipzig, 1929).

Wildberger, H.,   *Jesaja* (BKAT 10; Neukirchen-Vluyn, 1972-1982).

Willi, T.,   *Die Chronik als Auslegung: Untersuchungen zur literarischen Gestaltung der historischen Überlieferung Israels* (FRLANT 106; Göttingen, 1972).

Williamson, H. G. M.,   *1 and 2 Chronicles* (NCB; Grand Rapids and London, 1982).

"Review of S. L. McKenzie, *The Chronicler's Use of the Deuteronomistic History*", *VT* 37 (1987) 107-114.

Willis, J. T.,   "Samuel Versus Eli: I Sam. 1-7", *TZ* 35 (1979) 201-212.

Wilson, R. R.,   *Prophecy and Society in Ancient Israel* (Philadelphia, 1980).

Winckler, H.,   *Alttestamentliche Untersuchungen* (Leipzig, 1892)

Wolff, H. W.,   "Das Kerygma des deuteronomistischen Geschichtswerks", *ZAW* 73 (1961) 171-186.

Wright, G. E.,   "The Book of Deuteronomy: Introduction", *IB* 2:311-330.

Würthwein, E.,   *Die Erzählung von der Thronfolge Davids - theologische oder politische Geschichtsschreibung?* (ThS 115; Zürich, 1974).

                                  "Die josianische Reform und das Deuteronomium", *ZTK* 73 (1976) 395-423.

                                  Die Bücher der Könige: Das erste Buch der Könige, Kapitel 1-16 (ATD 11/1; Göttingen, 1977).

                                  Die Bücher der Könige: 1. Kön. 17-2. Kön. 25 (ATD 11/2; Göttingen, 1984).

Yeivin, S.,   "The Sepulchers of the Kings of the House of David", *JNES* 7 (1948) 30-45.

Yurco, F. J.,   "Sennacherib's Third Campaign and the Coregency of Shabaka and Shebitku", *Ser* 6 (1980) 221-240.

Zakovitch, Y.,   "יפתח = ברך", *VT* 22 (1972) 123-125.

Zenger, E.,   "Die deuteronomistische Interpretation der Rehabilitierung Jojachins", *BZ* N.F. 12 (1968) 16-30.

Zevit, Z.,   "Deuteronomistic Historiography in 1 Kings 12-2 Kings 17 and the Reinvestiture of the Israelian Cult", *JSOT* 32 (1985) 57-73.

Zimmerli, W.,   *Erkenntnis Gottes nach dem Buche Ezekiel: Eine theologische Studie* (ATANT 27; Zürich, 1954).

                                  Ezechiel (BKAT 13; 2 vols.; Neukirchen-Vluyn, 1969).

INDEX OF BIBLICAL REFERENCES

BEIHEFTE ZUR ZEITSCHRIFT FÜR DIE ALTTESTAMENTLICHE WISSENSCHAFT

GERALD T. SHEPPARD

Wisdom as a Hermeneutical Construct

A Study in the Sapientializing of the Old Testament

1980. Large-octavo. XII, 178 pages. Cloth DM 78,—
ISBN 3 11 007504 0 (Volume 151)

J. A. LOADER

Polar Structures in the Book of Qohelet

Edited by Georg Fohrer

1979. Large-octavo. XII, 138 pages. Cloth DM 65,—
ISBN 3 11 007636 5 (Volume 152)

PHILIP J. NEL

The Structure and Ethos of the Wisdom Admonitions in Proverbs

1982. Large-octavo. XII, 142 pages. Cloth DM 74,—
ISBN 3 11 008750 2 (Volume 158)

WILLEM S. PRINSLOO

The Theology of the Book of Joel

1985. Large-octavo. VIII, 136 pages. Cloth DM 74,—
ISBN 3 11 010301 X (Volume 163)

ANNELI AEJMELAEUS

The Traditional Prayer in the Psalms

LUDWIG SCHMIDT

Literarische Studien zur Josephsgeschichte

1987. Large-octavo. VI, 310 pages. Cloth DM 140,—
ISBN 3 11 010480 6 (Volume 167)

Prices are subject to change

Walter de Gruyter Berlin · New York

BEIHEFTE ZUR ZEITSCHRIFT FÜR DIE
ALTTESTAMENTLICHE WISSENSCHAFT

MARVIN A. SWEENEY

Isaiah 1—4 and the Post-Exilic Understanding of the Isaianic Tradition

1988. Large-octavo. X, 212 pages. Cloth DM 98,—
ISBN 3 11 011034 2 (Volume 171)

CHRISTOPHER R. SEITZ

Theology in Conflict

Reactions of the Exile in the Book of Jeremiah

1988. Large-octavo. Approx. 400 pages. Cloth approx. DM 148,—
ISBN 3 11 011223 X (in preparation)

ETAN LEVINE

The Aramaic Version of the Bible

Contents and Context

1988. Large-octavo. Approx. 290 pages. Cloth approx. DM 118,—
ISBN 3 11 011474 7 (in preparation)

SA-MOON KANG

Divine War in the Old Testament and the Ancient Near East

1988. Large-octavo. Approx. 290 pages. Cloth approx. DM 120,—
ISBN 3 11 011156 X (in preparation)

JOHN HA

Genesis 15

A Theological Compendium of Pentateuchal History

1988. Large-octavo. Approx. 290 pages. Cloth approx. DM 82,—
ISBN 3 11 011206 X (in preparation)

BARUCH MARGALIT

The Ugaritic Poem of AQHT

Text — Translation — Commentary

1988. Large-octavo. Approx. 590 pages. Cloth approx. DM 198,—
ISBN 3 11 011632 4 (in preparation)

Prices are subject to change

Walter de Gruyter Berlin · New York